# Chinese Capitalisms

# Social Transformations in Chinese Societies

## The Official Journal of the Hong Kong Sociological Association

*Editors*
Chan Kwok-bun, Cheung Tak-sing and Agnes S. Ku

*Book Review Editors*
Ruan Danching and Anita K. W. Chan

*Editorial Assistants*
Vivien W. W. Chan
Farheen Mukri

VOLUME 3
2007

# Chinese Capitalisms

*Editors*
Chan Kwok-bun, Cheung Tak-sing and Agnes S. Ku

*Book Review Editors*
Ruan Danching and Anita K. W. Chan

*Editorial Assistants*
Vivien W. W. Chan
Farheen Mukri

*Guest Editor*
Chu Yin-wah

BRILL

LEIDEN • BOSTON
2007

This book is printed on acid-free paper.

ISSN 1871-2673
ISBN-13: 978 90 04 16824 4



PRINTED IN THE NETHERLANDS

## CONTENTS

## ARTICLES



## BOOK REVIEWS

# FROM THE EDITOR

Publishing a scholarly journal is like establishing an honorable but unprofitable institution that travels down a long and winding road. Three years after its transfer to Brill Academic Publishers of the Netherlands from the Chinese University Press, this journal has seen several significant developments. English is now its publishing language, and it has gone international as a result of Brill's backing and quality submissions from renowned local and overseas sociologists. It now also features regular special issues on subjects of emerging significance, and within a year, it will go online. Yet, in the usual lifespan of a journal, ours is still in its infancy. A senior editor at Brill once told me that it takes around thirty years for a scholarly journal to reach maturity and achieve international prominence, though a slightly shorter duration, perhaps ten years, is needed to make it financially viable. Meanwhile, numerous new journals emerge, struggle, and die many a painful, premature death—which seems to be a fact of life, a kind of survival of the fittest, cruel but true.

Many of us in the business of publishing and editing a journal know that its operations depend on the goodwill of a community of intellectuals who are willing to submit their best works, do peer reviews of article manuscripts promptly and without bias, and volunteer to undertake the laborious task of putting together a special issue. The editors do the mundane work of writing letters to authors, reviewers and the publisher, conducting editorial meetings, raising funds and nurturing the financial health of the journal. It is indeed a labor of love, and involves a readiness to face up to public criticism.

Recently I was involved in a lively debate on the dilemma of local sociologists who are often persuaded to save their best works for journals and conferences in the U.S., for the practical reasons of what counts and what does not in times of assessment for promotion and tenure. In a deep and structural way, this dilemma is also the plight of editors of journals in Hong Kong if our university senior management, deans, heads of departments and, indeed, the University Grants Council, continue to favor journals and books published overseas in the English language. I know for a fact that Singapore, Taiwan, Japan, Thailand, and now even China, have taken important steps to put resources, both financial and intellectual, into producing quality journals, thus taking pride in essays published locally, while at the same time encouraging social scientists to publish their works in international outlets—a kind of two-legged existence. Hong Kong may have a lesson or two to learn from our neighbors in this regard.

The special focus of this issue is Capitalisms in Chinese societies, and it features essays by prominent sociologists: Nan Lin, Gary Hamilton, Kao Cheng-shu, Michael H. H. Hsiao, Ho Tsai-man, and Ku Chung-hwa. Also included are articles by Wu Xiaogang, Eric Fong, and Jonathan Unger. By coincidence, many of the contributors are from Taiwan, but they examine Chinese forms of capitalism as they have emerged and are redefining themselves under the nascent forces of globalization.

My fellow editor Cheung Tak Sing has retired, and this issue is his swansong. Many of you might know that Tak Sing has been instrumental in the journal's publication since Day One. He has been a vital source of energy, stimulation, and perseverance. Chinese literature being his first love, he tells me that he will spend the first few years of his retirement studying Chinese classic texts which, in the old days, were read by children who had just started their schooling. The editorial board will miss him sorely. Chu Yin-wah will replace Tak Sing, and her first contribution to the journal is serving as guest editor for this issue.

Agnes S. Ku, Chu Yin-Wah, and I serve as the journal's editors, with Ruan Danching and Wang Cangbai as the book review editors, and Vivien W. W. Chan and Farheen Mukri as editorial assistants. As a group we are currently working on ideas for our next issue—a special issue on the family. We have already considered several possibilities for particular directions but we welcome more suggestions and, of course, article submissions.

*Chan Kwok-bun*

## AUTHORS' BIOGRAPHIES

Chu Yin-wah is Associate Professor in the Department of Sociology at Hong Kong Baptist University. She has published on various aspects of economic and political development in East Asia. Presently, she is researching on South Korea's and Taiwan's effort to take on the challenge of the information economy as well as on various aspects of land rights movements in Greater China. Email: ywchu@hkbu.edu.hk.

Eric Fong is Professor of Sociology at the University of Toronto. He has published extensively in the areas of racial/ethnic residential patterns and ethnic businesses. His recent review paper on multiethnic cities appeared in the *Annual Review of Sociology*. Recent publications include *Inside the Mosaic* published by University of Toronto Press and *Chinese Ethnic Business* (with Chiu Luk) published by Routledge. Email: fong@chass.utoronto.ca.

Gary G. Hamilton is a Professor of Sociology and of International Studies at the University of Washington. He specializes in historical/comparative sociology, economic sociology, and organizational sociology. He also specializes in Asian societies, with a particular emphasis on Chinese societies. He is an author of numerous articles and books, including most recently *Emergent Economies, Divergent Paths, Economic Organization and International Trade in South Korea and Taiwan* (with Robert Feenstra) (Cambridge University Press, 2006) and *Commerce and Capitalism in Chinese Societies* (London: Routledge, 2006). Email: ggh@u.washington.edu.

Ho Tsai-Man is a Post-doctoral fellow in the Centre of Asian Studies, University of Hong Kong. She obtained her Ph.D. in Sociology at the Tunghai University, Taiwan. Her thesis tackled the transition and adaptation of a Taiwanese firm from a small and medium-sized scale to a giant supplier with the move of assembly lines to the Chinese mainland and of financial capital in the Hong Kong stock market. Her research interest includes globalization and its impact on Asia, and the development of capitalism in Chinese Societies. She is currently working together with other team members on a research project of three eminent families, namely the Rong, Gu (Koo), and Ho Tung families that have created business dynasties in the Chinese mainland, Taiwan, and

Hong Kong respectively. She is in particular interested in the dynamics between the various institutional conditions and the development of these three families. Email: tsaimanh@hkucc.hku.hk.

HSIN-HUANG MICHAEL HSIAO is the Executive Director of the Center for Asia-Pacific Area Studies (CAPAS) and Research Fellow of the Institute of Sociology, Academia Sinica, and Professor of Sociology, National Taiwan University. He has currently devoted his research efforts to civil society and new democracies, changing faces of middle classes in Asia, *Taishang* (Taiwan businessmen) in Southeast Asia, local sustainable development, and Hakka identity in Taiwan and Southeast Asia. His most recent books include: *Civil Society and Democratization in East Asia* (co-editor, in Japanese), *The Frontiers of Southeast Asia and Pacific Studies* (editor), *Capital Cities in Asia-Pacific: Primacy and Diversity* (co-editor), *Asian New Democracies: The Philippines, South Korea and Taiwan Compared* (editor), *The Social History of Social Movements in Taiwan since 1980s* (co-author, in Chinese), *The Social History of the Dynamics of Environment and Society in Taiwan since 1980s* (co-author, in Chinese), and *The Changing Faces of the Middle Classes in Asia-Pacific* (editor), among others. He also received the Distinguished Alumni Award from The University at Buffalo in 2005. Email: michael@gate.sinica.edu.tw.

KAO CHENG-SHU is Professor of Sociology at Tunghai University in Taiwan. He is also Vice Chairman of the Board of Trustees at Feng-Chia University in Taiwan. He specializes in sociological theory, historical sociology, and the sociology of Chinese economies. He is the founding director and a continuing associate of the Institute of East Asian Societies and Economies at Tunghai University. The Institute is the location of the most extensive archive of interviews with Taiwanese businesspeople. He is the author of many books and articles, including most recently *The Boss's Wife* (in Chinese) (Taipei: Lien Chin Publishing, 1999). Email: kao@thu.edu.tw.

KU CHUNG-HWA is Professor of Sociology at the Department of Sociology, National Chengchi University in Taipei (Taiwan), and also the Director of the Center of Third Sector in the same university. His endeavour is not confined to academic research, but extends to concern with public issues. Beside the teaching job, he volunteers to work in many non-profit organizations such as Citizen Congress Watch and National Association for the Promotion of Community University.

Professor Ku is especially interested in the sociological theory of Max Weber, and he is known as an expert in the research fields of civil society and non-profit organization. He has published books and articles about sociological theory, social capital and the development of the third sector in Taiwan. Email: chku@nccu.edu.tw.

KUNG I-CHUN is a sociologist and Professor of the Graduate Institute of Southeast Asian Studies at the National Chi Nan University, Taiwan. She is the author of *Immigrant State and Native Society: The Formation of Social Base of KMT State in Taiwan-1950–1969* (1998, in Chinese) and *Stepping Out: The Social Formation of Taiwanese Business in Southeast Asia* (2005, in Chinese). Email: ickung@ncnu.edu.tw.

NAN LIN is the Oscar L. Tang Family Professor of Sociology at Duke University. He is also an Academician and Distinguished Research Fellow at Academia Sinica, Taiwan, and member of the Sociological Research Association. He was formerly Vice President, the American Sociological Association, and Director of the Asian/Pacific Studies Institute at Duke. He holds honorary professorships at Nankai University, Renmin University, Fudan University, Tianjin Academy of Social Sciences, and Shanghai Academy of Social Sciences. His research interests include social capital, social networks, stratification and mobility, stress and coping, and Chinese societies. He is the author of *Social Capital: A Theory of Social Structure and Action* (Cambridge University Press 2001) and editor of *Social Capital: Theory and Research* with Karen Cook and Ronald S. Burt (Aldine de Gruyter 2001) and *Social Capital: An International Research Program* with Bonnie Erickson (Oxford University Press 2008). Email: nanlin@duke.edu.

SUN WENBIN is Honorary Research Fellow at the Centre of Asian Studies, University of Hong Kong, and is working at Central Policy Unit of the Government of the Hong Kong Special Administrative Region as Senior Researcher. Her major research interests cover areas related to the development of the private sector in the Post-Mao China, Chinese family enterprises in the Mainland, Hong Kong and Taiwan, and entrepreneurship. She received her degrees at the University of Bristol in Sociology, and since published a number of articles in the development of private enterprise in contemporary China, and comparative studies of family enterprises in the Chinese Mainland and Hong Kong. Email: wbsun@cpu.gov.hk.

JONATHAN UNGER, a sociologist, is Director of the Contemporary China Centre at the Australian National University. He edited *The China Journal* from 1987 through 2005. His research interests include rural social and political change, social stratification, family life, education, industrial relations, and associational activity. He has published more than a dozen books about China, including *Education Under Mao: Class and Competition in Canton Schools* (Columbia University Press, 1982); *Chen Village Under Mao and Deng* (co-authored with Anita Chan and Richard Madsen) (University of California Press, 1992); and *The Transformation of Rural China* (M.E. Sharpe, 2002). Email: Jonathan.Unger@anu.edu.au.

WANG HONG-ZEN is Professor and Director of the Graduate Institute of Sociology at the National Sun Yat-sen University in Kaohsiung, Taiwan. He has been working on ties between Vietnam and Taiwan since 1999. His research has focused on overseas investment, industrial relations, ethnic relations and recently on migrant worker and marriage migration issues. His paper co-authored with Australian National University's Dr. Anita Chan "The Impact of the State on Workers' Conditions—Comparing Taiwanese Factories in China and Vietnam" is awarded by *Pacific Affairs* the William L. Holland Prize. Currently he is working on the impact of global corporate social responsibility on industrial relations in Vietnam and China. Email: hongzen@gmail.com.

WU XIAOGANG is Associate Professor of Social Science in the Hong Kong University of Science and Technology (HKUST), and Research Affiliate of the Population Studies Center at the University of Michigan, Ann Arbor. His research interests include social stratification and mobility, education, labor markets and economic sociology, and statistical methods. His current work attempts to link the social mobility process with stratification outcomes and to provide a synthesis on the source/mechanism of inequality. He received his Ph.D. in Sociology from the University of California, Los Angeles, and has previously published in *American Journal of Sociology*, *American Sociological Review*, *Social Forces*, and *Demography*. He was the recipient of the National Academy of Education/Spencer Post-doctoral Fellowship (2006–2007), the Research Paper Award on Asia (2006) and the Asian and Asian American Early Career Award (2007) from the American Sociological Association. Email: sowu@ust.hk.

SPECIAL FOCUS: CHINESE CAPITALISMS

GUEST EDITOR: CHU YIN-WAH

# INTRODUCTION: FROM DESTITUTE TO *XIAO KANG* (WELL-BEING), MAYBE *DA GUO* (GREAT NATION): EXPLORATIONS OF CHINESE CAPITALISMS AND CAPITALIST ACTIONS*

Chu Yin-wah[1]

Issues pertaining to the emergence of capitalism in China have captured the attention of scholars for generations. Some have examined why, despite the prevalence of commerce and the emergence of banks, trademarks, and other seemingly capitalist institutions, a fully fledged capitalist system has not emerged in the country. Others have queried the Western centered concept of capitalism and contended that Chinese business actions are no less capitalistic in essence. Amid these debates, China's religion, imperial rule, state-bureaucracy, legal system, trade, commerce, industrial enterprise, currency, population, migration, and war-making have been subjected to detailed scrutiny. All of these have oftentimes intertwined with the nation's quest for wealth and political prowess. The rise of the so-called East Asian economic miracles fueled the debates in the 1970s, and so has the emergence of new theoretical perspectives or historical data. The literature is extensive; it is beyond the capacity of this short introduction (not to mention me) to recapitulate the empirically rich and theoretically complex debates.[2]

Of the five essays collected in this special issue, Ku Chung-hwa's is the only one to allude to the longstanding debates about why China has failed to develop capitalism on its own. Most contributors have

* Reference to this article should be made as follows: Chu, Yin-wah. 2007. "From Destitute to *Xiao Kang* (Well-Being), Maybe *Da Guo* (Great Nation): Explorations of Chinese Capitalisms and Capitalist Actions."

[1] The guest editor would like to thank Miss Beatrice Oi-yeung Lam for her highly competent editorial assistance and Miss Selina Wan for helping to translate Ku Chung-hwa's essay.

[2] Ku Chung-hwa's essay in this special issue alludes to some of these debates. Interested readers may like to refer to the works of Yu Ying-shi (1987), Susan Mann (1987), Bin R. Wong (1997), Liu Kwang-ching (1962), Philip Huang (1980), Gary Hamilton (1985), Peter L. Berger and Hsin-huang M. Hsiao (1988), Ambrose King (1978), Siu-lun Wong (1988), Alvin Y. So (1986).

chosen *not* to revisit these debates, and concentrate on present day mainland China or Taiwan and address issues emerging from contemporary theories of economic sociology or the political economy of development. The following will highlight the main arguments of the five essays, after which an effort will be made to compare their viewpoints on three themes: the relative importance of global or national forces, the relevance of the state and social relations, and the political implications of China's rise.

Lin Nan starts with an evaluation of whether China has developed the right institutions to warrant being labeled capitalist, goes on to identify the unique characteristics of China's capitalism, and concludes by examining the political and theoretical challenges posed by the rise of capitalism in the country. While contending that much of the "China-as-threat" discourse articulated in the American media has been mistaken, Lin argues that China's capitalism, characterized by the "state as capitalist" and the importance of social relations, has posed a challenge to accepted theories of capitalism in the West. Ku Chung-hwa's strategy of addressing Chinese capitalism is vastly different from Lin's. He seeks to reexamine Max Weber's China thesis in the light of China's recent economic expansion and, at the same time, evaluate the nature of China's capitalism with Weber's thought. While arguing that China is without a doubt capitalist, he is wary of its inability to cultivate a "spirit of capitalism" or the ethical political underpinning of capitalist actions. Gary G. Hamilton and Cheng-shu Kao have very different concerns. Their point of departure is the emergence of what they call a "demand-responsive economy" of which Taiwan is a prime example. Through the skilful analysis of seven-digit trade statistics collected by the U.S. customs service, astute examination of institutional changes in the U.S., and in-depth interviews with Taiwanese businessmen, they demonstrate that Taiwan's capitalist industrialization (inclusive of its internal economy and the effort of its people to make money) has been shaped by the sourcing efforts of global retailers such as J. C. Penny, Nike, Walmart, and the like. Equally concerned with the global dimension of Taiwan's capitalist development, Hsin-Huang Michael Hsiao, Kung I-Chun and Wang Hong-zen argue that due to Taiwan's semi-peripheral status, its businessmen can only adopt a "defensive globalization strategy". The details of such a strategy, including the extension of production networks and labour deployment tactics, are then illustrated through drawing on research conducted in Malaysia, Vietnam, and other Southeast Asian countries. Finally, Ho

C. Tsaiman and Sun Wenbin discuss Taiwan's capitalist development through an in-depth case study of the Koo family. In particular, they delineate the complicated interrelationships between government policies to redefine property rights, their implications for business risk-taking, and the entrepreneurial endeavours initiated by each generation of the Koo family as both a result of their bold innovations and the adept cultivation of social networks.

These five essays put forth complex empirical observations, nuanced theoretical generalizations, and provocative conclusions, the richness of which defies effort to summarize or compare them in any simple way. The following will nonetheless highlight a few points of contention among the essays. In so doing, I hope to arouse greater interest among readers and hence their craving to savor the essays.

### *Capitalist Development: Global or National?*

The notions of the "international division of labour", "global production network", "global commodity chain", and "globalization" have been very much in vogue within the social sciences in the last few decades. Some of these concepts were coined to make sense of the political economy of less developed countries; others were put forth to account for changes in the world at large. They contrast in their own ways with the ideas of "modernization" or "globalization skeptic", which maintain the fundamental significance of national forces, be they social, economic, or political. Although none of these concepts or approaches has been developed specifically for Chinese cases, they inform some of the essays collected in this special issue and in general constitute the backdrop against which all of the essays can be read.[3]

Despite differences in their political orientation, Hamilton and Kao, and Hsiao, Kung and Wang, give much weight to global processes in their essays. For Hamilton and Kao, Taiwan and other globally-engaged economies, such as China, are instances of the demand-responsive economy. Global retailers that source worldwide for consumer products

[3] However, few authors in this special issue consider the influence of global or national forces to be absolute; more often than not they are perceived to work dialectically. Also of interest is the fact that in their earlier studies of Taiwan's capitalist development Gary G. Hamilton and Michael H. H. Hsiao placed much more emphasis on national factors such as social networks and the developmental state.

have emerged in the United States since around 1965. These powerful retailers have not only provided an opportunity for Taiwan to industrialize, but have also shaped the momentum and internal structure of Taiwan's capitalist expansion (in particular, the predominance of small-and-medium enterprises, their specialization in "batch production", and strategy of networked expansion) as well as the "make-money" mentality among Taiwanese businessmen. Hsiao, Kung and Wang adopt a broadly world-systemic perspective and argue that Taiwan's "passive and defensive globalization strategy" since the 1980s has been shaped by the island-state's semi-peripheral status and the need of its businessmen to stay competitive. Affected by the cost increase associated with the Plaza Agreement, small-and-medium enterprises in Taiwan had to transplant their production networks to selected ASEAN countries and later mainland China. Adopting a dialectical mode of reasoning, these authors contend that investments in Southeast Asia also enable the Taiwanese businessmen to learn about new business models, intensify labour control, and expand their scale of production, which in combination with their R&D capacity has made them truly global competitors that cannot easily be replaced by more recent and cheaper competitors such as those from mainland China.

Though not denying the importance of global processes, Lin Nan, Ku Chung-hwa, Ho and Sun pay more attention to national factors in their essays. Ho and Sun's focus on entrepreneurship and the ways in which it has been shaped by state policies is only too obvious. As for Lin Nan, the weight he places on national factors can be seen from his definition of capitalism, view of the processes driving China's transition to capitalism, and the unique features of capitalism in China. Specifically, Lin defines capitalism as "a set of arrangements of social institutions that sustains the production, reproduction, and accumulation of capital" (p. 16). In his opinion, these institutions include calculating capitalists, free markets, wage labour, an expanding system, and a strong and supportive state. Despite the global reach of capitalism, as is implied in the idea of an expanding system, Lin's analysis of capitalism is anchored at the national level. For him, China's transition to capitalism has been made possible by the Communist state, which is the only state in China's history to have legitimized capital accumulation. It has also played a most crucial role in initiating reforms in various domains and actively taking up the role of a capitalist. Hence, Lin suggests that China's capitalism is distinguished by the dual features of the state as capitalist *and* the significance of social relations in coordinating the various institutions.

Finally, Ku Chung-hwa's concern with national forces is in part an outcome of his strategy to juxtapose China's recent experience with Max Weber's "China Thesis". In following Weber's footsteps, Ku examines the preconditions for the rise of capitalism in China. He does so by highlighting the changes initiated by the Communist state, not only after 1978 but also in the first thirty years of its rule. Significant developments include the transformation of the patrimonial bureaucracy, the launch of the Cultural Revolution, and the implementation of the one-child policy. In following Weber's footsteps, Ku also argues against a one-sided emphasis on material institutions. In this connection, he draws our attention to the flimsiness of interpersonal trust, stark social inequality, the suppression of civil liberty, and the Communist regime's heralding of a nationalist ideology as a means to subdue social discontent, which together illustrate the paucity of the development of a "spirit of capitalism" in China that is commensurate with its accumulation of material wealth.

### *State and Social Relations* (Guanxi)

A second major theme touched upon by the five essays is the complex interrelationship between the state and social relations and how together they have shaped the trajectory of development of Chinese capitalisms. Hamilton and Kao, Ho and Sun, and Hsiao, Kung and Wang have slightly different understandings of social relations, though they share the idea that such relations provide a valuable resource for individual businessmen to deal with imperatives imposed by the state. In their earlier works, Hamilton and Kao conceptualized and examined in great detail how state-society relationships in Taiwan have provided a fertile ground for the emergence of *guanxi*-based business networks. Because of the wide accessibility of their earlier works, they do not repeat their discussion of state authority and social networks in this essay. Instead, they present a few detailed case studies to illustrate how the Taiwanese people have mobilized social networks woven together by family, school-mates, co-workers, friendships and other socially-sanctioned ties to start and expand their businesses and capture the opportunities presented by the global retailers whose presence in Taiwan has in turn been made possible by institutional conditions that include changes in state policies and social situations.

As for Ho and Sun, their study of the Koo family suggests that while entrepreneurship is related to an individual's ability to innovate and take risk, it is also deeply social and political in nature. The authority of the state to define (and re-define) property rights is an important factor determining the legitimacy and hence risk level of an innovation. At the same time, social networks provide an important means by which to gain early access to economic and political information, and hence opportunities for new ventures.

In a way similar to Hamilton and Kao, Hsiao, Kung and Wang depart from the main concern of their earlier research: Taiwan's developmental state. In their essay here they investigate the influence of social relations, particularly those that involve cultural/ethnic identity, on the extension of production networks and the practice of labour deployment. On the one hand, they find that Taiwanese businessmen have relied on social relations to transplant their production networks developed at home to Southeast Asian countries. Apart from the importance of trust, the lack of possible synergy with local Southeast Asian or ethnic Chinese firms—a result of the industrial policies of Southeast Asian states—has also exerted its constraint. On the other hand, they find an unambiguous correlation between ethnic/cultural identity and the individual's position in the corporate hierarchy: Taiwanese at the top, ethnic Chinese with Taiwan connections serving as high-level administrators, ethnic Chinese and mainland Chinese with no Taiwan connections working as mid- to low-level managers, and local ethnic groups or migrant workers labouring on the shop-floor.

Ku Chung-hwa does not provide an explicit analysis of social relations (*guanxi*) in his essay. However, it is arguable that he holds a vision of the relationships between the state and social relations quite similar to authors of the three essays just examined. That is to say, at the same time that social relations serve the Chinese as a buffer to state domination, they can also be mobilized to influence state actions. However, not only has a strong civil society failed to take root among the bourgeoisie in contemporary China, social relations and trust founded on familiarity have also dwindled as a result of the 1949 socialist revolution, social mobilization thereafter, and the current effort to pursue wealth at all costs.

Among the five essays, Lin Nan provides the most systematic treatment and the most sanguine view of the relationships between state and social relations. As mentioned earlier, he considers China's capitalism to be characterized by the dual features of the state as capitalist and the integrating function of social relations. Although "in many capitalist societies the state also operates enterprises considered critical or essential for national survival... seldom have we seen a state itself acting as a capitalist entity competing in the domestic and international markets, as we are witnessing in China" (p. 38). Furthermore, instead of seeing a segregation of social relations from economic relations, Lin contends that social relations have served as the basis of economic activities in both Chinese and non-Chinese societies, though in the former case "relationship is everything" (p. 45). Most significantly, he differs from the other authors in postulating a close and synergetic relationship between the state and social relations in China. Specifically, he suggests that the country is moving toward "planned capitalism" wherein the government, labour, and industry will join hands to plan long-range initiatives. The Chinese state's exercise of adjustment and control (*tiao-kung*), in his view, demonstrates Peter Evans' idea of "embedded autonomy" and showcases how an assertive developmental state can adeptly combine planning and control with networking that goes beyond corporate and individual entities. Lin's vision of the Chinese state and his application of Evan's concept are theoretically and politically provocative, to say the very least. It is nonetheless a bold idea worthy of contemplation and careful scrutiny.

### *Chinese Capitalism: Political Ramifications*

Is there anything Chinese about this capitalism? Hamilton and Kao, Ho and Sun, and Hsiao, Kung and Wang do not expend much effort on exploring the issue. In the context of their essays, the most distinct characteristic of capitalism in Taiwan is perhaps that it is being driven by an already developed global economy, the country's semi-peripheral status, and its tortuous political history. Save for these, the capitalist practices so emerged are not much different from those of other latecomers to capitalism.

The two papers that focus on mainland China, however, devote much attention to the issue, with totally different conclusions. As noted above, Lin Nan considers Chinese capitalism to possess two unique characteristics: the state as capitalist and the importance of social relations. These two characteristics are considered to intertwine with the issues of civil liberty, political democracy, and social justice. In the first place, for many Western observers, one anomaly of capitalism in China is its departure from Western-style democracy. However, Lin contends that "empirical studies of capitalist societies have . . . uncovered diversity and differentiation in the actual institutional arrangements" (p. 25) and, in his view there is no such a thing as an ideal capitalist society. In the second place, Lin considers that China is seeking to develop a unique capitalist system that combines rapid growth with social stability, social justice, and gradually greater civil liberty. Although the fact that the Chinese state acts as a capitalist has its drawbacks, including the lack of checks and balances and the threat of nepotism, Lin believes that "the population is by and large supportive of the present system" (p. 39). Economic growth has benefited the majority of the population and most people are concerned with getting rich. Furthermore, the government has mobilized a nationalist ideology, and the general public tends to agree that only a strong and united China can face the severe international challenges posed by the United States and its allies. Above all, Lin contends that China is moving from "command capitalism" to "planned capitalism" whereby "government, labour, and industry jointly plan long-range initiatives" (p. 55). The unique characteristics of Chinese capitalism are precisely the means for the Chinese state and Party to exercise adjustment and control (*tiao-kung*) to ensure social and economic stability and justice. State control of critical sectors, the role of unions in collective bargaining, the new contract law, and plans to provide better rural medical care and financial assistance to students can all be seen as benchmarks of the emerging "planned capitalism".

Ku Chung-hwa has completely different observations to offer. He finds it shocking that socialist China can tolerate a level of inequality that even capitalist Taiwan would consider obscene. He deems it sad that the mutual trust built on familiarity and preexisting social networks should come into imminent decline in China. The lack of concern for the advancement of civil society and political democracy among mainland Chinese capitalists deeply disappoints him. In other words, he simply fails to observe the so-called joint effort of the government, labour, and industry that Lin Nan considers to be emerging in China. Like Lin, however, he observes repeated attempts on the part of the Chinese government to mobilize a nationalist ideology. Similarly, he observes widespread interest in making profits among the Chinese populace. But instead of seeing these as proof of social justice and stability in the country, Ku considers the nationalist ideology to be a tranquillizer to subdue popular resentment and a sense of injustice. He also considers the exclusive concern with making money to be a mark of the inadequacy of China's capitalism. To be specific, it is a capitalism that emerges exclusively on the basis of material institutions, which in the case of China have been made possible rather ironically by the socialist revolution and subsequent mass mobilizations that undermine traditional social relationships and reformed traditional political institutions. The void in the spiritual domain, in Ku's view, cannot be filled by the commercial promotion of Confucianism or other forms of "traditional culture". By reminding us of Max Weber's criticism of the politically immature German bourgeoisie, their yearning for the protection of a "new Caesar", and the tragedy of Nazi Germany that emerged a decade after Weber's death, Ku bodes the danger of the Communist Party's attempt to maintain its rule by mobilizing nationalist ideology.

Whose argument is more plausible? Lin Nan's recommendation that one should not too readily accept the American media's attempt to demonize China is correct enough. However, his sanguine reading of China's recent development and his tendency to accept at face value the policies of the Chinese government is unwarranted. Ku Chung-hwa's historical-analytical reading of China's recent history is appealing. His cautions about the extant inequalities in China are also more plausible than Lin's optimistic account. His caveat on the underdevelopment of the "spirit of capitalism" in China, especially the ethical political dimension of capitalist actions, is well taken. However, has it been proved beyond doubt that social relations founded on familiarity have been shattered altogether in China or that the Chinese bourgeoisie are completely devoid of civic consciousness? A recollection of the participants in the June 4th incident in 1989 will suggest otherwise. Similarly, is the concern with "profit-making" exclusive to people in mainland China? Hamilton and Kao describe the mentality of present day Taiwanese businessmen as being concerned with making money, both for themselves and for their business partners. Hsiao, Kung and Wang also report how Taiwanese businessmen have declared that human rights are a luxury for a people with low per capita income. In the light of these, one cannot rule out the possibility that the exclusive concern with making money may one day turn into the noble search for social and political betterment of everybody. History sometimes takes us by surprise. There is no guarantee that the quest for well-being (*xiao kang*) cannot one day become the foundation for the pursuit of a truly great nation (*da guo*).

## *References*

Berger, Peter L. and Hsin-Huang M. Hsiao (eds.) 1988. *In Search of an East Asian Development Model*. New Brunswick: Transaction Books.
Hamilton, Gary G. 1985. "Why no Capitalism in China?" *Journal of Developing Societies*
Huang, Philip C. C. 1980. *The Development of Underdevelopment in China: a symposium*. White Plains: Sharpe.
King, Ambrose Y. 1978. *Cong Chuan Tong Dao Xian Dai*. Taipei: Shi Bao.
Liu, Kwang-ching. 1962. *Anglo-American Steamship Rivalry in China, 1862–1874*. Cambridge: Harvard University Press.
Mann, Susan. 1987. *Local Merchants and the Chinese Bureaucracy, 1750–1950*. Stanford: Stanford University Press.
So, Alvin Y. 1986. *The South China Silk District: local historical transformation and world-system theory*. Albany: SUNY.
Wong, Bin R. 1997. *China Transformed: historical change and the limits of European experience*. Ithaca: Cornell University Press.
Wong, Siu-lun. 1988. *Emigrant Entrepreneurs: Shanghai industrialists in Hong Kong*. Hong Kong: Oxford University Press.
Yu, Ying-shi. 1987. *Zhongguo Jin Shi Zong Jiao Lun Li yu Shang Ren Jing shen*. Taipei: Lianjin.

# EMERGING CHINESE CAPITALISM AND ITS THEORETICAL AND GLOBAL SIGNIFICANCE*

NAN LIN[1]

## *Introduction*

In this essay, I argue that China hosts an emerging capitalist society. Studying the nature of this capitalism will allow us to evaluate and reassess the definition and theories of capitalism—a pivotal notion in the contemporary explanation of economic growth and associated ideas such as freedom and democracy. It will also afford us a better understanding of how this capitalism could impact the world economically, politically, and socially. Finally, it may help to identify clues about the mechanisms that are guiding China into the future. Specifically I will make the following arguments. First, capitalism consists of a set of social institutions that sustain the production, accumulation and reproduction of capital and these institutions include: calculating capitalists, free markets, wage labour, an expansive system, and a strong and supportive state. Theories ranging from self-interest—the psychological motive; exploitative reproduction—the sociopolitical motive; to institutional enticement—the cultural motive; and the networking imperative—the social motive: and they collectively explain how these institutions are coordinated. Second, China today strongly meets these requirements as a capitalist state. Capitalism in China, further, exhibits two relatively unique features: the state as capitalists and social relations (guanxi) embedding economic activities. Finally, I will consider theoretical implications of these institutional features for

---

* Reference to this article should be made as follows: Lin, Nan 2007. "Emerging Chinese Capitalism and its Theoretical and Global Significance".

[1] Portions of the essay have been presented at the conference "The Global Futures of World Regions," Seoul, South Korea, September 28, 2006; at the World Forum on China, Shanghai, China, September 22, 2006; and at the annual meeting of the American Sociological Association, New York, August 12, 2007. I am grateful for comments and suggestions from Yanjie Bian, David Brady, Choyun Hsu, Lisa Keister, Steve McDonald, William Parish and Joon-mo Son.

conceptualising and theorising capitalism, and for understanding global and domestic developments.

### *The Rise of China*

In January 2007, *Time Magazine* proclaimed the dawn of the Chinese century. While seen as premature by some, the rise of China as an economic power was not unanticipated. For a few scholars who have examined longer historical trends (Wong 1997; Frank 1998), the rise of the West in the past two centuries was the abnormality: for more than ten millennia the East has been the leading world power. Due to a combination of circumstances that occurred in the East and in the West (for Frank, the discovery of gold and silver in the Americas allowed Western economies to appropriate materials and wealth from China), the West took the lead in the world economy in the eighteenth century, but that is only a temporary change. Yet even though this perspective has gained some empirical validity, the causes for the anticipated re-emergence of the East are unspecified or unclear.

The rise of China has also been anticipated by scholars who have analysed Asian economic miracles for the past three decades. In the early 1990s, proponents of the "snowballing" or the "flying geese" process also projected that following the rise of Japan, and then the four tigers (Singapore, Hong Kong, South Korea, and Taiwan), China would inevitably join the Asian trend. But the process hardly anticipate or explain the speed and velocity of China's rise.

In less than two decades, China's per capita GDP has risen from less than 200 U.S. dollars to over 1,500 U.S. dollars. The poverty rate has dropped from over 60 percent to about 10–15 percent. During this period China lifted 300 million of its people out of absolute poverty (based on the one U.S. dollar a day threshold, set in 1993), even though 200 million remain below the poverty line (*Business Week* January 3, 2007). Xinhua reported that the number of impoverished people without adequate food and clothing declined from 250 million in 1978 to 23.6 million at the end of 2005. It claimed that the percentage of the population living in poverty had fallen from 30 percent to less than 3 percent.

According to the World Bank (2005) and the World Development Indicators, China's consumption is 29.7 percent of the world's rice, 24.4 percent of soy oil, 31 percent of cotton, 33 percent of tin, 29 percent of zinc, 29 percent of iron ore, 31.5 percent of steel and 12.6 percent of energy (coal and oil). Goldman Sachs (May 2007) has estimated that China will match the United States in GDP (in purchasing power parity terms) by 2020, and it may well become the largest economy in the world (in actual market exchange rates) by 2027 (*The Economist* 2007a).

During this short span of time, China has become a major manufacturer, consumer in the global economy, a major polluter, a furious competitor for energy resources, and a significant exporter of goods, services, and manpower. These trends have obvious impacts and consequences for the rest of the world: intellectuals, politicians, businesses, and the media have all been busy contemplating and analysing responses to the challenges posed.

Grave concerns about the rise of China go beyond its economic challenges. China does not seem to adhere to the ideals of freedom, democracy, and the free market that are considered central to economic development. As recently as ten years ago, some still hope that the Chinese political regime would become unstable and either "transition" into a Western-style democracy or collapse altogether (Chang 2001). The new "superpower" has clearly shaken the ideals and social order, real or imagined, of most Western observers and scholars. A hierarchy based on any number of economic and political criteria has been disrupted. Arrighi (2005) rightly pointed out that the rise of China is "a fundamental subversion of the very pyramidal structure of the hierarchy."

The phenomenal and sustained economic growth of China over the past two decades has raised fundamental issues about whether the economy is properly capitalistic, and if so whether that capitalism poses ideological and theoretical challenges to the norms of Western economics. Hence, I will (1) outline the received and updated definition and theories of capitalism; (2) argue that what is going on in China meets those conditions; (3) delineate the specific features of Chinese capitalism and how they both help and hinder its development; (4) discuss the implications of these features for the received wisdom on capitalism; (5) point out the implications of Chinese capitalism for the global system; and (6) sort through the confusion about the nature of the mechanisms that will lead China into the future.

### *What is Capitalism?*

The term "capitalism" may have first been mentioned by Marx when he questioned whether Russia could bypass the "capitalist" stage of development, but it is an intellectual invention of the 20th century, as Sombart (1902) may have been the first to properly use the term. To understand capitalism we first need to be clear about what capital is (see Lin 2001a, chapter 1). Marx identified it as part of the surplus value generated in the production, distribution, and marketing of commodities. Surplus value becomes possible because of the difference between labour cost (use value) and the value of the good produced (exchange value). When part of this surplus value is reinvested in the production of the same or different commodities in anticipation of generating more surplus value, it is called capital. The process by which capital is invested, reinvested, and accumulated is called capitalism.

More specifically, capitalism can be defined as *a set of arrangements of social institutions that sustains the production, reproduction, and accumulation of capital*. It is intrinsically social in that it both describes a social process and implicates social elements (institutions). Much of the historical analysis of capitalism has focused on the transition from feudalism to capitalism as experienced in Europe and North America in the past four or five centuries and has identified coalition processes among urban elites (e.g. intellectuals, nobles and merchants) and rural peasants, serfs and slaves in upending feudal systems and bringing in various capitalistic institutions (see Brenner 1976; Dobb 1947; Goldstone 1987; Gould 1987; Hill 1972; Hilton 1978; Kriedte and Schlumbohm 1981; Lachmann 1987, 1989; North and Thomas 1973; Tilly and Tilly 1971; Walzer 1965). The extensive discussion about the nature, logic, and history of capitalism has identified fundamental and nearly consensual, but incomplete, institutions as essential to capitalism (see examples in DiMaggio and Powell 1991; Heilbroner 1985; March 1989; Meyer and Rowan 1977; Miller 2005; North 1990; Williamson 1975, 1985; Zucker 1988). Heilbroner (1985:34–35) argued that capitalism was "not a material thing but a process that uses material things as moments in its continuously dynamic existence. It is, moreover, a social process, not a physical one." What, then, are the major institutions that are implicated? Integrating diverse and rich discussions, I identify the following institutions.

### *Calculating Capitalists*

First, there are the actors who engage in the generation and regeneration of capital—*the capitalists*. They are distinguished from waged labour. Labourers are mostly excluded from engagement in capital production and reproduction, primarily because when they claim a wage they forfeit their claim to the products and the means of production (property rights). Neither are wealthy actors automatically capitalists: there are many sources of wealth, such as inheritance or even work that does not involve reinvestment in production. As Adam Smith (1937) pointed out, it was the individual effort to pursue material benefit that promoted free enterprise and the market system, the foundations of the wealth of the entire community, or the nation. Even though Smith himself did not use the term "capitalism," his theory of self-interest and rational choice laid the foundation for much discussion about capitalism in the 20th century.

There is some paradox to being a capitalist. On the one hand, there is the drive to produce and reproduce wealth, part of which allows a certain lifestyle and leisure time for enjoyment. On the other hand, there is restraint on the use of wealth for pleasure, as part of it is reinvested in the capital production process. These dual characteristics, the drive for profit and asceticism, reflect in part the ever-calculating personality of the capitalist.

### *Free Markets*

Second, there are *markets* in which production, distribution, and consumption exchanges can take place. These markets form a circular network; each relies on and propels the others (see Lin 2001a, chapter 1). A production market requires an ample supply of material resources and human resources (the labour). The commodities produced must be distributed to consumers, and there must be markets where consumers can find the commodities. Efficient production markets generate commodities at a use value that can be sold at a higher exchange value (price) to produce surplus value in the distribution and consumption markets. Exchanges in these markets are further facilitated by financial markets which raise capital, buffer risk and expedite trade (through loans, stocks, bonds, derivatives, hedge funds, etc.).

All three types of market are never entirely free in the sense that each is dictated by the negotiation of prices between sellers and buyers and involves control or manipulation by these or other actors. A pure free market would inevitably fail, as actors would deny other actors access to resources, control of information, and so on to serve their self-interests and maximise their relative advantages. Contracts, organisations, and informal networking, which always exist in markets, inevitably reduce the freedom of the market. Government regulations, such as taxation, which was created to protect public goods such as roads and a safe environment, and to prevent fraud, further reduce the freedom of the market. Nonetheless, in an ideal and efficient market system, such "restrictions" are assumed to be kept at a minimum, and entries and exits are entirely voluntary and transparent.

### *Wage Labour*

A third necessary institution in capitalism is *wage labour*. Capitalism as a social system differs from other systems in that it cannot rely on free (or slave) labour; it allows the claim of "proper" compensation for labour: wages are paid to the labour force for work. However, this transaction favors the capitalist. Commodities tend to generate exchange values that exceed production costs. Labourers forfeit their claim to the means of production and produced commodities (Heilbroner 1985). The labourer has no property rights whatsoever in the production process, beyond wage and compensation for their labour time and effort. This peculiar transaction is, of course, essential for the production and accumulation of capital.

### *An Expanding System*

Fourth, capital accumulation dictates *an ever-expanding system*. The drive for profit requires capitalists to seek and expand the production of commodities and to generate profits through extensive and extending distribution and consumption markets. The process of production—in which costs must be paid for the labour and materials—and profit generation in the distribution and consumption markets become a relentless and continuous circulation and form the basis for competition. Thus "capital itself introduces a form of social war" (Heilbroner 1985:57). Likewise, Schumpeter stated that "capitalism stands and falls with entrepreneurship: if capitalism continuously presents new opportunities for profit it will thrive, otherwise it will die out" ((1946) 1951:81–86).

Expansion can be achieved through commodity diversification, increased production resources including labour, extended distribution channels and chains, ever-stimulated desires for commodities, and new consumers. Therefore capitalism, by definition, must continue to expand. Technological innovations are a necessity, as is the containment of production costs. But ultimately, capitalism needs ever-larger markets for resources, including labour, for production on one end, and for consumers on the other. Heilbroner stated, "Without the organising purpose of expansion, capital dissolves into material building blocks that are necessary but not sufficient to define its life purpose" (1985:26–37). Wallerstein (1979) pointed out that the essence of capitalism is in the capitalist's production of commodities for sale on the world market.

An expanding system presumably also overcomes the possible concern about a zero-sum game. By continuously expanding, collective wealth and therefore capital are increased. But the fact is that this expanding system creates an economic paradox. There has been continuing debate among economists as to whether economic growth or economic inequality should be a primary concern. By the expansion criterion described here, economic growth should have the priority. There is not necessarily any association (either positive or negative) between economic growth and income inequality, either theoretically or empirically. However, once economic growth becomes the priority, income inequality may persist or even increase. As will be seen later when looking at the historical data from China and other capitalist countries such as the United States, economic growth has been negatively associated with income equality over the last two decades.

### *A Strong and Supportive State*

Finally, there must be *a state—a governance institution* that is willing and capable of protecting, regulating, and promoting the coordination and functioning of capital accumulation, the markets, and wage labour. None of the institutions mentioned previously constitute a capitalist system by themselves, and there is no guarantee that they will simultaneously coordinate with one another. Some scholars have maintained that capitalism only needs a governance system that monitors the "natural" free market and allows it to function without interference or abuse. Rand ((1946) 1966), for example, stated that the only function of the government should be the task of protecting man's rights. In a capitalist system all human relationships should be voluntary.

Historical evidence, however, convincingly shows that to thrive, capitalism requires a strong governance system, and thus *a powerful state*. Some economists have admitted that the state intervention may be necessary for a backward economy to catch up and become a capitalist system (see, for example, Rosovsky 1961 on France, Germany and Russia; and Gerschenkron 1962 on Japan). However, analysis of broad historical data on capitalistic development demonstrates that a strong and supportive state is an essential ingredient for all capitalistic systems. Braudel (1977) stressed that capitalism, differing from a mere market system, triumphs only when it becomes identified with a powerful state. He cited the Italian city-states, Holland, and England as examples. The state guarantees that players follow the rules of the game. It ensures that the capitalists produce and reproduce commodities with acceptable practices of acquiring material resources and compensating labour. Commodities are channeled through distribution and consumption markets transparently and without price fixing, hoarding, or dumping. Also important is the state's role in arbitrating disputes over production, distribution, and consumption markets. While attempting to be even-handed, the state is ultimately responsible for protecting the capitalists so that capital accumulation can proceed (Johnson 1995).

Polanyi (1944; see also Polanyi, Arensberg, and Pearson 1957) made the essence of the state explicit. He identified the state and the market as the two central pillars of modern capitalism. To Polanyi, the two institutions are interconnected. The state plays a central role in determining the structure of property rights, the quality of financial institutions, and incentives for capital accumulation, investments, and entrepreneurship (see Heilbroner 1985 for elaboration). Of particular interest is the arbitration of disputes between capitalists and the labour. While in some capitalist states, unions are advocates of labour, the state is the ultimate arbitrator. It ensures that labourers never challenge capitalists for rights to the products of their labour and the means of production.

Many sociologists and political scientists have rightly stressed the significance of the state in modern industrialised societies, among them Wallerstein (1979), Evans (1995), Skocpal (1996), and Hobson (1997), Weiss (1998), Evans, Rueschemeyer, and Skocpal (2002). Historically, the United States government has not shied away from interfering with the market system to protect or save firms and industries. Some examples include its long-term farm protection policies, rescue of the automobile, steel and airline corporations, and international tariffs.

Examining the recent history of the United States, Fligstein (2005) pointed out that entrepreneurship and competition matter for the creation of new markets and industry but that they cannot occur without governments and stable social structures to support them. He showed that the U.S. government has directly affected market activities with laws and rules that determine tax policies, govern the use of equity and debt by corporations, regulate employment relations, enforce patents and property rights, and regulate competition or antitrust policy. It can act as a buyer of products and a provider of research and development funds to firms. It also makes rules that directly favor certain firms and particularly industries, often at the behest of the most powerful actors in those industries. The government, he pointed out, also built up public and private infrastructure that opened up possibility for new firms and industries to emerge. Heilbroner made this point clear:

> The state, both as defender and promoter of the economic realm, has played so prominent a role that even the most abstract scenarios of the system unwittingly assign it a central and indispensable place where they take as their unit of conceptual analysis *the state*.... Remove the regime of capital and the state would remain, although it might change dramatically; remove the state and the regime of capital would not last a day.... In this sense politics is prior to economics in that domination must precede exploitation.... All this mocks the conventional economic view that the public realm is somehow secondary or ancillary to the private realm, and that a market system can be adequately represented and even studied in models that omit the loss-absorbing, momentum-imparting political domain, with its curiously concealed economic functions. But it is precisely this concealment—the consequence of the fissioning of unitary empires into state and economy—that is another instance of the capacity of capitalism to enthrall and becloud the understanding of its members, in many respects the most powerful of the ways in which the nature of the system affects behaviour and belief (1985:105–6).

A strong state will protect a domestic market, protect capitalists, assure the supply of wage labour, create and implement rules for law and individual rights, secure networks and chains of trade, and advocate globalisation for the benefit of the domestic market and capitalists. It is a core element of capitalism. Yet, interestingly, the role of the state is largely absent or in the background in many economic analyses of capitalism.

*Contending Institutions: Private Property Rights and Democracy*

Two other institutions have also been associated with capitalism in scholarly literature: the private ownership of property and political freedom or democracy. The argument for the private ownership of property and its link to political development can be traced back to John Locke ((1764)1952). In the wake of the parliamentary struggle against the monarchy, Locke heralded the significance of the social contract whereby property rights must be spelt out and protected. Subsequent discussions extended this historically based argument into a broad argument for private ownership in a free or democratic society. Rand ((1946)1966), for example, defined capitalism as a social system based on the recognition of individual rights, including property rights, in which all property is privately owned.

However, the nature of property rights and its association with capitalism have remained equivocal. Property rights refer to a bundle of rights (Alchian and Demsetz 1973), including ownership, use rights, rights to transfer, and rights to exclude use by others (Heilbroner 1985). Some have argued that use rights rather than ownership are the central feature of property rights (Alchian 1965). Scholars have also argued that the exclusion of others from use rights rather than claims to property is more important. Others question the validity of private property rights in capitalism and suggest that public property rights (e.g., eminent domains) are essential for the production of public goods and infrastructure to benefit all.

Recently, De Soto (2000) directly linked private property rights (ownership) to capitalism or democracy. But evidence that private property rights produce more capitalist behaviour such as borrowing capital for investment remains unproven (*The Economist* 2006). Historically, capitalism has thrived with the ownership of the means of production but without the ownership of other properties such as land. Although Friedman (1962) hailed Hong Kong as a shining example of capitalism, the government owns all land and only grants allotments for private ownership in the New Territories under the Small House Policy.

The linking of political freedom or democracy to capitalism is also a rather recent intellectual formulation. Friedman probably made the first link, proclaiming "the role of competitive capitalism…as a system of economic freedom and a necessary condition for political freedom" (1962:13). But he also cautioned that "it is clearly possible to have economic arrangements that are fundamentally capitalist and political arrangements that are not free (1962:10). Subsequent discussions tend to forget this causal conjecture and even reverse the sequence so that, for some, democracy is now seen as a precedent or necessary ingredient of capitalism. There is little theoretical foundation or historical evidence that democracy leads to capitalism and, according to Heilbroner (1985:126–129), "capital itself has no inherent dependence on or affinity to political freedom.... It is an elemental proposition of democracy that every voting citizen has the right to cast but one vote, whereas it is an equally elemental proposition of capitalism that every market participant may rightly cast as many votes as his or her wealth permits". Differential voting weights, as practiced in shareholding rights among different types of shareholders, illustrate this distortion of democracy well (*The Economist* 2007b). The dual- or multiple-class share system allows capitalists to exercise much greater power in corporate decisions. In fact, recent evidence suggests that "savvy autocrats have learned how to cut the cord between growth and freedom, enjoying the benefits of the former without the risks of the latter (Mesquita and Downs 2005).

Nevertheless, there is some evidence that capitalism promotes democracy. In Britain, voting rights were granted to all male citizens in urban areas in 1867, and extended to all male citizens in rural areas in 1928. It was not until 1928 that women were allowed to vote, long after the industrial revolution was over and capitalism reached maturity. In the United States, white males passing certain property and religious tests could cast votes in the years 1810–1820, and the tests were abolished in 1830. After the Civil War, the Fifth Amendment granted African Americans the right to vote in 1870. Women were not granted suffrage until the Nineteenth Amendment was passed in 1920. It is thus important to remember that it is capitalism that may lead to democracy, rather than the other way around. One possible reason why capitalism enhances the likelihood of democracy is that it brings about a middle class that has collective resources and challenges the prevailing authority (Rueschemeyer et al. 1992).

## *Theories of Capitalism*

What mechanism brings the social institutions of capitalism together and coordinates them in an orderly fashion? No single theory that can explain how they coordinate, but there are four "general theories", each of which explains an important part or component of capitalism: self-interest—the psychological motive; exploitative reproduction—the sociopolitical motive; institutional enticement—the cultural motive; and the networking imperative—the social motive.

Self-interest. The dominant theory of capitalism focuses on individual behaviour, with a historical base of Britain's rise as an industrial power, and incorporates Adam Smith's explanation that the pursuit of self-interest necessarily promotes the public good. When everyone has the opportunity to pursue their own interests, exchanges are based on the supply of and demand for goods, and an optimal transaction based on the negotiated price will result. Without external influences, these transactions maximise the flow of production and consumption of goods, and create the optimal flow of goods and wealth for the entire society. While Smith did not employ the term "capitalism" to characterise the arrangement of social institutions, his argument laid the foundation for much of the subsequent discussion of capitalist development.

Exploitative Relations of Production. Karl Marx focused on the process by which production was accumulated—the rate of exploitation. Capitalists' exploitative relations with labour, the extent to which they extract surplus value from the use value of labour, determine how much capital could be reinvested in production. Capitalists not only control the means of production but also the arrangements of the institutions (wage labour, markets) that sustain and promote the accumulation of capital, with the state serving the interest of the capitalists.

The Cultural Enticement. Max Weber (1947) focused on the evolution of religious institutions in Western Europe, and argued that the Reformation resolved the tension between devotion to work and ascetics. The joining of the sacred (ascetics) and the secular (profit making) unleashed productive forces and channeled profits into further production rather than pleasure—thus developing the spirit of capitalism. Weber modified Marx's theory by identifying a process in which surplus value could be generated by labour as well. By combining ascetics and profit making, it is at least conceivable that some labourers may generate surplus value and convert part of it into capital. In this consideration, it can even be argued that Weber preceded, even though he did not anticipate, the development of neo-capitalist theories such as human capital, cultural capital and social capital (see Lin 2001a, chapter 1).

NETWORKING AND CHAINS OF COMMODITIES. The networking motive joins the desire for profits with the practical necessity of locating resources and markets through chains of production (commodity chains), distribution, and consumption (value chains). Wallerstein's (1979) world system exemplified the significance of chains in production and consumption. Braudel's analysis of networks characterised the market system beyond local boundaries (1977). Castells (1996, 1998) saw networking afforded by the new electronic media and the Internet as allowing capitalism to reach its summit. Such trust-based networks, more than anything else, ensure that the flow of resources and commodities transcends geographical limitations and imperfect information flows. Without these often informal relational configurations, capitalists would find it impossible to generate and accumulate capital. Even today, many regional alliances (e.g., the European Union) find it necessary to rely on networks to sustain their expansion to other parts of the global economy.

None of the abovementioned theories can explain capitalism by itself, but they each describe a sub-process of capitalism. Self-interest explains the effort, action, and choices of actors in the drive for profit and wealth. Exploitative production characterises the mechanism by which capital is retained and regenerated. The cultural and institutional mechanisms allow for the masses to participate in the capitalist processes. The networking mechanism explains the linkage from the production process to the distribution and consumption processes in the ever-expanding system. It is in fact, the combination of these psychological, political, cultural, and social mechanisms that bring the actors together and submit their forms of behaviour and practices to a set of rules and arrangements expected in capitalism. It is not surprising that more recent observers have noted the multifaceted nature of capitalism. For example, after the analysing economic development in East Asia, Hamilton and Biggart (1988) argued that it could best be understood in terms of a combination of market, culture, and authority.

## *Multiple Models of Capitalism*

Similar to the multiple theories that describe the mechanisms of capitalism, empirical studies of capitalist societies have also uncovered diversity and differentiation in the actual institutional arrangements (see Esping-Anderson 1990). In fact, if rigorous criteria are used, no single society throughout history fulfills all of the requirements of capitalism as defined and theorised. Each society molds and transforms but never revolutionises available institutions to promote capitalism.

The initial models of capitalism were formed around Marx and Smith's observations of British economic development in the 17th and 18th centuries. That development was organised by medium and large firms, backed by industrialisation with the invention of the textile mill and the steam engine, and the subsequent development of more advanced transportation, communication, and military technologies, coordinated by a powerful state with a military force that reached around the globe. The subsequent emergence of the United States, with its British institutional legacy, allowed the development of an Anglo-Saxon model of capital, characterised by an emphasis on entrepreneurship, less restrictive government regulations, and free trade; this has been labeled as liberal market-driven capitalism. There is also a continental European model of Germany, France, and others, as well as Japan, which has been labeled coordinated capitalism and is characterised by coordination between the state and large corporations.

Capitalistic states can also be grouped by certain theoretical or practical criterion. Esping-Anderson (1990) has used the term "welfare regime" to classify three types of capitalism, depending on the degree of state welfare provision or the de-commodification of labour. A liberal regime, as exemplified by the United States, offers minimal policy intervention; a conservative regime, as exemplified by Germany, provides selective welfare services to stratified groups; and a social democratic regime, as exemplified by the Scandinavian countries, exercises a broad welfare policy. The extent and nature of state intervention has also been used by Monsen and Walters (1983) to characterise command capitalism, planned capitalism, regulated capitalism, democratic socialism, and pure market capitalism, with states capable of moving from one type to another.

Within each model or classification of capitalism, more refined capitalist states have been identified, such as the East Asian model of Japan and South Korea (see Albert 1991/1993; Arrighi 2005). Finer analyses would further reveal that each society within a category shows certain different or unique features.

Other models have been based on the historical reconstruction of economies such as those of the Italian city-states. Venice has been described as a type of capitalist city-state where merchants traded over oceans with chains of exchanges for resources, backed by a powerful navy. Portugal, Spain, and Holland represented more extensive powerful colonial capitalist states where naval forces in conjunction with merchants extended trade and colonialism to several continents, including the newly "discovered" America.

Because of the close association of a scholar with the empirical system under observation, it is no surprise that each scholar has a favourite model of capitalism. Smith highly valued the British system of the 18th century. Likewise, Weber favored the Western European model. Even today, scholars freely express their preferences for a particular model. Baumol, Schramm, and Litan (2007) thought a combination of the American (entrepreneurial) and European-Japan (big-firm) models was the best. Most Western scholars tend to agree. Favoritism aside, historical and theoretical discussions lead to the inevitable conclusion—capitalism is an ideal that undergoes constant modifications as variations of systems emerge and evolve. Each capitalistic society is an evolving system. As timely opportunities and constraints appear and path dynamics evolve in interactions with the world, a society changes the institutional elements or their coordination to survive and persist. Thus, there is no ideal or "typical" capitalist society.

However, this absence of an ideal society does not erase the more universal underpinnings of capitalism. Each capitalist society must exhibit the presence of capitalists who seek to produce and reproduce capital, the presence of markets for production, distribution, and consumption, the availability of wage labour, and the presence of a state that maintains, protects, and promotes the institutional arrangements, the interests of the capitalists, and the expansiveness of the system. Thus, determination of whether a particular society is capitalist or not should be based on the extent to which that society has met the fundamental definition and essential elements or the consensual features described above. Only then is it necessary to identify its unique features and speculate on how those features may be projected into the multiple configurations of capitalism.

### *Is China a Capitalist Society?*

In accordance with the institutional arrangements already outlined, China is an emerging capitalist system, with characteristics that are nevertheless different from those of other capitalist societies.

Calculating Capitalists. There are several indications that capitalists are emerging in China. The first is that the amount of wealth held by the top executives in corporations is approaching the level generally associated with capitalists in the West. The top fifty executives in China were worth 50 billion yuan (5.1 billion U.S. dollars) by the end of 2006, thanks largely to the booming stock market (*Xinhua* January 2, 2007). None of the top fifty was worth less than 200 million yuan, and half of them were worth more than 500 million yuan each.

The number of large corporations is increasing, and the capital and assets of those corporations are growing. Huawei now employs over 25,000 workers, sells technical equipment in over seventy countries, and generated revenue of 5 billion dollars in 2004. Other internationally known corporations such as Haier, a white goods company, and Baosteel, the country's top steelmaker, are already listed among the top 500 global companies by *Fortune*.

By 2006 China had become the third largest automobile producer in the world. Shanghai Automotive Industry Corp (SAIC) aims to be among the world's top six car companies by 2020. Chery and Geely, two semi-government automakers, are planning to export automobiles to the United States in three to five years. GM and Volkswagen are producing more cars in China than anywhere else in the world except the United States and Germany respectively, and making more money there. It is certain that much of the present production relies on low-cost labour and low-level technology. China has a long way to go before catching up with the advanced countries in the mass of capital and dynamics of corporations. Further, in many areas, foreign or foreign-invested companies take the lead. However, this may augur well for China's future as skill levels improve and the level of technological innovation gradually catches up.

Another clear indication of capitalism in China is the rise of the middle class, a class of individuals who have accumulated sufficient wealth to enjoy leisure and luxury. According to the National Bureau of Statistics of China (*China Statistical Yearbook* 2005), in 2004, 95.9 percent of urban households owned washing machines (37.3 percent of rural households), 90 percent owned refrigerators (17.8 percent of rural households), 133 percent owned color televisions (75.1 percent of rural households), 47 percent owned cameras (3.7 percent of rural households), 11 percent owned mobile phones (34.7 percent of rural households), and 2.2 percent owned automobiles. McKinsey & Co. (2006) estimated that the ranks of the lower middle class (defined as earning an annual income of 25,000–40,000 yuan) will reach 290 million in 2011, and 520 million by 2025. It also estimated that 100,000 yuan would buy a lifestyle in China equivalent to 40,000 U.S. dollars in the United States in 2005.

Yet another indicator is the structural shift of the economic sectors. Between 2001 and 2005, the state sector decreased by 48.2 percent, currently claiming fewer than 190,000 enterprises. The collective sector has likewise experienced a decrease of 46.9 percent, with less than 450,000 enterprises remaining. In contrast, the number of stockholding companies have increased 35.2 percent, private companies 49.7 percent (now more than 2 million), foreign companies 9.6 percent (more than 150,000), and other types of companies 66.5 percent (more than 75,000). The state intends to trim state-owned corporations and concentrate on building thirty to fifty state firms into globally competitive multinationals by 2010. The top three oil companies, PetroChina, Sinopec, and CNOOC, are buying oil and oil fields and building pipelines around the world, often in competition with each other. Boasteel plans to become the third largest steelmaker in the world by 2010.

Free Markets. China has established substantial free markets for production, distribution, and consumption of commodities over the past two decades. According a recent World Bank report (Winters and Yusuf 2007), exports from China of goods and services in 2004 accounted for 5.7 percent of the world's total, behind only the United States (11.2 percent) and Germany (9.1 percent). By 2006 China had become the second largest exporter in the world, next to the European Union and surpassing the United States, according to a World Trade Organization report. Between 2005 and 2020 its share of growth is expected to be 15.4 percent of the world's total growth, surpassing all other nations including the United States at 9.9 percent. However, it should be noted that about 60 percent of China's exports are goods produced or assembled in China by multinational companies (*International Herald Tribune* February 9, 2006).

Export industries have also shown significant shifting patterns in the past decade (United Nations Commodity Trade Statistics, accessed via the World Bank's World Integrated Trade Solution software). Twenty-six percent of China's exports in 1995 were textiles, but by 2004 textiles exports only accounted for 16 percent of the total. Iron and steel also decreased from 3.5 percent to 2.3 percent. On the other hand, electrical equipment rose from 5.9 percent to 10 percent. Vehicles accounted for 1.8 percent in 1995 and 2.8 percent in 2004. Thus, the shift has moved away from labour-intensive products and raw resources to more technologically advanced products. As of 2004, exports of goods and nonfactor services accounted for close to 45 percent of GDP (World Bank, World Development Indicators database).

China's domestic market continues to grow as well. By October 2006, its retail sales amounted to 199.8 billion yuan, a surge of 14.3 percent from the previous year. In 2004 its imports of goods and services accounted for 4.8 percent of the world total, trailing only the United States (16.5 percent) and Germany (8.2 percent). The World Bank estimates that China's share of growth between 2005 and 2020 will be around 11.0 percent, trailing only the United States (at 15.4 percent). In 2006 alone, China received 63 billion U.S. dollars in foreign direct investment (FDI) (*Xinhua* January 14, 2007). Imports of capital (in terms of foreign direct investment), firms, technical and other personnel, and energy resources have also been remarkable. Currently China ranks second only to the United States in the amount of annual FDI. In 2005, 70 percent of the top 200 enterprises in the world had made investments in China. Recently, China also did away with tax advantages for foreign firms and investments; foreign and domestic firms can now compete on an equal footing.

China became the factory of the world by the early 2000s. In the past decade it has emerged as the consumer market of the world. Joining WTO has continued to affect the openness of the Chinese market. Foreign banks have been encouraged to invest in Chinese banks. More recently, foreign banks have been allowed to register locally. It is only a matter of time before China's financial sector and stock market will be as open as many other capitalist states in the world. Some have argued that China's market is more open today than those in Japan and South Korea in terms of the extent of relaxation of tariffs and commodity protection. For example, the United States has recently demanded that South Korea open its market to American automobiles—a non-issue in China.

The automobile industry provides a striking example of China becoming both an import and export market. China surpassed Japan to become the world's second-biggest vehicle market in 2006, and sales rose 25 percent to 7.22 million units. China now has more than 100 automakers. Honda, DaimlerChrysler, GM, and Ford have all invested heavily in manufacturing and assembling cars in China, to the tune of 21 billion U.S. dollars. China is Volkswagen's largest overseas market, and has made GM's Asia-Pacific region its most profitable. The estimation is that the passenger car market, around 5.24 million in 2007, will grow by 40 percent to 7.3 million vehicles by 2010.

An ever-increasing, though still relatively small, portion of the cars produced in China will be made by Chinese firms rather than by joint ventures. Chinese automobile companies have bought foreign car companies wholesale, including the manufacturing plants for engines and transmissions. For example, Nanjing bought MG Rover in 2005, transplanted the plants wholesale from England, and within a year started producing MG cars in China. Chongqing Changan Automobile Co. also began making its internally designed model, the Benben compact, in September 2006. Chery showed off thirty new models in April 2007 and Geely showed fourteen new models at the same time. Chery outsold Shanghai-GM in March 2007, the first Chinese firm to overtake the Detroit flagship venture in monthly sales. By 2007 China was exporting more automobile parts to the United States than most other countries, passing Germany and trailing only Japan (*Herald Tribune International* June 6, 2007). Chery reached an agreement with Chrysler in July 2007 with the aim of supplying up to 100,000 sub-compacts per year to the United States within three years.

Over the past decade China's foreign trade surplus has been on the rise. By the end of March 2007, its foreign reserves had exceeded 1.2 trillion U.S. dollars. Since July 21, 2005, China has relaxed its currency peg to the U.S. dollar, shifting the yuan from 8.20 to 7.10 per dollar by February 2008. It seems that China has decided to make slow adjustments over a period of time to limit the possible effects of hot money pouring into the country with a substantially devalued currency, which could render it a semi-colonial state as it was during the foreign economic, political and military domination of the late 19th and early 20th centuries.

The equity market has also been moving ahead at a measured pace. After some rules were relaxed, the stock market shot up in 2006 to a composite value of more than 1 trillion dollars, an annual increase of 130 percent (*The Economist* April 24, 2007). The market continued to surge in 2007, with the Shanghai market index reaching 4,000 in May, an increase of 85 percent over 2006. As of May 2007, an estimated 96.8 million Chinese are participating in the stock market. By April 2007, bank savings deposits had decreased to 17.37 trillion, while the stock market value exceeded 17.43 trillion by May 17. Although corrections are expected, the long-term perspective seems positive—more Chinese are becoming rich, and their wealth will partly be recycled to produce more capital.

China is also ambitious in the world market. In 1990 China's exports amounted to 2.5 billion U.S. dollars. By 2002 its cumulative exports had increased to 35.5 billion dollars, and by 2005 to 57.2 billion. By late 2006 Chinese exports were the third largest in the world, behind only Germany and the United States (*Financial Times* March 23, 2007). In fact, China will become the largest exporter in the world by 2008.

Wage Labour. China is currently the most populous nation in the world and enjoys an ample supply of labour. While the distribution of education across the population is uneven, the general literacy and education level are good for a developing country. The relatively low wages also afford competitive advantage to manufacturers in producing commodities in the world market. The cheap labour has so far allowed products made in China to be extremely competitive in the world market. Despite a tightening labour supply in certain industries, the massive population in the interior and rural areas will keep wages in China low in comparison with labour in North America and Europe for many decades to come.

Eventually, some argue, China's population and cheap labour advantage will be reduced. Within the next five years, India's population will surpass that of China; from that point on, China's population will be aging with increasing speed. The expectation is that if current trends and policies hold, the aged population will reach 400 million by 2040, bringing with it a reduction in labour supply. However, the current trends and policies need not remain unchanged. The one-child policy is likely to be reassessed and moderated in the near future. The retirement age may also be extended and become more flexible. Thus, the only real threat to wage labour relative to other countries is rising wages and benefits.

An Expansive System. China recognises the vast and expansive domestic market, and is making systematic plans to build up infrastructure to facilitate its growth. Urbanisation is taking place at a brisk pace of 0.8 percent per year, and economic development has been expanding to the interior regions and cities (*New York Times* November 21, 2006). Along the upper reaches of the Yang-tze and Pearl rivers, cities and industries are sprouting up. Wuhan is becoming a major industrial, commercial and financial center. Chengdu-Chongqing is emerging as another gigantic commercial center. An entirely new development zone is being developed in Northeast China to match the still growing Shanghai-Jiangsu region and the Pearl River delta. Dalian in the Northeast and Qingdou in Shangdong are fast emerging as high-tech centers, following the developments in Shanghai and Beijing regions.

In 2005 China announced that it would renovate or expand twenty regional airports with an investment of 5 billion yuan. It has also started developing large cargo and passenger airplanes with of the aim of competing with Boeing and Airbus for the Chinese market in ten to fifteen years, and with an eye toward the world market.

Existing harbors are being upgraded and new harbors built. From 2005 to 2010, China will invest over 400 billion yuan to improve its ports (*Bloomberg News* November 2, 2005) and highways. In 2006 China had seven of the world's twenty busiest shipping terminals. A deep-water port is being built from scratch in Hangzhou Bay, Zhejiang, 27.5 km from Shanghai. In 2007, South Korea built 41 percent of all ships delivered, but Chinese yards signed 56.6 percent of the total number of new contracts in the first quarter of 2007, with the South Koreans accounting for only 26.1 percent. The projection is that China will overtake South Korea as the largest ship builder by 2015 (*China National News* May 19, 2007).

China currently has a 45,400 km of express highway (Ministry of Communications January 2007) at both national and local levels, the second longest in the world behind only the United States. It will build another 5,000 km in 2007 to complete the 36,700 km trunk lines of its national highway network. The national network will probably reach 50,000–55,000 km by 2010. In 2007 it will also upgrade up to 300,000 km of rural roads. China's railroad construction is also expanding at a frantic pace. Currently, it has a network of 76,000 km and will reach 90,000 km by 2010, the longest mileage among all nations.

These infrastructure projects will continue to fuel the growth of domestic markets and the internal capacity for manufacturing and service industries. But China has also aggressively sought out resources and markets globally. It has started exporting cars, vans and trucks to Africa, Latin America, and Iran. China-made Hondas have now been successfully launched in Europe. Many multi-national automotive companies no longer see China as a sales market only, but are making it an important manufacturing, outsourcing, exporting, and regional research base.

To supply the increasing energy needs of its population and industry, China has ventured to Africa, the Middle East, Russia, and South America for oil exploration and purchases. Uganda, Sudan, Ethiopia, Iran, Russia, Azerbaijan, and Venezuela, among others, have all signed agreements with China for joint oil explorations and/or supply.

The strategies for China's overseas expansion are two-pronged. On the one hand, China makes investments in resource exploration, refinement, and transportation, in cooperation with local governments and firms, sharing the benefits and profits. It also demands that local markets be opened to Chinese goods and services, and promises to allow local goods to be imported to China. On the other hand, China has extended foreign aid and technical support to many countries in the third world. With its ample foreign currency and state treasury, it is helping to build hospitals, schools, roads, railways, and technical and personnel assistance in Africa, Latin America and the Middle East. Chinese firms, almost all of them state enterprises, have been given the actual construction and assistance contracts along with Chinese managers, technicians, and workers. Chinese entrepreneurs also followed by setting up shops and trading companies in these countries. Chinese-manufactured commodities are being supplied and in many instances saturate the local markets, with their relatively inexpensive price tags and reasonable quality. China also promises to not interfere with local politics or ideologies.

China's expansion into Africa over the past decade illustrates these strategies well. There were 450 Chinese investment projects in Africa in 2004 (Winters and Yusuf 2007). In 2005, Africa exported goods valued at 20 billion dollars to China and imported goods valued at 15 billion dollars from China. By 2006 there were more than 700 Chinese companies in Africa. China has become the continent's third largest trading partner, after the EU and the United States, but closing in on the United States fast. It is buying copper and cobalt from Congo and Zambia; iron ore and platinum from South Africa; timber from Gabon, Cameroon, and Congo-Brazzaville; and oil from Nigeria and Angola, Sudan, Equatorial Guinea, Gabon, and Congo-Brazzaville. A Chinese firm is engaged in coal mining prospects in Algeria, and intends to export coal to Morocco and Spain.

About 70 percent of Sudan's exports go to China. The biggest oil refinery in Sudan was expanded in 2006 to double its capacity with an investment of $341 million from China and construction by Chinese firms. Of Sudan's $2 billion in oil exports, half was sent to China. In 2006 a Chinese state-owned company agreed to pump more than $2 billion into a major, loss-generating refinery in northern Nigeria, Africa's leading oil producer, in exchange for drilling rights in four sought-after oil fields.

Similar strategies and initiatives, on a relatively smaller scale, are being undertaken in Southeast Asia, Latin America, the Middle East, and Central Asia. Venezuela has promised to substantially increase oil exports to China (from the current 150,000 barrels a day to 1/2 million a day in five years, and perhaps up to 1 million barrels a day by 2012). China has also signed a free trade agreement with Chile, with special interest in its copper mines. China wants natural gas from Bolivia and agricultural products from Brazil and Argentina. It has agreed to purchase mid-range airplanes from a Brazilian company. It will build a railroad for Cuba. China is now the second largest trading partner of Peru and Brazil, the third largest of Chile, and the fourth largest of Argentina. Trade with China now falls within the top ten for Paraguay and Uruguay (Malik 2006).

China is now the biggest trading partner for the EU, Southeast Asia, and East Asia (Japan, South Korea, and Taiwan). Regional alliances are also being promoted by China. The ASEAN countries plus three (China, Japan, and South Korea) are discussing the establishment of a free-trade zone, parallel to the EU. The Shanghai Cooperation Organization Conference is an example in which China, Russia, and the Central Asian states of Kazakhstan, Kyrgyzstan, Tajikistan, and Uzbekistan have formed an alliance of mutual assistance, resource exploration, and other exchanges. India, Pakistan, Iran, and Afghanistan have recently joined as observers with the potential for membership in the near future. China is actively befriending Japan and South Korea, in particular de-emphasising Japan's atrocities during the Second World War.

A Strong And Leading State. China provides a clear example of how a strong government participates in the development and growth of capitalism. In fact, the state was responsible for initiating that development. In the early phase of reform (1978–1989), the state allowed the market mechanism to emerge in rural development, and followed with policies that gradually allowed public institutions and enterprises to be diversified into pseudo-independent enterprises. Other public enterprises were allowed to be truncated into public and "private" enterprises to contain public and bank debts. Collective enterprises in rural areas were allowed to pass into private (largely local cadre) hands (see, for example, Lin 1995; Lin and Ye 1998). Urban housing was gradually released to private ownership. Job assignments were gradually replaced by a job market. At every step, the state watched the dynamic changes and implemented policies to encourage market mechanism.

Domestically, the state has implemented rules and regulations consistent with international standards in the monitoring and regulation of economic transactions and trades, the stock market, financial and banking services, and property rights—rules largely developed by capitalist states for capitalist states. Since joining the WTO in December 2001, China has been trying to meet various deadlines for market access for goods and services. Among the key commitments to be undertaken by China are the following: (1) the provision of non-discriminatory treatment to all WTO Members; (2) the elimination of dual pricing; (3) the removal of price controls; (4) the revision of existing domestic laws and the enactment of new legislation to comply with the WTO agreement; (5) the freedom of internal trade with three years of accession; and (6) the removal of all export subsidies on agricultural products.

China still lags significantly in meeting these commitments. However, fundamental steps have been taken. In early 2007 China allowed a number of foreign banks to register domestically without the requirement of allying with any Chinese bank. The first five such foreign applications were approved in early 2007. Foreign enterprises no longer enjoy any tax or tariff breaks, putting them on an equal footing in competing with domestic enterprises in the local markets. The stock market, still primitive by international standards, has also undergone changes. Foreigners can now purchase stocks previously reserved only for domestic parties. Significant, but still minor, shares of the public companies whose stocks are largely in the hands of public owners (the state or local governments) are now being released to the market.

### *Unique Features of Chinese Capitalism*

Chinese capitalism is at an early stage of development. However, the trends over the past twenty years are clear and significant. By most of the universal criteria discussed earlier, China has the appropriate institutional arrangements to be labeled capitalist. Nevertheless, Chinese capitalism is different from other forms, with two institutions in particular making the difference.

State As Capitalist. Given its past, it is not surprising that the state holds a commanding position in the political and economic arenas in China. As the country evolves toward capitalism, the state-economy synchronicity remains significant. Over the past decade the state has begun to separate itself from economic enterprises. The initial step was to segment state enterprises into the critical and non-critical sectors. The critical sector included industries and enterprises considered vital to the state, such as mining, defense, energy, transportation, and communication. The non-critical sector was further sorted into debt-laden and non-debt laden enterprises. Much effort was made to release debt-free enterprises to non-state operators, and arrangements were made to reduce the obligations of debt-laden enterprises, either by reduction of work and employment or changes in management, production, and so forth to gradually reduce debt. So far, the strategies seem to be working in general; over the past four or five years the level of debt among state enterprises has been greatly reduced. By the end of 2005 the four state-controlled asset management companies had disposed of 839.75 billion yuan of non-performing assets, according to the China Banking Regulatory Commission. At that time the State-owned Assets Supervision and Administration Commission announced that it planned to complete payment on all bad debts within four years.

However, the state retains a significant presence in the manufacturing sector. As of 2004 state enterprises accounted for 36.7 percent of manufacturing enterprises (National Bureau of Statistics of China, *China Statistical Yearbook* 2005). These state-owned enterprises accounted for 47.8 percent of manufacturing sales revenue and 41.1 percent of employees in the sector.

The state has also invested in nominally non-state enterprises in significant industries such as automobile manufacturing. It is difficult to estimate the extent of this penetration because the control and investment in enterprises are not transparent. For example, all major banks in China are under state control, but this only became apparent to many foreign observers recently when the CEOs of three leading banks, all former state bureaucrats, were replaced with other state bureaucrats. Many known "private" brands such as Haier, Lenovo, and Chery are in fact backed by the central and/or a local government.

The state as capitalist has also directly or indirectly tried to invest in foreign companies. Lenovo is one example, with its large state share ownership and its purchase of IBM's PC division. In 2005 CNOOC, a state-owned petroleum company, made an offer of 18.5 billion U.S. dollars to purchase Unocal, but the deal was blocked by the U.S. government. More recently, the Chinese government has moved into the global equity market. With its foreign exchange surplus exceeding 1 trillion U.S. dollars and growing by about 20 billion dollars per month, the Chinese government established the State Foreign Exchange Investment Company in 2007, through which it purchased $3 billion worth of non-voting shares (or about 9 percent of total shares) of Blackstone, one of the largest private equity firms in the United States.

The state's capitalistic nature cannot be appreciated by simply examining the behaviour of the state-owned companies. Many more enterprises "lean" on state or collective institutions, meaning that although they have been "officially" separated from public institutions they are largely filled with former state employees and retain close relationships with their originating work unit, in terms of personnel, resources, capital, and networks of supply and distribution.

Further complicating the relationship between the state and the economy is the participation of the Party. It is extremely difficult to separate the Party from the state: the presence of one inevitably indicates the presence of the other. The presence of the state in an enterprise also indicates the presence of the Party apparatus in the enterprise. Most private firms of reasonable size incorporate the Party apparatus through the presence of a Party secretary and an office. More recently, the Party has used official unions as surrogates in foreign firms and joint ventures, most notably in Wal-Mart, which has resisted the presence of unions elsewhere in the world.

It should be noted that the state's strong presence in China is not unique. In all capitalist societies, the state cooperates and coordinates with firms and capitalists. In many capitalist societies the state also operates enterprises considered critical or essential for national survival, and industrial sectors bearing on the development of military weapons, transportation and communication, energy exploration and development are either directly under the state's jurisdiction or under close supervision and command of the state. As such, they are much less likely to be subject to market rules. However, seldom have we seen a state itself acting as a capitalist entity competing in the domestic and international markets, as we are witnessing in China.

What are the implications of this feature? On the positive side, it allows for the fast accumulation of capital at the macro-level. The state has direct access to surplus value as long as its enterprises make profits. The surplus value further affords quick reinvestment in the production cycle. The direct participation of the state also reduces the opportunities for the enterprises to avoid taxes. In fact, tax revenue increased by 20 percent between 2004 and 2005, and by another 21.9 percent between 2005 and 2006. This "surplus" capital allows the state to make heavy investments in target areas that are vital for further development—infrastructure, education, communication, and the development of vital sectors such as high tech industries and the military industry.

More recently, the state has begun to address issues of inequality. In its current five-year plan, launched in 2006, more emphasis has been given to rural and regional development, the development of the service sector, and an energy-saving, environmentally friendly, and socially harmonious society focused on the quality of life, health, and public safety.

On the negative side, however, is the lack of checks and balances. The state presumably regulates and monitors the operations of the economy and the capitalists. Now it is both a referee and the player in the game. Despite efforts to discharge the responsibility of being the regulator by sending investigative teams to trouble spots and organisations, and initiating major investigations into the corruption at high levels of the government and state-owned businesses, the state finds itself in an awkward position—encouraging and tolerating regional and local government participation in capitalism while monitoring and regulating their activities. The state simply does not have the resources to conduct such independent work. This will remain a serious problem in the near future.

Another consequence of the joining of the Party, the state, and the economy is that nepotism often gets in the way of proper supervision and regulation. As of 2006, most of the top capitalists in China are children of high-level cadres. According to one unconfirmed report (Chinesenewsnet.com September 3, 2006), on social and economic conditions produced by researchers at the State Council, the Central Party School and the Chinese Academy of Social Sciences, 2,932 of the 3,200 richest persons were children of those cadres, and among the top executives, between 85 and 90 percent were children of the cadres. They held key positions in finance, foreign trade, land development, large construction projects, and the stock market.

Yet despite these problems, the population is by and large supportive of the present system. No doubt strong Party and state control account in part for the lack of resistance. Other factors may also explain why the public is willing to tolerate this odd linkage. For one, the state keeps reminding the population that it is for national interest and national development. The public is often reminded that China still faces severe international challenges, particularly from the United States, which is seen as the superpower that dominates, sometimes with force, in the global arena. The Chinese people are frequently reminded that Taiwan is an inalienable part of China and that the United States is the principal factor maintaining the continued separation of Taiwan from the mainland. Bilateral security treaties that the United States has established with Japan, Australia, and South Korea, and the intrinsic American sympathy for India, the largest democratic nation in the world, makes China feel that it is surrounded by the United States and its real and potential allies. The population is indoctrinated with patriotism and loyalty to the state. It is convinced that only a strong and united China can defend its own interests and ensure its ultimate survival.

The overall economic growth and its benefits to a majority of the population also contribute to this loyalty. Hunger and disease no longer threaten the great majority of the population. Rather, getting rich has become the focus. Ten years ago, laid-off workers from state firms seemed to be creating a potentially explosive threat to the stability of the country, but the rapid and continued economic growth and the emergence of many small firms has substantially increased permanent and temporary employment. It is impossible to find precise information about unemployment rates in China. Most official reports stated that by 2007 the urban unemployment rate was between 6 and 4 percent. Some (e.g., Rand) estimated that the actual rate for the total labour force was about 23 percent (taking into account rural as well as urban rates and including "disguised" unemployment—those reported as employed but have no income). So far, the economic opportunities seem to have contained possible discontent from the unemployed or underemployed. Ideologically and materially, the population has been convinced that strong state participation in the economy benefits the nation and its people.

Social Relations (*Guanxi*). *Guanxi* is a reciprocal relationship that mixes utility and sentiment. For critical observers, it represents a transaction cost that reduces the efficiency of market exchanges. Guanxi, practiced universally in varying degrees, may induce corruption and fraud, and, to some scholars, need to be replaced by market and free trade practices. However, evidence has shown that in fact *guanxi* is used among Chinese even when the markets are quite open and competitive (Bian 1994, 1995, 1997, 2000; Bian et al. 2005; Lai 1995; Lin 1989, 1995, 2001, 2003). In Hong Kong, Singapore, Taiwan, and other communities where ethnic Chinese participate in local and global market competition, *guanxi* is often seen as offering a competitive advantage (Bian and Ang 1997; Hwang 1987; King 1985, 1982/1988). *Guanxi* is a useful lubricant for buffering hard times and sharing profits. More importantly, social relations are the foundation for social capital—

resources embedded in social networks that can be accessed and mobilized for instrumental or expressive returns (Lin 2001b).

During the Asian financial crisis in the late 1990s and early 2000s, much of Southeast Asia and Northeast Asia suffered heavily and has only recently recovered. Yet Hong Kong, Singapore, and Taiwan were relatively less affected. One argument for this difference was that in these ethnic Chinese communities, corporate relationships were not abandoned. Instead, the cost of reduced work was shared by all and lay-offs were minimised. These overseas communities also benefited from their continued participation in the markets in China, which were relatively immune from the crisis because it managed its currency and financial institutions almost independently from the rest of the region. As China continued to grow in its domestic and international trade, these communities participated and benefited from that growth. During the crisis many ethnic Chinese firms and entrepreneurs in much of the affected areas shifted their capital and investment to China through their ties.

This practice applies not only to individual capitalists, but also to the state itself. China is establishing economic transactions with other states around the globe, but at every step it wishes to maintain and promote friendly relationships and shared benefits. Thus China gives out aid when and wherever it is necessary. It expects reciprocity of relations and sentiment and sees such *guanxi* and economic cooperation as going hand-in-hand.

## *Implications for Theory*

What does a study of Chinese capitalism contribute to the theoretical analysis of capitalism in general? As discussed previously, two institutions that feature in Chinese capitalism deserve more attention: the state as capitalist and the utility of social relations.

### *The State Managing Capitalism*

The foregoing overview of Chinese capitalism suggests that the role of the state deserves greater attention in the analysis of capitalism. While many scholars have pointed to the role of the state in discussing economic development and capitalism, its centrality in the development and maintenance of capitalism deserves stronger emphasis in theoretical discussions. The dominant theories of capitalism have thus far either dismissed or deemphasised the role of the state. Yet capitalism depends on a strong state for its preservation and development. The British Empire enjoyed such a strong state, as does the United States. China is now enjoying it. But why did capitalism fail before in China?

### *Why Capitalism Failed before in China*

It can be argued that various elements of the current institutional arrangements have been in place before in China. Chinese merchants throughout history understood the need to reinvest surplus value in production to accumulate capital (Arrighi 1996; Redding 1990). What was missing was state legitimisation of this ideology. Since the Han Dynasty, when the state established a national examination system and instituted Confucian ethics as the principal way of selecting and rewarding bureaucrats at all levels, society was stratified according to a moralistic ideology that downgraded profit making and placed merchants near the bottom of the social hierarchy. Even merchants were indoctrinated into this ideology, trading their wealth for bureaucratic positions and literate status and encouraging their sons to focus on training for examinations. Instead of business and commerce, capital was thus largely invested and re-invested in land ownership, but land accumulation was constrained by the rules of succession, which dictated the division of property among sons (Hsu 2007; Lin 1989).

Another major consequence of the state-commerce split in spirit and practice was the restraint placed on economic expansion. The state identified a geographic boundary for the centre of the civilized world, beyond which the Chinese were not encouraged to go. Dynasties consistently constrained and even forbade economic expansion beyond its borders, and merchants were punished for venturing outside the boundaries (Wong 1997). Arrighi called this the "introverted" system of capitalism (2005). Faure (2006) showed that during the Ming and Qing dynasties (1368–1644, and 1644–1911) Chinese merchants had to rely on informal and private contracts to sustain trade and mobilise resources. Without the state's participation and support, such informal institutions could not resist the onslaught of Western capitalists in the 18th and 19th centuries.

The centrifugal and contradictory ideology of the state and society has been sustained even into the 20th century. Following Hong Kong and Singapore, both of which had developed state capitalism under British rule, and Taiwan which followed suit when the KMT abandoned the idea of "recovering" the mainland and began focusing on economic development and allowing capitalists to develop through special economic and technological zones, China finally decided to focus on "modernisation." In the early 1980s, Deng Xiaoping proclaimed that "it does not matter whether it is a white cat or black cat as long it catches the mice," and followed through with his southern inspections in 1992 that legitimated capitalistic developments in the special economic zones in the wake of the disastrous Tiananmen Incident that had deterred economic growth.

A second, and equally important, ramification of the state managing capitalism in China is that it acts as a capitalist itself. It is true that in capitalist countries most states are capitalists to varying degrees in that they manage or own certain corporations. State ownership of these corporations and enterprises is largely based on the premise that they hold vital resources for the survival of the state. As such, their operations tend to retreat from market competition. The Chinese state, in contrast, has shown a tendency to operate enterprises in the competitive market. Chinese state-capitalistic corporations show no sign of retreating from the market and every sign of aggressive competition. Chinese banks, largely owned by the state or local governments, are operating as typically private enterprises, listing in stock markets, entering into joint ventures with foreign banks, and entering into foreign markets. Ministries and local governments continue to incorporate local and private enterprises under their wings. This blurring of the demarcation between the public and the private and between the government and enterprises is a significant deviation from practices in other capitalist countries.

### *Social Relations Embedding Capitalism*

The other interesting institution highlighted in the study of Chinese capitalism is *guanxi*, or social relations. Conventional wisdom, with exception of the recently developing behavioural economics, in the analysis of capitalism separates economic and social relations. Polanyi (1944) believed that capitalism was a historical anomaly because unlike previous economic arrangements, capitalism social relations were defined by economic relations (see Heilbroner 1985 for elaboration). Polanyi further thought that in the great transformation of human history, rules of reciprocity, redistribution, and communal obligations were far more frequent than market relations. He did not contemplate the possibility that capitalism and social relations could be complementary rather than antagonistic, and his view was formed before the economic rise of East Asia. Much of East Asia, including China, has always valued social relations. Within the constraints and opportunities offered by the protection of the state and the operation of a free market, they consolidate reciprocity and mutual benefit with relational rules (Redding 1990) to accrue and reproduce capital. The cost of sub-optimal profit in these socially based transactions is well compensated for by the benefit of long-term payoffs and the rewards of reputation and social standing (see Lin 2001a, chapter 9).

Even in other countries, social relations have not been replaced by capitalism, as Polanyi pessimistically forecasted. Indeed, with the advent of the Internet and other cyber-technologies, social relations and social networks are at the forefront of capitalistic development. Cyber networks (Lin 2001a, chapter 12), or social relations and social networks in cyberspace, have become the foundation of entrepreneurship. AOL was probably the pioneering enterprise in this regard (Swisher 1999), when Steve Case focused on the development of online forums and beat out the more economically oriented competitors (Lin and Gao, 2000). Google established a network-based ranking system, again initially without regard to economics. MySpace and FaceBook carried it a giant step forward. Economic payoffs followed. Second Life, the online game in which real firms establish virtual presences to do real business, is another example. Thus, in this most modern and technologically innovative social system, cyber networks are the primary goal of development and economic relations follow. Wikipedia is a shining example of collective and networking production, without regard so far, for economic returns.

A major contribution of neo-economic sociology, as Granovetter (1985) pointed out, is that economic activities are all embedded in social relations. However, the centrality of *guanxi* in certain societies and the fact that social relations and networks precede economics in cyber networks all point to a different theoretical proposition: that social relations serve as the foundation for economic activities. Zelizer (2005) challenged the assumption that markets undercut solidarity-sustaining personal relations and described these "circuits of commerce" where intimate and interpersonal relations control and sustain transactions for communal benefits. In this view, *guanxi* represents generalised circuits of commerce as it transcends geographical and temporal boundaries. *Guanxi* can and must be maintained across time and space to allow its utilisation as transactions demand.

This articulation about the importance of social relations does not deny the possibility of economic transactions with actors outside the circle. Actors within the circle continue to search for and establish relations with actors outside to seek and expand profits. However, the expectation is that such economic activities will be followed by the development of *guanxi* to maintain and expand future transactions. External partners are expected to become part of the *guanxi* network if transactions are to be maintained and expanded. Only when such relational commitment has been made will economic activity be continued. It is only with *guanxi* that economic activities afford the sharing of profits in good times and sharing of losses in bad times. Abandoning partners in times of crisis is seen as shameful and damaging to one's reputation. Once one's reputation is damaged, others treat future transactions with guarded suspicion and one is given lower priority in choices. In this sense, *guanxi* adds value to economic transactions. *The Economist*, in describing how Western banks play the game of courting in seeking recognition and profit in China, quoted a seasoned British banker in Hong Kong, "in this part of the world relationship is everything" (*The Economist* "The Art of Courtship," May 19, 2007).

## *Globalization for Whom?*

The world economic order is clearly going through a major transformation. According to *The Economist* (January 21, 2006), the thirty-two emerging economies are producing more than half of the world's output measured in purchasing power parity terms, and they also account for more than half of the increase in the global GDP in current-dollar terms. All of these countries grew in both 2004 and 2005, while in the previous three decades at least one of them suffered recession in a particular year. It took fifty years during the industrial revolution for Britain and the United States to double their real incomes per head; China has achieved that in a single decade. While this comparison must be contingent on market and technological constraints in different historical periods, China is quickly establishing itself as a major player in the global context, as the largest trading partner of the European Union, Southeast Asian countries, Japan, and South Korea.

There are two competing theories about what the new world order will be like. One theory espouses that any new economic power will simply increase global economic growth and bring global benefits. The other theory, prevailing among politicians and media in the West and gaining converts among scholars as well, is that China constitutes an economic, political, and technological threat to the existing world order and to the leadership of the United States. There is some evidence that the rise of a new economic power also increases global economic growth. A new economic power does not necessarily imply the demise of an older economic power. During the 20th century, for example, Europe did not really suffer as a consequence of the emergence of American capitalism. Without World War One and World War Two, Europe would have enjoyed continued economic growth. In fact, after each of the two wars Europe recovered quickly, although with help from the United States, and assumed its growth. Thus, the assumption is that the emergence of Chinese capitalism, perhaps along with other developing economic powers such as India, Russia, and Brazil, will increase the economic pie and each may gain a share. This does not negate the fact that some of the current leading economic powers (e.g., United States, Britain, and the EU) may make room for China and others and even eventually cede their leadership. Nevertheless, there is no reason for them to suffer economically.

One variation of this theory even argues that the rich countries do not have to cede their leading positions. By upgrading their technologies and promoting innovations, these countries may cede the labour-intensive and low-skilled work to the emerging economic powers but will retain their comparative competitiveness by moving on to manufacturing and producing high-value and high-skill work—the Ricardian school of thought. Further, the rise of new economic powers will have increased the labour pool, the talent pool, the sharing of resources, and the consumer demands. Presently rich economies could share these pools.

Others, especially those in developing countries, see China's rise as a good counterbalance to the United States and the European Union, which are seen as imposing Western ideologies and other demands not necessarily consistent with local religions, cultures, and economic needs. In their eyes, China provides an alternative partner in development and, at least can serve as a bargaining chip for soliciting and obtaining aid from other countries.

Yet the emergence of Chinese capitalism has created deep conceptual turmoil. Many theoreticians are confronted with the need to reassess and even revise their views about how the world evolves and will evolve. As most of these theories and theorists have used certain types of models and ideologies, the need for reassessment and reinvention will be uncomfortable at best and downright painful for others. What makes this phenomenon more discomforting for most observers is the fact that China remains a socialist state after the world has proclaimed the triumph of Western liberal democracy following the collapse of the Soviet Union and most other forms of state socialism in the early 1990s, and has congratulated the United States not only for its supremacy as a world economic power but more importantly as the unchallenged world leader in ideology.

The Ricardian theory of comparative advantage is under challenge, at least from proponents of outsourcing (see Samuelson 2004 and rebuttals by Amiti and Wei 2004 and Bhagwati, Panagariy and Srinivasan 2004). The underlying challenge from China and other emerging economic powers will be that they have no intention to simply carve out economic niches by making only labour-intensive and low-technological products. Both China and India now produce more engineers and high-tech scientists, and they are working on the forefront of science and technology. Increasingly Chinese and Indian scientists and engineers are obtaining patents in the United States and elsewhere, and claim their share of publications in the top scientific and engineering journals around the world. In 2004 China ranked fifth in the world with 57,400 theses listed in the science citation index (SCI). Microsoft has established twenty (soon to be twenty-two) innovation centres (it has about 110 around the world) in cooperation with local universities and companies in China, where it has the most comprehensive research and development system outside of its headquarters in Seattle, with 1,200 engineers (*China Daily* April 21, 2007). On his visit to China in April 2007, Bill Gates proclaimed that the growth of the country's software industry would stun the world. Zhang Yaqin, vice-president of Microsoft in charge of development activities in China, said that "a trend that is taking place is a shift from 'made-in-China' to 'innovated-in-China,'" as the country builds up its innovation efforts.

Similar to the United States, China can count on its enormous domestic market to buffer any possible international trade disputes and problems. Currently, three quarters of Chinese exports are assembled goods with components shipped in from abroad. Yet domestic consumption accounts for an ever-increasing portion of produced goods and commodities. Foreign investments and firms inevitably bring advanced technologies to China, so that reliance on imported components will be eased.

Instead of seeing China's emergence as higher water that will carry all vessels, it is seen as a real threat to the Western economies and what they represent politically and ideologically. This superpower mentality and fear account for some of the currently arranged security pacts the United States has signed with Japan, South Korea, Australia, and many of the Southeast Asian countries and its stance on Taiwan. Johnson (2006), quoting official source, stated that the United States maintains 737 military bases around the world in 2005. It sees itself as the guardian of the free market and democracy that cannot be challenged. The terrorist attacks on New York and Washington on September 11, 2001 made this matter event more urgent. While the United States has had its hands full dealing with terrorists in the Middle East and elsewhere, China, with its communist ideology, growing military prowess, and ever-expanding reach, is viewed as challenging the supremacy of the United States as a world leader. The fact that China often signs cooperative agreements with authoritarian states in Africa and Latin America, while the United States and the European Union has shied away from such aid or provides aid with many constraints and conditions is troubling to many in the West. Also, doubt has been cast as to whether the United States can upgrade its technologies and innovations to remain relatively competitive as China occupies the labour-intensive sectors (*Business Week* May 30, 2005). With China becoming more innovative and upgrading its technology, the United States is also worried about the significant trade and exchange imbalance and losing professional and technical jobs. The fact that China is building aircraft carriers is also seen as a threat to the United States' supreme position in the Pacific, Northeast Asia, and Southeast Asia, and to the situation in the Taiwan Strait.

To a great extent, this perceived threat is exaggerated. From certain perspectives, China is far from a world power. Many indexes still place China as comparable to England and United States in the late 19th century or early 20th century (even in purchasing power parity terms). As *Time Magazine* (January 22, 2007) correctly pointed out, China is still a poor country (GDP per head in 2005 was 1,700 U.S. dollars, compared with 42,000 U.S. dollars in the United States) whose leaders face so many problems that it is reasonable to wonder how they ever sleep. The country's urban labour market recently exceeded by 20 percent the number of new jobs created. Its pension system is nonexistent. China is an environmental dystopia, with the air of is cities foul beyond imagination, and clean water scarce. Corruption is endemic and growing. Protests and riots by rural workers are measured in the tens of thousands each year. The most immediate priority for China's leadership is less how to project itself internationally than how to maintain stability in a society that is going through the kinds of social and economic changes that have led to chaos and violence in the past.

At the same time, there is little evidence that developed economies have suffered as China's economy has grown. On the contrary, the United States and the European Union countries have continued to thrive economically. Despite recent housing slumps and concerns over energy costs, the United States continues to show economic growth, a relatively low unemployment rate, and low inflation rate (*Reuters* June 8, 2007). However, the newly gained benefit is largely unshared by workers (wages have not increased meaningfully in the United States for the past two decades). A recent report by the Congressional Research Service showed that CEOs make, on average, 179 times as much as rank-and-file workers. Seeking and maintaining skilled workers either through better education systems or immigration policies remains largely unresolved. Weakness in the manufacturing sector, unless corrected, will eventually harm economic growth. Most of these issues may not be corrected even with improved trade relations and demands with China and other developing economies. Interestingly, these problems may suggest the necessity of a stronger role for the state, not a weaker role (*The Economist* January 21, 2006). The question of how to encourage more saving, to re-equip the labour force for the new economy, and to develop new industries and services demands national policies and plans for existing and potential economic powers alike.

### *From Command Capitalism to Planned Capitalism?*

In a farsighted statement in 1984, Deng Xiao-ping laid down the conceptual and practical grounds for defending the reform that was unfolding at the time while insisting that China was still following the socialist path (1984). He stated that in the advanced stage of socialism—communism—the principle of "from each according to his ability and to each according to his needs" would be applied. However, at the primary stage of socialism, Marxism as defined by Deng, the focus should be on the development of productive forces and the creation of an "overwhelming" abundance of material wealth. This two-stage formulation simultaneously defended the introduction of capitalist elements and remained in the process of an evolving socialism. It fended off possible ideological reactions and even revolt from conservative elements and pragmatically allowed the reform process to continue. It was a brilliant conceptual innovation.

During this primary stage, capitalist features were not only possible but perhaps necessary. At the time Deng envisioned it would take twenty to thirty years to attain a GDP per capita of 800 U.S. dollars and raise total GDP to one billion U.S. dollars. During this period, Deng also wanted to eliminate poverty and enrich 90 percent of the population instead of 10 percent. Zhao Ziyang, Jiang Zemin, and Hu Jintao, subsequent party general secretaries, have all reaffirmed these goals. But how long will China need to move to the advanced stage of socialism?

By all measures, the goals Deng set for the primary stage were attained by the late 1990s and early 2000s, except for one—equal distribution of wealth throughout the population. Should China take the next step to the advanced stage of socialism? Before his retirement as the party general secretary in 2002, Jiang Zemin proposed that China needed another twenty years to accomplish the goals set out by Deng. But in February 2007 Premier Wen Jia-bao emphasised that China would remain at the primary stage of socialism for generations, perhaps for 100 years. The goals for socialism were not only to unleash productive forces, but also to create social fairness and justice in a "prosperous, strong, democratic, civilised and harmonious modern socialist society." Thus, Deng's economic goals, the releasing of productive forces and the creation of wealth, have been now supplemented by the social and political goals of fairness and justice, and even democracy. The long-term vision is reinforced and goals are expanded.

If the current state of affairs lasts one hundred years, then the issue of identifying the mechanisms that will or will not bring the primary stage of socialism to the advanced stage of socialism will lose its urgency. But as an academic exercise, we should be curious about alternative courses for China that may extend from the current trends into the next decade or two. Two such trends can be identified: (1) ongoing and growing capitalistic development, and (2) the evolving nature of that capitalism—from command capitalism to planned capitalism.

### *Capitalist Trends*

Some recent developments have far-reaching implications for the growth of capitalism in China. The number of capitalists is increasing, as is their capital, and they have been welcomed into the Party. Likewise, the private sector is continuing to grow. Markets are also growing with strong state support. A new labour contract law was also approved for implementation in January 2008, requiring employers to provide written contracts for all employees. Part-time contracts can be renewed once and then those employees must become regular employees. At almost the same time, the state advised local (provincial) governments to implement minimum wage guidelines. These were seen as a major advance in protecting labourers in the increasingly free labour market. The financial market is also expanding. The stock market is growing in terms of capital, number of investors, and participation of Chinese corporations. Almost all of the giant corporations, including the three big banks, the petroleum companies, steel and other industrial corporations, have either listed or are on the verge of declaring IPOs. These companies are investing and reinvesting capital and intend to be global players. The projection is that China will host the most IPOs in 2007, with capital raised exceeding $52 billion, easily surpassing Hong Kong, London, and New York (*Financial Times* July 4, 2007). Foreign banks are allowed to take minority, usually non-voting, shares in banks. They are also allowed to take majority shares or even ownership in some regional and local banks. Foreign banks and financial institutions are also gradually being permitted to issue credit cards and loans (including mortgages), either in conjunction with Chinese institutions or on their own in some localities.

To put the private and public sectors, and domestic and foreign firms on equal footing, tax laws are also being revised and improved. The export tax waiver for Chinese firms has been lifted. Real estate will attract taxes, first for all corporate buildings and then apartment buildings. The tax advantage for foreign firms will be eliminated on January 2008, raising the corporate tax rate from 15 percent to 25 percent.

A far-reaching new property law was accepted by the National People's Congress and enacted into law in 2007. It gives protection to private as well as public (state and collective) properties and against unreasonable land seizures especially in rural areas, which are a major source of unrest and protest. The law stipulates that the state continues to own all mines, rivers and seaboards, urban land, forests, mountain ranges, grasslands, uncultivated land and beaches, legally designated wild animals and plants, wireless wave channels, legally designated artifacts, defense resources, and infrastructures such as power, communication, and oil pipelines. Also, the collectives (local governments) continue to own legally designated land, forestry, mountain ranges, grasslands, uncultivated land, beaches, constructions, production equipment, irrigated lands and irrigation, infrastructure such as education, science, culture, health, and sports facilities, and other designated properties. Agricultural land is collectively owned and can be contracted to farmers for up to thirty years. Non-agricultural land used for buildings can be owned and used for profit by individuals. Land for housing can be owned and used by individuals for up to seventy years. Private individuals can own legally designated incomes, housing, daily life necessities, production tools, and raw materials, as well as savings, investment, and its profits. All property owners—the state, the collectives, and individual or private entities—enjoy equal protection under the law. This is a significant step toward permitting and protecting the private ownership of property.

Social reforms are also making progress. For example, recently the state, through its Patriotic Catholic Church, responded rather positively to the pope's desire for a better relationship between it and underground churches. Civil society has received a surprising boost from the mushrooming of housing owners' associations in cities around the country. As private ownership of housing grows, these associations allow apartment owners in residential buildings to form collectives that protect their property rights, negotiate for service contracts, and engage in dialogue with local government units. It is not farfetched to speculate that they may also exercise some power in local elections as blocks of voters in the future.

Transparency in governance has also gained ground. Cadres are now subject to closer supervision, training, and evaluation. Major cadre training schools have been established around the country where cadres receive more up-to-date management training. As of 2006, all major administrators (from bureau and county-level up) in state and Party offices must include all sources of income in their individual annual reports.

Political reforms are evolving slowly but surely, with remarkably open debates on certain issues. Over the past two years, a group of cadre-scholars at the Central Party School has been engaged in the formulation of political reforms. A draft statement supported the authority of the

Party but raised issues on allowing religious freedom for Party members, reducing bureaucratic levels and the number of bureaucrats, developing more NGOs, and electing members to the national legislature. In October 2006, Yu Keping, former deputy director of the Central Translation Bureau and supposedly a protégé of Hu, wrote an article entitled "Democracy is a good thing." He argued that while there were limitations to democracy and a price to be paid, under democracy officials should be elected and authority is constrained by the people. It was published in *Beijing Daily* on December 29 and widely reprinted, drawing severe criticism and counterattacks from doctrinal politicians and scholars. In a February 2007 interview with the *Southern Metropolis Daily* in Guangzhou, Zhou Ruijin, a retired editor of the *People's Daily*, urged a faster democratic reform to overcome the serious social and economic problems of wealth inequality, waste of natural resources, deteriorating environments, a weakened social welfare net, and rampant corruption. He advocated expanded local elections and improved civil society. Xie Tao, a retired vice president of Renmin University, praised Sweden's Social Democratic Party as a model for China's Communist Party in a piece published in the liberal-leaning journal *Yanhuang Chunqiu*. Further debates ensued in the *People's Daily*; rebuttal came in a statement on May 10, stating that "the democratic socialism is not suitable to China's situation" and that democratic socialism was not authentic Marxism. Subsequently, the paper published a statement on June 4 from Nie Yunling, a professor and authority on Western communism, who warned that China should not uniformly follow the changes and transformation in communist parties in Western democratic societies. Kao Fang, a senior professor from Renmin University, published a piece in *Southern Weekend* on the long history of changes in democratic socialism and scientific socialism in the West, and concluded that communism and social democracies shared origins, ideology, and politics. Others have joined in the discussion and debates. Cai Kuo, a political science professor from Nankai University, suggested that there were aspects of social democracy that China could learn from.

These debates could not possibly have taken place over such a protracted period and such a wide range of institutions and media without tacit permission and even encouragement from the senior political leadership. The debates reached a climax on June 25, 2007, when in his speech at the Central Party School Hu took a stand on the issue of political reforms. As expected, he took the middle ground. Declaring that he would follow the socialist path, he stated "four insistences":

liberating thoughts, reform, open and scientific development, and social harmony. He also suggested that political institutional reform would follow the principle of elevating and adjusting to people's desire to participate in politics. This stand keeps the socialists at bay and yet leaves open discussion on political reform. The "elevation and adjustment" statement is the most intriguing. On the one hand, it keeps the Party in the leading role of elevating political participation among the populace. At the same time, it reminds Party cadres and thinkers to pay attention to what the people desire and adjust their positions accordingly. This stand will certainly be featured in the forthcoming congress of the Party scheduled for the latter part of 2007.

## *Capitalism with Chinese Characteristics*

These trends and clues guide us in considering and evaluating alternative courses that China may undertake in the next decade or two and to assess their viability. One course is the process of moving toward the advanced stage of socialism. While it is not clear what mechanisms will be required to facilitate this movement, we may assume that the fundamental requirement for the advanced stage of socialism is the public ownership of capital. Once capital is built up during the primary stage, then ownership of capital will revert to the public. The state is holding firm on certain economic sectors, either through outright ownership or owning the majority of the shares. But the larger trends have been the shrinking of the state sector and the expansion of the non-state sector. There is little evidence that any initiatives have been taken toward implementing the advanced stage of socialism in the next two decades.

Another course would be to segment the socialist and capitalist portions of society. One portion of society that can take advantage of capitalist development would be allowed to produce and reproduce capital on its own, while the state would focus on the remaining portion to ensure that social and economic justice and equality would be maintained. Essentially, this would be social capitalism, as exemplified in Scandinavian countries. Current trends cannot reject this alternative outright, but it would require significant evacuation of the state and the Party from much of society. The likelihood of this course for the next two decades is remote.

We can also rule out several other alternative courses. State capitalism typically implies that the state is the sole capitalist, which is no longer the case in China. Authoritarian capitalism conventionally refers to a dictatorial governmental rule over all economic development, such as in Nazi Germany. This does not fit the current trend in China. Instead, China is in the process of moving from command capitalism toward planned capitalism. In command capitalism, the central government dictates and guides industrial and economic practices. In planned capitalism, government, labour, and industry jointly plan long-range initiatives (Monsen and Walters 1983). In China, interactions and joint efforts of the government, industry, and society seem to be emerging. Evans (1995) uses the term, embedded autonomy, to describe an assertive developmental state which also networks with society. China showcases the nuance of such networking beyond corporate and individual entities and drives home how planning and control dictate such networking.

The state and Party in China have always exercised their authority with adjustment and control (*tiao-kung*). *Tiao-kung* manages economic growth and social stability so that it will not overheat or subvert their authority, or reduce social stability and harmony. In other words, the state and the Party not only monitor and regulate developments, but they guide developments at a pace that maintains social and economic stability and justice. For example, while the state continues its general retreat from all economic sectors, it will continue to control sectors deemed critical, such as major energy resources, defense and security, and important research and development. It also intends to develop thirty to fifty major state-owned firms to compete in the world market. In the new labour contract law, a provision designates unions as the collective bargaining unit for negotiating salary and benefits for employees, yet all unions report to the All China Federation of Trade Unions, an organisation with deep ties to the Party and the state. A certain degree of control is thus assured.

More importantly, adjustments and control allow the state to continue to invest and implement macro-projects to facilitate economic growth, social development, and societal safety and security. China has plans to build vital infrastructure such as highways, railways, airports, harbors, and communication lines. Rural and regional development is also receiving higher priority than before. Education received a larger budget in 2007, exceeding 3 percent of GDP, an annual growth rate of 8 percent. Financial assistance for colleges and vocational school students increased from 1.8 billion yuan in 2006 to 9.5 billion yuan in 2007, and over 20 billion yuan in 2008. Tuition and fees are waived for up to six years of education for all students in rural schools. Tuition is waived for all teacher training in the six national normal universities. There are more than ninety normal colleges and universities at the local and regional levels that have yet to benefit from this new policy.

Ambitious plans are being made to cover medical care in more than 80 percent of the rural counties. In 2007 the state invested more than 10 billion yuan to subsidise this plan. Plans are also being made for aged care. This may entail a social security system based on individual accounts, along with contributions from firms and the government.

In response to the increasing emission of greenhouse gases, the state is launching a major environmental initiative in 2007 that will eventually close a massive section of old heavy industry (e.g., iron foundries and steel mills), ban the wasteful use of land, including the building of golf courses and free-standing homes, and implement energy-saving projects in various industries. It will also increase imports of energy, raw materials, and advanced technologies and build up the service sector.

Local governments are encouraged to take the initiative in economic and social development, but at the same time certain privileges and forms of authority have reverted back to the state. The new property laws set guidelines and limits on whether and how land, especially agricultural land, can be appropriated from peasants and properly compensated. Local governments have also been served notice that evaluations of their performances will now encompass social development and environmental protection. The state and the Party also maintain strict control over the appointment and removal of regional and provincial leaders.

Adjustment and control at the more macro-level are exercised through five-year plans that set the course of focus and development. A constant feature of the Chinese regime, five-year plans were originally adopted from the practice of the Soviet Union. For a while the planning aspect was de-emphasised, and in 1993 the term "planned economy" was deleted from China's Constitution, but it has come back in full force during the Hu-Wen era. It is an instrument with both policy and development directives. This middle-range strategy allows periodical investigation of the needs and demands of the people and society, and micro- and macro-level responses and adjustments in strategies and tactics in the formulation of policies and their implementation (Hsu 2007). The interaction and feedback between the state and society are effected in the planning process. The process also allows a gradual shift of macro-strategies and goals.

Such may be the case of the current five-year plan, which claims several firsts. It is the first time specific indicators and targets have been identified, and the first time that social development, rather than economic development, has assumed priority in the number of indicators and targets (fifteen versus seven). Employment, social security, poverty reduction, education, medical care, environmental protection, and safety are given priority. Chapters are devoted to rural development, development of the service sector, resource conservation, the development of science and human resources, institutional reforms (including finance, taxation and markets), further openness and foreign-trade and capital expansion, and the promotion of a harmonious society. Among the economic institutional indicators are the value added percentage of the service sector, the employment percentage in the service sector, research and development as a percentage of GDP, and the urbanisation rate. It is clear that planning is taken seriously and that priority is currently given to social justice and welfare. Both the public and private sectors are to be mobilised to achieve these goals.

The focus of the current five-year plan is on the "construction of a Xiaokang society," with the term *Xiaokang* ("moderate prosperity" or "well-off society") having historical significance. Over two millennia ago, Confucian scholars compiled and narrated two visions of societal development in the *Book of Rites*. In the long term, they envisioned a world of great harmony, *Datong* ("universal harmony"). In the short term, they pictured a society of good living and wealth, *Xiaokang*. In lieu of great harmony during *Xiaokang*, society achieves moderate prosperity by following moral principles (propriety and justice), with all individuals claiming their rightful positions and performing their rightful duties. The state defends society. Wise men, following moral principles, being trustworthy and exercising legal authority, are in charge of the state. Those in authority who do not follow these principles can be removed and viewed by the people as pariahs. In *Datong*, the ultimate way, the world belongs to the public, where the wise and able are elected, trust and harmony prevail, and men care for not only their kin, but for all, including the young, the old, the handicapped, the sick, and the isolated. Resources and properties are not hidden by individuals; volunteerism is assumed. There is no trickery, corruption, or thievery. No doors ever need be closed.

Linking Xiaokang to development in China was another of Deng's brilliant innovations. In 1979 he clarified that unlike what it might mean in the West, modernisation in the case of China must refer to *Xiaokang*. It is clear that in Deng's conception the primary stage of socialism substantially overlapped with *Xiaokang*, where the principal goal was to achieve a certain level of overall prosperity while society maintained stability and harmony under the leadership of the state. The goals identified for *Xiaokang* and *Datong* are strikingly similar to those identified for the two stages of socialism advocated by Deng, Hu, and Wen. The significance of this indigenising socialist ideology cannot be overlooked. *Xiaokang* and *Datong* stress order, equality, and harmony, and teach respect for authority and concern for all. They are consistent with the visions outlined for the primary stage of socialism. At the macro-level, they legitimate the authority of the state and the Party, not so much based on political ideology as on their wise and competent management of society's well-being and the people's desire for better lives. At the micro-level they expect that indigenously valued social relations will promote and sustain harmony. They offer an authentic Chinese justification for permitting greater political, economic and social participation.

This course, from command capitalism to planned capitalism, offers a softer and indigenised version of ideology and projects harmonious social relations. As long as the state and the Party act on behalf of the well-being of all the people, protects China's interests in the world, and adjusts itself to meet the people's demands and desires, there is every reason to believe that they will remain supported by the people. This shift does not require abandoning any prevailing ideology. After all, the socialist and democratic ideals advocated are all embedded in *Xiaokang* and *Datong*, which predate Marx by more than two thousand years.

## *References*

Albert, M. (1991/1993). *Capitalism Against Capitalism (Capitalisme Contre Capitalisme)*. London/NY: press.

Alchian, A. (1965). "Some Economics of Property Rights." *Il Politico* 30(4):816–29.

Alchian, A. and H. Demsetz. 1973. "The Property Right Paradigm." *Journal of Economic History* 33:16–27.

Amiti, M. and S. Wei. (2004). *Fear of Outsourcing: Is It Justified*. NBER Working Paper No. 10808. National Bureau of Economic Research.

Arrighi, G. (1996). "The Rise of East Asia: World Systemic and Regional Aspects." *International Journal of Sociology and Social Policy* 16(7):6–44.

——. (2005). "States, Markets and Capitalism, East and West." Pp. 110–145 in *World of Capitalism: Institutions, Governance and Economic Change in the Era of Globalization*, edited by M. Miller. London: Routledge.

Baumol, W., C. Schramm, and R. Litan. (2007). *Good Capitalism, Bad Capitalism*. New Haven, CT: Yale University Press.
Bhagwati, J., A. Panagariy, and T. N. Srinivasan. (2004). "Economics of Outsourcing." *Journal of Economic Perspectives* 18(4, Fall): 93–114.
Bian, Y. (1994). "Guanxi and the Allocation of Jobs in Urban China." *The China Quarterly* 140:971–99.
——. (1995). "China: Getting a Job in a Web of Guanxi." In *Networks in the Global Village*, edited by B. Wellman. Boulder, CO: Westview.
——. (1997). "Bringing Strong Ties Back In: Indirect Connection, Bridges, and Job Search in China." *American Sociological Review* 62(3):366–85.
——. (2000). "Getting a Job Through a Web of Guanxi in Urban China." In *Networks in the Global Village*, edited by B. Wellman. Boulder, CO: Westview.
Bian, Y., and S. Ang. (1997). "Guanxi Networks and Job Mobility in China and Singapore." *Social Forces* 75:981–1006.
Bian, Y., R. Breiger, D. Davis, and J. Galaskiewics. (2005). "Occupation, Class, and Social Networks in Urban China." *Social Forces* 83(4):1443–68.
Braudel, F. (1977). *Afterthoughts on Material Civilization and Capitalism*. Baltimore: Johns Hopkins University Press.
Brenner, R. (1976). "Agrarian Class Structure and Economic Development in Pre-Industrial Europe." *Past Present* 70:30–75.
Castells, M. (1996). *The Rise of the Network Society*. City: Press.
——. (1998). *End of Millennium*. Malden, MA: Blackwell.
Chang, G. G. (2001). *The Coming Collapse of China*. New York: Random House.
De Soto, H. (2000). *The Mystery of Capital: Why Capitalism Triumphs in the West and Fails Everywhere Else*. New York: Basic Books.
Deng, X. P. (1984). "Build Socialism with Chinese Characteristics." *English, People's Daily* (Beijing), 30/6 *A Talk with the Japanese Delegation to the Second Session of the Council of Sino-Japanese Non-Governmental Persons*.
DiMaggio, P. J. and W. W. Powell. (1991). "Introduction." Pp. 1–38 in *The New Institutionalism in Organizational Analysis*, edited by Walter W. Powell and Paul J. DiMaggio. Chicago: University of Chicago Press.
Dobb, M. (1947). *Studies in the Development of Capitalism*. New York: International Publishers Co.
Esping-Anderson, G. (1990). *The Three Worlds of Welfare Capitalism*. Princeton, NJ: Princeton University Press.
Evans, P. (1995). *Embedded Autonomy*. Princeton, NJ: Princeton University Press.
Evans, P. B., D. Rueschemeyer, and T. Skocpal (eds.). (2002). *Bringing the State Back In*. New York: Cambridge University Press.
Faure, D. (2006). *China and Capitalism*. Hong Kong: Hong Kong University Press, 07/03/30.
Fligstein, N. (2005). "States, Markets, and Economic Growth." Pp. 119–43 in *The Economic Sociology of Capitalism*, edited by V. Nee and R. Swedberg. Princeton, NJ: Princeton University Press.
Frank, A. G. (1998). *ReOrient: Global Economy in the Asian Age*. Berkeley, CA: University of California Press.
Friedman, M. (1962). *Capitalism and Freedom*. Chicago: University of Chicago Press.
Gerschenkron, A. (1962). *Economic Backwardness in Historical Perspective*. Cambridge, MA: Beknap Press of Harvard University Press.
Goldstone, J. (1987). "Cultural Orthodoxy, Risk and Innovation: The Divergence of East and West in the Early Modern World." *Sociological Theory* 5 (Fall):119–35.
Gould, M. (1987). *Revolution in the Development of Capitalism*. Berkeley, CA: University of California Press.
Granovetter, M. (1985). "Economic Action and Social Structure: The Problem of Embeddedness." *American Journal of Sociology* 91:481–510.

Hamilton, G. G. and N. W. Biggart. (1988). "Market, Culture and Authority: A Comparative Analysis of Management and Organization in the Far East." *American Journal of Sociology* 94:S52–94.
Heilbroner, R. (1985). *The Nature and Logic of Capitalism*. New York: W. W. Norton.
Hill, C. (1972). *The World Turned Upside Down*. Hammondsworth: Penguin.
Hilton, R. (ed.). (1978). *Transition from Deudalism to Capitalism*. London: Verso.
Hobson, J. M. (1997). *The Wealth of States*. Cambridge: Cambridge University Press.
Hsu, C. (2007). Personal communication.
Hwang, K. K. (1987). "Face and Favor: The Chinese Power Game." *American Journal of Sociology* 92(4, January):944–74.
Johnson, C. (1995). Japan: Who Governs?: The Rise of the Development State. New York: W. W. Norton.
——. (2006). *Nemesis: The Last Days of the American Republic*. NY: Metropolitan Books of Henry Holt and Company.
King, A. Y. C. (1985). "The Individual and Group in Confucianism: A Relational Perspective." Pp. 57–70 in *Individualism and Holism: Studies in Confucian and Taoist Values*, edited by D. J. Munro. Ann Arbor: Center for Chinese Studies, the University of Michigan.
——. (1982/1988). "Analysis of Renqing in Interpersonal Relations (Renqi Guanxi Zhong Renqing Zhi Fensi)." Pp. 319–45 in *Psychology of the Chinese (Zhongguren de Xinli)*, edited by K. S. Yang. Taipei, Taiwan: Guiguan Press.
Kriedte, P., Medick, H., and J. Schlumbohm. (1981). *Indiustrialization Before Industriailization*. Cambridge: Cambridge University Press.
Lachmann, R. (1987). *From Manor to Market: Structural Change in England, 1536–1640*. Madison, Wisconsin: University of Wisconsin Press.
——. (1989). "Origins of Capitalism in Western Europe: Economic and Political Analysis." *Annual Review of Sociology* 15:47–72.
Lai, G. (1995). "Work and Family Roles and Psychological Well-Being in Urban China." *Journal of Health and Social Behavior* 36(1, March):11–38.
Lin, Nan. (1989). "Chinese Family Structure and Chinese Society." *Bulletin of the Institute of Ethnology* 65:382–99.
——. (1995). "Local Market Socialism: Local Corporatism in Action in Rural China." *Theory and Society* 24:301–54.
——. (2001a). *Social Capital: A Theory of Social Structure and Action*. London and New York: Cambridge University Press.
——. (2001b). "Guanxi: A Conceptual Analysis." Pp. 153–66 in *The Chinese Triangle of Mainland, Taiwan, and Hong Kong: Comparative Institutional Analysis*, edited by A. So, N. Lin and D. Poston. Westport, CT: Greenwood.
——. (2003). "Job Search in Urban China: Gender, Network Chains, and Embedded Resources." Pp. 145–71 in *Creation and Return to Social Capital*, edited by H. Flap and B. Volker. NY: Praeger.
Lin, N. and Bai Gao. (2000). "Cybernetworks and a Social Capital-Based Economy." Presented at the Annual Meeting of the American Sociological Association, August 16, 2000, Washington, D.C.
Lin, N. and X. Ye. (1998). "Chinese Rural Enterprises in Transformation: The End of the Beginning." *Issues and Studies* 34(11):1–28.
Locke, J. (1952/1764). *The Second Treatise of Government*. Indianapolis: Bobbs-Merrill.
Malik, M. (2006). *Power and Interest News Report*, *China's Growing Involvement in Latin America*. City: Press.
March, J. G. (1989). *Rediscovering Institutions*. New York: Free Press.
Mesquita, Bruce Bueno de and G. W. Downs. (2005). "Development and Democracy." *Foreign Affairs*, September/October: Pp.
Meyer, J. W. and B. Rowan. (1977). "Institutionalized Organizations: Formal Structure as Myth and Ceremony." *American Journal of Sociology* 83:340–63.

Miller, M. (ed.). (2005). *Worlds of Capitalism: Institutions, Governance and Economic Change in the Era of Globalization*. London and New York: Routledge.
Monsen, R. J. and K. D. Walters. (1983). *Nationalized Companies: A Threat to American Business*. NY: McGraw-Hill Irwin.
North, D. C. (1990). *Institutions, Institutional Change and Economic Performance*. Cambridge: Cambridge University Press.
North, D. C. and R. Thomas. (1973). *The Rise of the Western World*. Cambridge: Cambridge University Press.
Polanyi, K. (1944). *The Great Transformation*. Boston: Beacon Press.
Polanyi, K. and C. M. Arensberg, Pearson. (1957). *Trade Market in the Early Empires*. Pearson, New York: The Free Press.
Rand, A. (1946/1966). *Capitalism: The Unknown Ideal*. New York: The New American Library.
Redding, S. G. (1990). *The Spirit of Chinese Capitalism*. New York: Walter de Gruyter.
Rosovsky, H. (1961). *Capital Formation in Japan 1968–1940*. New York: Free Press.
Rueschemeyer, D., E. H. Stephens, and J. D. Stephens. (1992). *Capitalist Development and Democracy*. Chicago: University of Chicago Press.
Samuelson, P. (2004). "Why Ricardo and Mill Rebut and Confirm Arguments of Mainstream Economists Supporting Globalization." *Journal of Economic Perspectives* 18(3, summer):135–46.
Schumpeter, J. A. (1946/1951). "Capitalism." Pp. 184–205 in *Essays*, edited by J. A. Schumpeter. New York: Addison-Wesley.
——. Skocpal, T. (1996). "Unravelling From Above." *The American Prospect* 25 (March–April):20–25.
Smith, A. (1937). *The Wealth of Nations*. New York: Modern Library Edition.
Sombart, W. (1902). *Der Moderne Kapitalismus (Modern Capitalism)*. Leipzig: Duncker & Humbolt.
Swisher, K. (1999). *AOL.COM*. New York: Random House.
*The Economist*. (2005). "China Wants to Build World-Class Companies. Can It Succeed?" January 6.
——. (2006a). January 21.
——. (2006b). "Or Property and Poverty." August 24.
——. (2007a). "Our Company Right or Wrong." March 15.
——. (2007b). "Come In Number One, Your Time is Up." April 14.
——. (2007c). "The Art of Courtship." May 19.
Tilly, C. and R. Tilly. (1971). "Agenda for European Economic History in the 1970's." *Journal of Economic History* 31:184–98.
Wallerstein, I. (1979). *The Capitalist World Economy*. Cambridge: Cambridge University Press.
Walzer, M. (1965). *Revolution of the Saints*. Cambridge, MA: Harvard University Press.
Weber, M. (1947). *The Theory of Social and Economic Organizations*. New York: Oxford University Press.
Weiss, L. (1998). *The Myth of Powerless State*. Ithaca, New York: Cornell University Press.
Wen, J. (2007). "Our Historical Tasks at the Primary State of Socialism and Several Issues Concerning China's Foreign Policy." Beijing March 4.
Williamson, O. E. (1975). *Markets and Hierarchies: Analysis and Antitrust Implications*. New York: Free Press.
——. (1985). *The Economic Institutions of Capitalism*. New York: Free Press.
Winters, L. A. and S. Yusuf (eds.). (2007). *Dancing with Giants: China, India and the Global Economy*. Singapore: Institute of Policy Studies, World Bank.
Wong, R. B. (1997). *China Transformed, Historical Change and the Limits of European Experience*. Ithaca, New York: Cornell University Press.
World Bank. (2004). World Development Indicators database.

Zelizer, V. A. (2005). "Circuits Within Capitalism." Pp. 289–321 in *The Economic Sociology of Capitalism*, edited by V. Nee and R. Swedberg. Princeton, NJ: Princeton University Press.

Zucker, L. G. (1988). "Where Do Instituional Patterns Come From? Organizations as Actors in Social Systems." Pp. 23–49 in *Institutional Patterns and Organizations: Culture and Environment*, edited by L. G. Zucker. Cambridge, MA: Ballinger.

# THE "SPIRIT" OF CAPITALISM IN CHINA: CONTEMPORARY MEANINGS OF WEBER'S THOUGHT*

Ku Chung-hwa

## I. *Introduction*

China's Property Law was passed on 16th March 2007 in the Fifth Session of the Tenth National People's Congress (NPC). Among the 2,889 representatives in attendance, 2,799 cast their votes in favor of the bill, thus putting an end to a debate that has lasted for some thirteen years. The Law provides a written recognition of the system of private property rights, and at the same time echoes the revision of Article Number Thirteen that was made during the 2004 Constitution Reform, which states that "citizens' legally owned private property is not to be infringed." The question remains as to whether the legislative changes signify China's wholesale retreat from socialism and move toward the adoption of the capitalist path. It may be that China's institutional transition has a long way to go, and in view of the numerous unresolved problems, the passing of the property bill may well intensify political conflicts and social unrest.[1]

There is already a rich plurality of theses on the policies and implications of China's economic reform that spans various academic disciplines. This essay attempts to apply the theories of the German sociologist Max Weber (1864–1920) to understand China's experience of moving toward a market economy and capitalism. Weber's magnum

* Reference to this article should be made as follows: Ku, Chung-hwa. 2007. "The "Spirit" of Capitalism in China: Contemporary Meanings of Weber's Thought".

[1] As a Taiwanese scholar researching legislative changes in China has commented, "the statement 'Workers of the world, unite!,' which appears on the back cover of all Chinese translated versions of *The Communist Manifesto* should remove the exclamation mark, replace it with a dash, and follow with the phrase 'together we become property owners'. This might better echo the reality of the institutional reform in the Chinese economy" (Wang 2007:8). The Property Law still emphasises that at the primary stage of socialism, the country insists on a fundamental economic system that seeks development through relying principally on collective ownership, accompanied by various alternative ownership systems. It thus epitomises the deep-seated contradiction between private property and collective property that is not easy to resolve.

opus *The Protestant Ethic and the Spirit of Capitalism* is now one hundred years old, and although it still provides us with a lucid account of capitalism, is now challenged by situations that were unforeseen when it was written, one of which is China's rapid economic growth in recent years. To understand the relationships between Weber's theory and empirical experience, it is necessary to re-examine Weber's perspective on what constitutes capitalism. Of particular importance is his emphasis on "economic ethic" (Wirtschaftsethik) and "spirit" (Geist), which we can use to ponder whether the Chinese economy has fully established the mechanisms of a capitalist system, both materially and spiritually. A re-interpretation of Weber's thought will not only enable us to arrive at the truth of the so-called "rise of China," but will also enrich our analytical perspective on the changes that are taking place in the world.

Where China's choice of development approach is concerned, the sixty years since the founding of the Peoples' Republic of China in 1949 can be divided into two major periods. In the first 30 years, China was under the tremendous influence of Mao Zedong, who incessantly pursued the radical road of collectivism and even launched the Cultural Revolution with a view to attaining the ultimate ideal of communism. This dream of a "New China" was shattered with Mao's death and the disbanding of the Gang of Four. What followed was Deng Xiaoping's "Reform and Openness" program, which was announced in 1978, an approach that Chinese leaders have continued to follow despite the 1989 Tiananmen Incident. Indeed, they have continued to open up the market, induced a massive inflow of foreign capital, achieved rapid economic growth year after year, and made China one of the locomotives of global capitalism.

China's pursuit of a market economy is a perplexing chapter in its history. The Chinese Communist Party (CCP) has ideologically adhered to the superiority of socialism, yet it has thoroughly implemented the market logic of capitalism, so much so that it has become more tolerant than capitalist countries (such as Taiwan) of the social inequalities induced by the widening income gap. In addition, alongside the thorough "commercialization" (Weber's term) of economic life, the people of China seem to have become increasingly accustomed to the values of capitalism. Does this assimilation process lend support to the claims made by the modernisation theory, developed during the height of the 20th century Cold War that the entire world is converging toward the Western capitalist model? What sea change has occurred in China that has allowed it to convert from being a steadfast opponent of Western imperialism to the most loyal bastion of capitalist production and consumption? What accounts for such a drastic change, and can we really conclude that China has become capitalist from top to bottom? When Weber first analysed the social structure and cultural content of traditional China, he articulated a range of conditions that were unfavorable to the emergence of capitalism. Is it really possible that all of these conditions have disappeared?

Given this background, the *problematique* of this essay is to re-examine Weber's theory of capitalism and evaluate it against China's experiences in recent years. In so doing, I aim to determine whether it is possible to identify the blind spots to provide a more appropriate evaluation of China's social and economic situations and address the questions that have been raised in the foregoing. In other words, this essay intends to bring together the last two decades of critical discussion of Weber's theory from academics worldwide—and China in particular, to juxtapose his theory with China's actual socioeconomic development, and to evaluate whether his theory can account for China's economic performance. Weber once suggested the use of two yardsticks—"causal explanation" and "meaning adequacy"—to evaluate research outcomes in the social sciences. Through the investigation of theories and the interpretation of empirical experience, this essay hopes to provide readers with a deeper understanding of the spiritual facets of China's economic growth, while at the same time endowing Weber's theory with a more contemporary meaning.

## II. *Continuity and Change in Weber's "China Thesis"*

What is generally known as "Weber's Thesis" refers primarily to the viewpoints delineated in *The Protestant Ethic and the Spirit of Capitalism*. The concern with Weber's Thesis among Western scholars has not diminished over time: in 2001 and 2002 alone, two new English translations of the work were added to the collection (Weber 2001, 2002).[2] In a similar

[2] Weberian scholar S. Kalberg has corrected the new translation mistakes made by T. Parsons' earlier translation, thus returning to Weber's original thought. This belongs to the domain of "de-Parsonizing Weber" (for the background to "de-Parsonizing Weber" in American sociology, see Ku 1992: 30–33; for reviews on the two newly translated books, see Kaelber 2002). Other discussions, such as that of J. Cohen's (2002), have provided a detailed examination of the discursive mechanism of Weber's Thesis,

vein, one can regard Weber's *The Religion of China: Confucianism and Taoism* as his "China Thesis". However, Weber's cross-cultural comparison of non-Western religions has long been viewed as a negative case study secondary to his thesis, because his analysis of world religions such as Confucianism, Taoism, Hinduism, Buddhism, and Islam was merely used to justify his claim that only the "economic ethic" of Protestantism was capable of instigating the spirit of capitalism, thus facilitating the emergence and growth of capitalism in the West. It is also because of Weber's strategy of raising only negative questions, such as "why (there is) no capitalism in China (or India, Saudi Arabia...)?" that his research on the non-Western world can be accused of Eurocentrism, raising doubts about his methodology and value stance.

Gary Hamilton, for instance, considers Weber's approach of asking negative questions to be misleading, and proposes that only by employing a China angle to explain its history can one understand how China has become China (Hamilton, translated by Chang et al. 1990). Hamilton's critique of Weber, in line with the recent turn toward a "China-centered history" among Western sinologists, may represent a more balanced approach to historical study. However, it has obliterated Weber's original intent, preventing readers from having a full understanding of Weber's sociological *problematique* and distorting the inspirational value of comparative research.[3] A deeper level of critique involves the contention that Orientalism largely constitutes the hidden assumption and foundational ideology of Weber's China analysis, leading him to describe China as being in stasis. If we can transcend the confines of the ideology of Orientalism and involve an element of chronology, then we can discover the webs of development and transformation in traditional Chinese society (Yang 1987:249). At a time when the discourse of post-colonialism has been made popular by scholars such as Edward Said, such a criticism certainly makes sense.

---

including Weber's understanding of Benjamin Franklin and whether the anxieties of the Puritans were really so extreme. In a different vein, S. Pierotti (2003) collects together the doubts raised by different scholars and helps to clarify Weber from a historian's perspective, arguing that Weber's Thesis can stand up to rigorous testing. In general, discussions of Weber's Thesis in the last few years have not gone beyond the scope of analysis provided by *Weber's Protestant Ethic: Origins, Evidence, Contexts*, a volume edited by H. Lehmmann and G. Roth (1993). The simplified Chinese character version was published in 2001.

[3] See the debate between Chang (1995) and Ku (1999) for Weber's methodological issues in this respect.

Nonetheless, Weber's "China Thesis" should not be understood as an analysis of stasis. In treating the huge amounts of historical materials regarding China, Weber actually provides an implicit assessment of whether China possesses an alternative rationalism, and whether China can possibly develop a unique model of rationalisation. Ultimately, given that Weber's China study is only a part of his series on "The Economic Ethic of World Religions" (Die Wirtschaftsethik der Weltreligionen), it should not be read in isolation but considered in relation to the entire collection. Thus, grasping Weber's dynamic narrative of a world history of which China is an integral part is perhaps an effort that must be made to sustain Weber's scholarship.[4]

In the century since Weber's Thesis was first presented to the world, it has been borrowed, appropriated, and misinterpreted in various ways across different times and space. In carrying on Weber's scholarship in different locations, we can also see how cultural specificities have led to the divergent emphases or interpretations of the Thesis.[5] Relative to Weber's Thesis, which was examined to different degrees from the outset, the China Thesis has rarely been subject to objective evaluation, largely because Weber had no chance to witness the sort of circumstances that would lead China to a modernised, Westernised, and rationalised mode of capitalistic development. His argument in *The Religion of China: Confucianism and Taoism* merely attempts to answer the historical question as to why capitalism had emerged exclusively in the West. Insofar as China served as a point of comparison, he naturally refrained from asking the question of how China was to develop capitalism. With the dissolution of the Soviet Union and the Eastern bloc, China progressively integrated into the global division of labor, with the deepening of capitalist economics in China becoming more apparent. At least from the economic perspective, few can deny that China has

---

[4] On this point, see Jian (1988). In addition, the author believes that the use of "ideal-type" constitutes the core of Weber's methodology, thus resulting in a static approach to the appropriation of historical materials. Weber was rather liberal and open in his argument for the rationalisation of world history, which rescues him from the pitfalls of Hegelian philosophy. For this reason, the author does not agree with these two interpretations of Weber's China Thesis and believes that we can uncover the positive contributions of Weber's theories on China's historical and contemporary situations (see Ku 1987, 1992).

[5] For instance, Professor Schwentker, who teaches at Osaka University, has traced the history of Weber in the field of social sciences in Japan, providing an in-depth understanding of how the spirit of capitalism in Japan has been understood and interpreted in different eras. See Schwentker (2005).

become a stronghold of capitalistic globalisation. However, that China has become a global factory and a consumer giant implies not only a transformation of the country's original outlook, but also the world's perception of China. Since the 1978 Reform, annual economic growth in China has averaged around 10%, and in 2006 its GDP amounted to US$2,684.7 billion, ranking it fourth in the world. Its foreign exchange reserves, which are now in excess of US$10,000 billion, have become the largest in the world, and its total import/export volume is ranked third globally. China's success story, however, remains a mystery to the world, which finds it difficult to decipher its internal dynamics and trajectory of development.

This essay brings the neglected spiritual dimension into its scope of analysis, outlining whether the uniqueness has been created at the level of economic ethics during China's journey toward capitalism, and whether this cultural product enshrines an alternative universality that will allow China to become a great nation that can compete with the West. In his conclusion to *The Religion of China: Confucianism and Taoism*, Weber classifies the traditional Chinese civilisation as embodying a "rational adaptation to the world" in contrast to the "rational mastery over the world" epitomised by Protestantism. This view is now challenged by new experiences, and whether it can still be justified is a point of contention. The question hinges directly on whether Weber's Thesis has been properly understood and developed. The following dissects three perspectives in which Weber's Thesis has since its inception affected the issues that are explored in this essay, and how it has triggered a new wave of contemporary discussion and historical interpretation.

When one reviews the significance of Weber's China Thesis, especially in terms of its "history of reception" (Rezeptionsgeschichte), it is notable that there have been few direct responses to *The Religion of China: Confucianism and Taoism*. On one hand, the topic is too removed from the mainstream academic pursuits of the West, and except for those who possess expert knowledge, is extremely difficult to follow. Unsurprisingly, only a handful of book reviews emerged up to the 1930s, and the English translation of 1951 received little attention (Ku 1987). However, with the propagation of the modernisation theory, a few scholars began to absorb the implications of Weber's argument. They contended that the Confucian tradition has hindered the modernisation of China, and that only with the thorough destruction of traditional culture could modernisation ensue (Levenson 1958). This line of argument foreshadows the debate that was spearheaded by Ambrose King and others on the Confucian ethic and economic development. Modernisation became a prominent stream of study during the 1970s in Taiwan, and the dichotomy of tradition and modernity that was popular at that time seemed to advocate the renunciation of tradition in favor of modernisation. However, in his *From Tradition to Modernity* (*Cong Chuantong Dao Xiandai*), King emphasises repeatedly that modernity is the "remaking" of tradition, noting that "the task of 'cultural remaking' in China's modernisation project will involve a rational 'choice'.... This 'selective transformation' will entail four major choices: 1) accepting certain new cultural traits; 2) rejecting certain new cultural traits; 3) preserving certain traditional cultural traits; and 4) selectively discarding certain traditional cultural traits" (King 1978: 213– 214). However, he does not elucidate how these choices are to be made in practice. When the economic growth of the Four Dragons of Asia became acknowledged by the West, King (1983) published his paper "Confucian ethic and economic development" (Rujia Lunli Yu Jingji Fazhan: Weibo Xueshuo De Chong Tan) and launched an attack on Weber's China Thesis. Inspired by the massive success of the Asian economic miracle, he proposed that the impressive economic development of some Asian countries posed the greatest challenge to Weber's China Thesis, and in particular his comments on the Confucian ethic. Consequently, King proclaimed that the "Confucian ethic is the cultural explanation to the puzzle of East Asian socioeconomics" (King 1983: 75), and used it to answer his question how tradition can be reconciled with modernity.

King's viewpoint on the positive effect of the Confucian ethic on Asia's economic development is somehow adapted from Robert Bellah's structural-functionalist position. King aimed to search for the "functional equivalent" of the Protestant ethic. In *Tokugawa Religion*, Bellah uses Weber's Thesis as an analogy to explain the significance of religion for Japan's economy. King also sought to apply this method of analogy to the four dragons with a view to revising Weber's China Thesis and reinstating the Confucian ethic. However, as many scholars have pointed out, Weber was not concerned with how capitalism spread to non-Western cultural areas once it had emerged, but how the West had broken away from the fetters of tradition and acquired the impetus for rationalisation. Hence, King's *problematique* does not necessarily have to implicate Weber, for it is an irrefutable historical truth that China had not generated capitalism spontaneously. Weber's China Thesis therefore is not necessarily shaken by King's act of rectification (Yang and Tu 1987).

Another prominent work is Yu Ying-shih's (1987) *Zhongguo Jinshi Zongjiao Lunli Yu Shangren Jingshen* (*The Religious Ethic and the Spirit of Merchant in Early Modern China*), in which he tries to demonstrate that one can detect in both the Neo-Confucianism of the Song and Ming Dynasties and in Zen Buddhism a turn to "*innerweltliche* (inner-worldly) asceticism" that is comparable to the Protestant ethic of the West. He also posits that the "Way of the Merchant" practiced by the strata of scholar-merchants during the Ming and Qing Dynasties matches Weber's portrayal of the spirit of capitalism. As such, Yu believes his study has corrected that of Weber. Of course, Weber was a layman to Chinese history where the mastery of historical materials and historical facts are concerned, and cannot compare with a true professional in the field. Although Yu's book has aroused much interest in researching China's merchant culture, he has not necessarily refuted Weber's China Thesis. Rather, he seems to have superimposed Weber's concepts on Chinese religious thought, while oversimplifying the complex relationships between the Protestant ethic and the spirit of capitalism. Furthermore, Yu fails to provide evidence at the behavioural level of how Chinese religious thought facilitated the rationalisation of means-end relationships. Attempts as such are not normally deemed successful.[6]

Second, it is worth mentioning that, in recent years, a few distinguished scholars have emerged in the disciplines of sinology and history in the West; in using new historical materials and perspectives, they seem to have formulated a new vision of "Weberian-type questions". The most representative of these scholars are Bin Wong and Kenneth Pomeranz. Wong's (1997) book *China Transformed: Historical Change and the Limits of European Experience* uses China as the focal point to examine the development of different regions in the world. He contends that China and Europe were very similar before the 18th century in terms of agricultural production and the degree of commercialisation, and that there was no sign of stasis in either (Wong 1997). Pomeranz (2002) built on Wong's premises to write *The Great Divergence: China, Europe,*

[6] See Chart (1992) for an in-depth review. In his conclusion on Yu, Chart remarks "his (Yu Ying-shin's) type of cross-cultural comparison does not work out well for either of the two sides compared. On the one side, in reducing it he distorts Weber's historical ideal-type of "inner-worldly asceticism" and disregards its dimension as a social action. On the other side, he attaches pseudo-Weberian labels to his Chinese data, thereby obscuring their meaning".

*and the Making of the Modern World Economy*, analysing why the East and the West have followed different routes of development since the 19th century. Undertaking a holistic assessment and evaluation of economic materials, he studies the impact of long-distance trade on domestic ecological and human resources, and concludes that whereas Europe's success in colonising the Americas enabled it to overcome its ecological constraints and develop industrial know-how, the Chinese government could only cope with the problem of population increase by inducing out-migration from the center to the periphery, thus achieving balanced regional growth. He concludes that one can better understand why Europe was able to breakout from its contemporaneous climate and cross the threshold to industrialism if one applies the regional economic unit in reconstructing the background of the rise of modern capitalism (Pomeranz 2000).

A *problematique* of this sort naturally links with the research conditions to which Weber was subject when he first formulated his thesis. If he could have made use of the materials that are available nowadays, would the causal relationships in his argument remain unchanged? Would Weber have abandoned his thesis, and agree that material and geographical conditions can in themselves account for the rise of capitalism only in Europe? The ever-advancing front of cross-cultural comparative research should inspire us to re-think some of the seemingly affirmed answers and seek more information to bring us closer to the historical truth. However, it should be noted that such historical materials are loaded with numerous assumptions and specific interpretive visions. If they can be used at all, in the absence of an *a priori* agenda, to engage in a comprehensive dialogue with Weber, they may be able to incite a splendid fusion of horizons that generates a more balanced judgment of the roles performed by ethical and spiritual factors. The debate on the Confucian ethic and economic development should perhaps be situated in a wider context, and it must be questioned whether there is any need to search for a concrete functional equivalent of the Protestant ethic in China. Perhaps as an alternative we should instead try to uncover whether any spirit or ethic can be sketched after China's thirty-something years of economic reform, and to determine how distant or different it is from Weber's ideal-type of "the 'spirit' of capitalism".

Finally, this essay represents an effort to sustain Weber's Thesis. However, it does not confine itself to Weber's focus on the two-way relations between religion and economy. Rather, it also considers the social scientific theories that have emerged in the last century, such as neo-institutionalism, civil society, civilisation, and the more recent discussion within economic sociology as to how economic activities are embedded in social networks. These theories will help to generate more concrete classifications and observations of the phenomena that have emerged in the process of China's economic development. Of particular importance is the academic study of "trust", which has become more mature and will definitely help to elucidate the abstract concepts of "spirit" and "ethic" formulated by Weber. Although Weber was able to "objectify" the development of Western culture through his detailed study of Protestantism, he was only able to invoke the general notions of Confucianism and Taoism when discussing China. Not only has this problem remain unresolved until now, it has been exacerbated by the decline of religion in China and the fading of the literati or "carriers" of Confucianism, such that there are now no ready-made substitutes for the key elements of the Protestant ethic. In spite of this, this essay undertakes a painstaking investigation utilising all of the available clues to identify the spiritual factors that have accompanied China's economic restructuring.

From this, it is hoped that an assessment can be made as to whether the relationships between capitalism and the rule of the Chinese Communist Party (CCP) can become symbiotic, or, as the Chinese saying has it "as close as lips are to teeth," or whether the two are no more than strange bedfellows awaiting an inevitable spilt. This essay situates Weber's concerns in contemporary China to deal with the dual challenges that arise from the connection of theory to practice. On the one hand, it uses Weber's idea that capitalism needs the support of spiritual elements to challenge the explanation for Chinese economic development; and on the other hand, it employs Weber's method of cross-cultural comparison to take on the challenge posed by China's economic transformation.

In sum, a survey of the literature inspired by Weber's Thesis leads to the conclusion that China's recent economic growth is a mega phenomenon compared with that of Asia's four dragons in the 1980s. In stimulating a greater space for imagination, it is hoped that this essay models Weber's quest for knowledge and gives new life to his China Thesis.[7]

---

[7] In China, the first book to systematically discuss Weber's China Thesis was perhaps Du Xuncheng's (1993) *Zhongguo Chuantong Lunli Yu Jindai Zibenzhuyi: Jian Ping Weibo*

## III. *Continuity and Fracture: What Changes Have Occurred to "Traditionalism" in Chinese Social Structure?*

By the time Weber had shifted his attention from occidental history to non-occidental history, the non-occidental regions had mostly been penetrated by Western powers, and, in the mode that historian Arnold Toynbee termed "challenge—response", had undergone tremendous transformations. For example, the 1911 revolution involved the replacement of the Qing Dynasty by Republican China, yet Weber said not a word on this momentous issue when he published *The Religion of China: Confucianism and Taoism* in 1915: what concerned him was China's state form and social structure, which had seemingly remained unchanged for the past two thousand years.[8] Perhaps right from the beginning, Weber was less interested in determining how modernisation had expanded to all corners of the world, focusing instead on questions pertaining to world history, such as how the West became the West of today and why capitalism emerged exclusively in the West, but not who would command the future world or which culture would be the next to ascend. As a matter of fact, Weber was rather reserved when confronted with

*Zhongguo De Zongjiao.* In its conclusion, Du reveals that whenever he heard of "people questioning Weber's theories on the premises of the economic development of Asia's Four Little Dragons," he immediately thought that "the condition of Asia's Four Little Dragons has yet to refute Weber's theory. For Weber had pointed to China's condition as a whole, rather than addressing some regions in China or its neighboring countries, in building up *The Religion of China: Confucianism and Taoism.*" This "gives rise to the idea of assessing Weber's theories by referring to the conditions of contemporary China" (Du 1993:211). For the successors to Weber's other classics, see Su (1989) and Liu (1996). In searching for related research materials within the China region, one can find many journal articles that touch upon Weber's assessment of traditional Chinese culture and whether his theories are serviceable for the establishment of a new ethos and social values. For example, He (2005) in "Weibo Zhongguo Mingti Yu Dongya Zibenzhuyi De Fazhan" maintains that it is desirable to "depart from the Weber Thesis" and construct a "new theoretical framework of cultural explanation". There are also studies like "Weibo Rujiao Lunli Yu Zibenzhuyi Fazhan Lilun Jieshi" (Yu 2004). In an essay "Shichang Jingji Lunli Jingshen Tan Xi–Weibo Xinjiao Lunli Yanjiu De Shidai Jie Du," Gao (2003) discusses ways to strengthen one's understanding of the cultural background of the market economy in China. Other theses include "Shichang Jingji Yu Chuantong Lunli De Chuangzaoxing Chong Gou" (Xu 2006), "Weibo Wenti Yu Zhiye Lunli" (Cui 2005), and "Qin Jian, Lunli Yu Dongya Fazhan Bian Xi" (Zhang 2003). All of these works symbolise an increasing concern among China's young scholars as to the relevance of Weber's Thesis to contemporary Chinese situations.

[8] In 1920, Weber increased the size of the original book by nearly half and expanded it into *The Religion of China: Confucianism and Taoism*, which became the first piece in his *Sociology of Religion*.

such practical problems. Nevertheless, in the conclusion to *The Religion of China: Confucianism and Taoism*, he asserts, "the Chinese in all probability would be quite capable, probably more capable than the Japanese, of assimilating capitalism which had technically and economically been fully developed in the modern culture arena. It is obviously not a question of deeming the Chinese (to be) 'naturally ungifted' for the demands of capitalism" (Weber 1952: 248).[9] If we follow the logic of Weber's China Thesis, we should perhaps ask whether, having been opened up by the West by force for more than a hundred years (taking the Opium War as a starting point), the conditions have become ripe for China to assimilate capitalism. We should question the changes that have occurred to those elements—be they structural, institutional, material, or spiritual—that were considered by Weber to be unfavorable to capitalism. Can we contend that capitalism, subsequent to its globalisation and China's conversion to a market economy, has reached the state where, as Weber describes, "this nullity imagines that it has attained a level of civilization never before achieved", and that "history" has approached "the end"?[10]

It is impossible to handle all of the related overly complex empirical information within the confines of this essay. All that we can do is to retrace the extensive use of "ideal-types" by Weber in *The Religion of China: Confucianism and Taoism* making reference to the most central ideal-types of "traditionalism", and concisely examine whether all of the negative traits originally identified by Weber have undergone fundamental changes. Only armed with this information can we judge

[9] Interestingly, when Weber mentions the Japanese in *The Religion of India: The Sociology of Hinduism and Buddhism*, he describes them as "a people among whom a stratum of the character of the samurai played the decisive role could not attain a rational economic ethic on their own, quite apart from all other circumstances, especially the closure against the outside. Nevertheless, the feudal relationships making for recallable, contractually-fixed, legal relationships offered a basis much more favorable to "individualism" in the occidental sense of the word, than did Chinese theocracy. With relative ease Japan was able to take over capitalism as an artifact from the outside, though it could not create capitalism out of its own spirit" (Weber, translated by Kang and Jian 1996: 444; Weber, translated by Gerth and Martindale 1958:275). From this, one can see that Weber holds a flexible view of the transplantation of capitalism and does not believe that any nation would be inherently incapable of accepting capitalism.

[10] The "End of history" was proposed by the Japanese-American scholar F. Fukuyama, who adopts a Hegelian vision of history and argues that human beings have become united under liberal democracy and the market economy with the collapse of the Soviet Union and Eastern Europe and the socialism that they espoused. As there is no longer any large dispute, history comes to an "end" (Fukuyama, translated by Li 1993).

whether capitalism has taken root in China and whether China has demonstrated its ability to assimilate the spirit of capitalism? Of course, the method of ideal-types tends to simplify historical truth, yet this has its advantages: we can take charge of the complicated by grasping the simple. Weber identified, by relying on this approach, several elements that he believed prevented China from developing capitalism spontaneously. They include the following:

1. The lack of specific, acknowledged, formal, and reliable legal base to protect the free development of the industry and commerce.
2. The lack of a professional and efficient bureaucracy.
3. The lack of a rational monetary economy and fiscal policy.
4. The lack of an independent and autonomous class of citizens.
5. The lack of self-governing city.
6. The lack of mutually competitive political entities (because of grand unification under a ruler) and the absence of a "reasonable" concept of war.
7. The lack of connection to overseas colonial subjects.
8. The lack of rational systems for administration and law enforcement.
9. The lack of a system directed to professional education and training.
10. The lack of rational science and technology.
11. The lack of rationally organized enterprises.
12. The lack of a rational system in accounting and book-keeping.
13. The lack of a method to direct daily lives that is unique to salvation religions (e.g. inner-worldly asceticism).
14. The lack of restraints from the instinctual "desire for profits" that threatens to destroy all rational modes of accumulation.[11]

These are the major elements pointed out unequivocally by Weber. As it would be impractical to examine each of them in detail, the following portrays the current situation in China focusing initially on the elements that pertain to the institutional level. This is followed by an analysis of the "spirit" level, which is the main theme of this essay.

Comparing China's condition at the beginning of the 21st century with that of a century ago, no one could deny that China has undergone profound changes. Traditional Chinese society, although one should no longer describe it as having been "in stasis"—in the same way that

[11] The summary relies mainly on Ku's (1987) PhD thesis and the work of Sun (1987:212). Due to the reliance on different editions of Weber, the original sources are omitted here.

Western history no longer designates the Medieval Period as the "Dark Ages"—was nonetheless set in a "pre-industrial" and "pre-Newtonian" state before its considerable contact with the West. The country showed no signs of moving toward modernity, but was instead engrossed in the self-imagination of the "Middle Kingdom," considering all surrounding states to be barbaric and obliging visiting ambassadors from the West to observe the hierarchical relationships typified by the paying of tribute and *kowtowing* to the Chinese emperor.[12] Only after it had experienced a series of dreadful defeats in the Opium War, First Sino-Japanese War, Boxer War, Second Sino-Japanese War and disillusion regarding socialism's ability to bring wealth and power did the political leaders of China decide to "cross the river by grasping the stone" by cautiously introducing market mechanisms and inserting China more firmly into the economic system of global capitalism.

The tremendous transformation that has been experienced by China following its economic reform far out-weighs that experienced by the Asian Dragons, which renders it necessary to re-examine the relationship between tradition and modernity. British sociologist Anthony Giddens has put forth the concepts of "de-traditionalisation" and "post-traditional society," in which he intended to describe the societies of the West, provide a lucid account of the chronic pains experienced by China.[13] As is well known, under the rule of the CCP, China not only engaged in a massive political struggle to purge the traditional land-owning and propertied classes and intellectuals, but also launched the unprecedented Cultural Revolution with the battle cry of "shatter the four 'olds' and launch the four 'news'" (*Po Si Jiu, Li Si Xin*), proclaiming as they did so the "complete eradication of Confucianism" so as to establish a "new China" totally extraneous to tradition. The radical Cultural Revolution thoroughly destroyed the legitimacy of tradition at both the institutional and behavioral levels. Juxtaposed against the characteristics of traditionalism identified by Weber, we can make at least two major observations.

---

[12] See Peyrefitte (translated by Mao et al. 1993) for the confrontations and consequences of the history of communication between China and the West.

[13] Here, I borrow Giddens' concepts to describe the series of de-traditionalisation campaigns launched by the CCP since it came into power (see Beck, Giddens and Lash 1994; Heelas, Lash and Morris 1996).

First, the Communist ideology is diametrically opposed to clan ties, which Weber considered to be the root of Chinese traditionalism. The power of the clan, extant in the social, political, economic, and cultural levels of Chinese society, suffered wave after wave of callous attack and purgation under Communist rule. After Mao Zedong established the People's Commune, which successfully transformed traditional village communities into factory-like production units, the functions of traditional family, lineage, and clan were more or less eliminated. Henceforth, China became a "unit-society," which replaced the tradition of self-governance (Li 2004). One might venture to say that from a sociological standpoint China has relied on external power to forcefully transform its social structure from "community" (*Gemeinschaft*) to "society" (*Gesellschaft*). This is symbolised by the severing of connections founded primarily on blood-ties and their replacement by the functional ties associated with bureaucratic relations, which has led to the disappearance of customs, institutions, and cultures that were attached to tradition. These incidentally were the overwhelming images outsiders acquired of "Red China" under the rule of Mao, perceiving him to have bred a new type of human being who unquestioningly obeyed the party-state and discarded without hesitation cultural traditions that had persisted for several thousand years.[14] Most intriguing is the implementation of the one-child policy following China's great upsurge in population; this further destroyed the clanship network, such that even though many traditional customs were revived after the economic reform, they could no longer be founded on a traditional social structure centered on clan and lineage.

A second anti-tradition force that cannot be ignored concerns the political transformation from "patrimonial bureaucracy" (Patrimonialbuerokratie) to "party bureaucracy," or the termination of the tradition of "family rule" (*Jia Tianxia*) at the national level and the re-creation of the literati into a loyal and specialised (*You Hong You Zhuan*) administrative machinery that formally matches Weber's definition of a bureaucracy. Despite the presence of "one-party rule" (*Dang Tianxia*) and the absence of democracy, China has freed itself from the mode

[14] There seems to be inadequate debate on the historical interpretation of the Cultural Revolution. The Chinese government considers it a taboo subject and has prohibited its discussion, even when it reaches its fortieth anniversary.

of the "pre-modern state" that is characterised by inefficiency and the inability to utilise organisational strength. The CCP has also established its legitimacy through the centralisation of violence and the process of nation-building. Under such "modern" conditions, China has been able to thoroughly implement its policies of economic reform since 1978. All of the institutional characteristics that Weber identifies as impeding capitalist development, and specifically "the lack of specific, acknowledged, formal and reliable legal base to protect the free development of the industry and commerce," "the lack of a professional and efficient bureaucracy," "the lack of a rational monetary economy and fiscal policy," "the lack of rational systems for administration and law enforcement," "the lack of a system directed to professional education and training," "the lack of rational science and technology," "the lack of rationally organised enterprises," and "the lack of a rational system in accounting and book-keeping," have all been overcome in the process of policy implementation.

In other words, China's traditionalism has been annihilated by conscious political force under the dictatorial rule of the CCP, the original purpose of which was to help attain the sacred goal of constructing a Socialist China. Yet when the strategy of a planned economy proved ineffectual and unsustainable, Deng Xiaoping's pragmatism which gained a new legitimacy and experimentation with a socialist market-economy also bore economic fruit. If we were to analyse this from the angle of historical causality, we would have to admit that had it not been for the violence of the Cultural Revolution, it might not have been possible to eradicate China's thousand-year traditions and the conditions that Weber considered impeded capitalist development. In this case, it is not possible to tell for sure whether China would have proceeded smoothly along the route of economic reform without undergoing a political revolution. Chinese scholars would also find it harder to boast that the "China model" is superior to the "Russian model."[15]

Thus far, it has been maintained that under the guiding principles of Chinese economic reform, China has successfully implemented commensurate reforms in its market economic institutions. The Property

[15] The Russian model means "politics first, economics later", whereas the Chinese model means "economics only, no politics." Chinese scholars have in general criticised the Russian experience so much that even the "Color Revolution" in the Central Asian countries has given rise to much caution among Chinese leaders (see Song 2005).

Law highlighted at the beginning of this essay demonstrates how the deepening of reform has gradually reached the level of fundamental value and ideology. From the viewpoint of neo-institutionalism, the series of reform measures has engendered the effects of "path dependency" that are not confined to external, observable institutional changes. China has indeed managed to transplant the capitalist institutions that Weber considers relatively easy for China to assimilate, such as the law, finance, a monetary system, trade, and the organisation of the enterprise. Nevertheless, what concerns us most is whether China has created the "spirit" of capitalism at the same time. We must invariably ask whether there have been major changes to the other non-material conditions identified by Weber, such as "the lack of an independent and autonomous class of citizens," "the lack of self-governing city," "the lack of a method to direct daily lives that is unique to salvation religions (e.g. inner-worldly asceticism)," and "the lack of restraints from the instinctual desire for profits, which threatens to destroy all rational modes of accumulation." The extent to which China has been baptised by capitalism as the country undergoes economic development, and whether, at the level of spirit and ethos, China has nurtured its own modern-compatible cultural values demand answers. Ultimately, we must ponder whether the uniqueness that China manifests will become a potential threat to the "universality" of modern civilisation.

## IV. *Has China Developed a "Spirit" or "Ethic" Compatible with Capitalism?*

The literature is too scant to permit a fair judgment of the changes in spirit or ethic that have taken place in the last thirty years and the many twists and turns that have occurred in the process of China's economic reform. The Tiananmen Incident in particular begged the question as to whether China would continue to pursue the Deng Xiaoping way. The real watershed at which China unveiled its capitalist guise can be dated to 1992, when Deng put forth the Opportunity Thesis (*Jiyun Shuo*) after his southern tour. As a mere fifteen years have passed since then, it is too soon to pass final judgment, yet it is hard to imagine that China's market economic reform will be reversed. Furthermore, if capitalism is given the opportunity to deepen, will a Chinese-style economic ethic emerge to provide the system with a spiritual pillar? Although Weber believed that the asceticism inherent in the Protestant ethic would slip away by the time capitalism became an iron cage, the ethos that will typify future China remains a central issue to be faced by humankind in the 21st century. China is a huge country, and the spiritual factors that have affected its economic actions and even institutional dynamics remain to be determined. In this vein, I now review the struggles that China has faced in the past few years.

After succumbing to the West and suffering the catastrophe of continued invasion and humiliation, China underwent several rounds of large-scale enlightenment campaigns. The most prominent was the May Fourth Movement of 1909, which signified the awakening of the intelligentsia. Its fanatical proposal to adopt a thorough-going Westernisation can also be regarded as the intellectual sea-change that prepared the way for the rise of the CCP. With the outbreak of the Sino-Japanese War, struggles for national survival took priority over enlightenment, the latter indirectly helping the CCP to wipe out the Kuomintang (KMT) and establish the People's Republic of China. The new authority adopted Marxism as its guiding principles and slashed all connections to the doctrines of Confucianism at the spiritual and conscious level. Borrowing Michel Foucault's viewpoint and Norbert Elias' "Theory of Civilization Process", one can say that the so-called "*Ah-Q-ism*"[16] that so characterised the Chinese became disciplined by the doctrinal principles of Communism, developing a tendency to exercise self-restraint and eliminating many types of uncivilised behavior. Although the Chinese ruling stratum has not always followed through with its oft-proclaimed goal of constructing a spiritual civilisation and have often stopped short at the level of outward compliance, to a certain extent a paradigm shift has occurred at the spiritual level. Nowadays, the imagery of the average Chinese no longer carries the uncivilised connotations of "disease-ridden Asian," "opium smoker," or "coolie", but unfortunately Communist collectivism has not engendered a substantive improvement in people's livelihood. The ensuing nightmare of backwardness ignited the so-called "*River Elegy*" (*He Shang*) fever among Chinese intellectuals in 1987 in response to a six-episode television series entitled *River Elegy* that was produced by Su Xiaokang

[16] Lu Xun, who is known as the "father" of modern Chinese literature, created the figure of Ah-Q in his famous novel "The True Story of Ah-Q" (Ah-Q Zheng Zhuan). Ah-Q is considered to be the personification of the negative traits of the Chinese national character. The term "*Ah- Q-ism*" was coined to signify the Chinese penchant for calling defeat a "spiritual victory."

and others. The fever has been likened to the May Fourth Movement, in that it reflected the desire for modernisation and had a bearing on the 1989 Tiananmen democratic movement.

If we consider the reflection of *River Elegy* to be an extension of the May Fourth spirit, then it is somewhat ironic that the democratic movement, which was sustained by the assembly in Tiananmen Square and the erection of the Goddess of Democracy statue, was to end so tragically on June 4 with a bloody suppression. This seems to restage the tragedy of survival taking precedence over "enlightenment," only this time the object of the survival campaign was the political rule of the CCP, rather than the nation. After the June 4 Incident, China's ruling stratum seems to have gradually developed a strategy of separating politics from economics. That is to say, "left [politics] moves far left, while right [economics] moves far right" [*Zuo (Zhengzhi) De Geng Zuo, You (Jingji) De Geng You*], and rapid economic growth has become the foundation of political legitimacy. In view of this situation, China's ruling stratum has put forth successive official ideological frameworks, including Jiang Zemin's "Three Lectures" (*San Jiang Shuo*) and "Three Representatives" (*San Ge Daibiao*) and Hu Jintao's "harmonic society" (*Hexie Shehui*), all of which epitomise the need to maintain stability at all costs, or the consolidation of CCP rule. In none of these frameworks can we find a trace of the spiritual element of capitalism. Perhaps we have to examine, at the societal level, the intellectual activities and modes of behavior of its people to determine whether China shows any sign of developing a spirit or ethic that is compatible with capitalism.

As has been mentioned, in attempting to build on Weber's argument about the elective affinity between the Protestant ethic and the spirit of capitalism, scholars have sought to identify the functional equivalents in non-Western cultures. Examples include Japan's Tokugawa religion and China's Confucian ethic. However, after many revisions, the colossal concept of the "Confucian ethic" has been reduced to the "family ethic" or "folk religious tradition." As in the cases of Taiwan, Hong Kong, and Singapore, it has been impossible to demonstrate that the Confucian ethic has, as was the case with Protestantism, performed the critical functions of providing rational guidance to daily lives and creating institutional innovation. Although they may make reference to the traditional virtues of hard work and frugality and Confucianism's adaptability to transplanted modern economic institutions, those who accord excessive commendation to Confucianism may become trapped in a labyrinth of obscurity that leads to the creation of yet another myth

(Ku 1999; see also Wong 1992; Yang and Tu 1987). Just as important, the contributions rendered by the expansion of economic opportunity, the increase in material inducement, and the efficient accumulation of capital seem to be pertinent to China's economic growth, and it is hard to rely on Confucian ethic as an explanation. This is also why we have not seen a resurgence of the debate on the Confucian ethic and economic development.[17]

However, following through with Weber's logic and considering all social actions to be guided by both cultural and material interests leads us to conclude that historical interpretations in favor of either idealism or materialism are necessarily one-sided and fail to represent the whole truth. This explains why Weber expends half of his book *The Religion of China: Confucianism and Taoism* on discussing Chinese money, city, guild system, hydraulic construction, conception of deity, central monarch, patrimonial bureaucracy, organisation of the sib, self-government in villages, and patrimonial legal structure. Only after he has dealt with these "sociological foundations" does Weber go back to his main thesis and start to analyse the Chinese literati, examination system, Confucian education, gentleman ideal (*Junzi Lixiang*), culture of officialdom, views on economic policy, and "Confucian life orientation". Weber emphasises that, if we were to consider the material conditions alone, even though China has structures that are unfavorable to the rise of capitalism, it also has some that are favorable ones compared to European countries. Examples include the import of precious metal, rapid population growth, freedom of migration, the absence of a

[17] See footnote 7 of Du's commentary. In another example, Xia (2005:251) contends in his book *Dongya Xiandaixing Yu Xifang Xiandaixing* that "from a cultural point of view, although Western modernity and Asian modernity share many similarities in material and spiritual factors, Western modernity and Asian modernity have noticeable differences. The main difference lies in Asian modernity's connection with the remnants of traditional Confucianism or values of post-Confucianism". Compared with Ambrose King's overstatement of the Confucian ethic, Xia's effort to use "the remnants of traditional Confucianism or post-Confucianism" to discuss the connection between Chinese traditional culture and capitalism is more practical and appropriate. After all, since China underwent the baptism of Marxism-Leninism, it is more difficult to consider Confucianism as the mainstream spiritual power. In addition to the various academic discussions, the Tianjin Academy of Social Sciences published in 2004 Qi Yanchen's *Zibenzhuyi De Lingyi Tiaotui*, which held Weber's economic ethos in great esteem. He contends that Qing-era China had lost the opportunity to communicate with the West, and at the same time inherited Confucianism's contempt for wealth accumulation. Together with political intolerance, this served to cut China off totally from capitalism, and as a result China remains a "society full of moral risk". To change this, one must "[have] honesty before respecting to one's occupation".

law against usury, a utilitarian view of the search for this-worldly wealth, and recurrent internal trade. Hence, the real obstacle to the rise of capitalism in China should, to a larger extent, be attributed to spiritual factors. This is particularly significant in the last chapter, in which Weber compares Confucianism with Puritanism and constructs the two contrasting ideal-types of "rational adaptation to the world" (Rationalismus der Weltanpassung) for Confucianism and "rational mastery over the world" (Rationalismus der Weltbeherrschung) for Puritanism. With this, Weber sought to demonstrate that China and the West stood at the extreme ends of two opposing spiritual values or worldviews. Furthermore, China was deeply entrenched in "a garden of witchcraft" (Zaubergarten) from which it was unable to extricate itself. Weber's portrayal of China is of course no longer relevant now that China has made up its mind to "assimilate" and has been so successful in its adoption of the capitalist market mechanism. However, as has been noted, the concern here is not to ask why Weber does not tell us the truth about Chinese history or why he does not ask positive questions, but to adopt his *problematique* to investigate the present status of China's spirit or ethic. Only in this way can we further predict the future of capitalism in China.

It would be hard to identify a series of ethical rules for the Chinese in contemporary China. This is so regardless of whether we make a comparison with what Weber did in his day to ascertain the general ethical codes of traditional Chinese culture, or whether we adopt the concept of *habitus* put forth by the French sociologist Pierre Bourdieu. In the past, the "guide to daily lives" (Lebensfuerung) had mostly been manifested in the "carriers" of the literati or clan leaders, who were the embodiment of the beliefs and attitudes of Weber's traditionalism and became the basis for his construction of the ideal-type "rational adaptation to the world." The behavioural codes of the Chinese in contemporary China, as social psychologist Zhai Xuewei maintains, while operating in more or less habitual ways, have been interrupted by the intervention of "everyday relationships" (*richang xing de guanxi*) and "everyday authority" (*richang quanwei*). As a result, the codes such as institutions, the law, and rights that are considered important and formal in the West have been taken less than seriously in the daily interactions of the Chinese. Hence, in China, "there is yet to constitute a more stable mode of modernity" (Zhai 2006:182).

To further compare with Weber's time, his observations on the Chinese religion, deviations notwithstanding, at least provide a reference point for Western religion, thus making it possible for him to draw a comparison between Confucianism and Puritanism. Today, however, Confucianism exerts its impact in the form of remnants and has no more than an indirect effect on the values and behavior of the Chinese. Meanwhile, other religions have gone underground and cannot be followed publicly. Events surrounding the Falun Gong, furthermore, have led the government to consider folk religions as a source of social instability that must be monitored and suppressed. The suppression of religious needs is a necessary consequence of the domination of the socialist dogma.

From the experiences of the Soviet Union and Eastern Europe, we know that it is hard to eradicate religious belief. As long as the ruling power no longer uses antitheism to attack religion, but meets basic human rights such as the freedom of thought, speech, and religion that are implied in a democratic system, then religion will play a positive role in civil society and constitute the core content of culture in any capitalist country. The Chinese government's suppression of religious freedom is another obstacle that prevents outsiders from gaining a better understanding of the spiritual world of the Chinese. Despite the fact that numerous people have made individual efforts to search for religion, this is quite different from Weber's notion of a world religion (*Weltreligion*) that provides guidance for believers in their daily activities and has an impact on the economic ethic.

If the Chinese official ideology cannot proactively create a spirit that is compatible with capitalism and, at the same time, the Chinese people lack religious-derived systematic guidance in their daily lives, then where else can we locate the pillar for China's spirit or ethic? To some extent, we can say that the behavioural style and economic ethic of the Chinese have not only experienced a "fracture" (*Duanlie*) from traditionalism, but that, as pointed out by Chinese scholar Sun Liping, this "fracture" also constitutes a big shock experienced by the Chinese in the 1990s. Similarly, Qiu Jianxin uses the case of a circulating credit union (*Hui*) in the Chongchuan Township to vividly describe how the culture of trust has suffered a fracture as traditional social connections have been changed by the transition to a market economy, leading to a serious case of *Hui* breakdown (Qiu 2005; Sun 2003). Qiu writes that the "breakdown of the circulating credit union at the Chongchuan Township demonstrates that we live in a time when social capital is being eroded. The social capital being eroded is our traditional culture, the foundational structure of our economy and our country...with social transformation we must locate a new mechanism of trust, one that transcends the trust of the traditional society which is narrow-based and confined to close relations. Otherwise, the force of modern life will stage more spectacles of "slaying the familiar" (*Sha Shu*) and put to death the trust based on it" (Qiu 2005:299–300).

Viewed from this perspective, regardless of whether or not China adopts political democracy, the fundamental crisis that confronts it on its road to capitalism is its inability to mould a sustainable modern mechanism of trust, and in particular its inability to shift from "personal trust" to "system trust" as emphasised by the German sociologist Niklas Luhmann.[18] Here, history teaches us a hard lesson. The Cultural Revolution radically severed the roots of "traditionalism," providing an opportunity for Western capitalism to press forth into China without being hindered by traditional factors, yet some traditional virtues were also disastrously eradicated during this process: the proverbial baby really was flushed away with the bath water. The "spiritual vacuum" that was generated by the Cultural Revolution cannot possibly be compensated by China's economic-driven efforts to promote cultural tourism or Confucianism.[19] Compelled by its illusory imaginings of its "great nation" status, China has been unwilling to openly accept universal values such as human rights, freedom, democracy, and peace, which has led to its being pressed into service as an archetype in Samuel Huntington's *Clash of Civilization*. This seems to imply that no matter how far China develops its capitalist market economy, it cannot completely assimilate itself into the essence of "modernity" embodied by the West. As Yu Ying-shih comments, in recollecting China's tradition, the CCP conjures up images of the Qing dynasty's imperial rule, hegemonic domination,

[18] See Luhmann (1973). Research on trust has gained increasing popularity in China (see Wang 2002; Zheng 2001; Zheng and Peng 2003). Lin Nan has also formed a research team to conduct a more systematic investigation in this area.

[19] Yu openly states that since Deng Xiaoping's economic reform in the 1990s, China has sought to find a new national identity through a reinterpretation of history. Popular culture has also demonstrated a tendency to embrace tradition: Chinese intellectuals seek to return to the humanistic tradition of Confucianism, and the general public greatly desires to practice the lineage system, to refurbish genealogical charts, and to worship at their ancestral graves. Nevertheless, this tendency carries political connotations, and has become the CCP's tool for cultural strategy and control. This is because Marxism is no longer convincing. In view of this, tradition is only used as a tool for patriotism. Yu comments that Chinese political rulers and traditional culture are strange bedfellows, and cannot generate an appropriate national identity (Central News Agency 2007/4/25).

and the rejection of democracy. Hence, we cannot tell for sure whether China's determination to go its own way will benefit or pose a threat to modernity.

More noticeable is the escalation in recent years of China's nationalist sentiment and pride, which has somehow become a means of filling the spiritual vacuum. Weber pointed out during his inaugural lecture "Nation-State and Economic Policy" that the nation-state is not purely a superstructure, but is a psychological foundation that is deeply ingrained in the hearts of the people, including the economically suppressed. The function of political leaders is precisely to shoulder the nation-political consciousness (Weber 1997:80). In light of this, Chinese political leaders seem to nicely fulfill the psychological needs of Chinese "citizens," and Beijing's hosting of the Olympic Games in 2008 will in particular provide timely satisfaction to the nationalistic sentiments and confidence. Nevertheless, Weber also provided in the same speech a profound reflection on the "bourgeoisie" of Germany, severely criticising all levels of the German bourgeoisie for being politically immature, unable to shoulder their own political responsibilities, and resigned to wishing for the protection of a "new Caesar." Weber held that the political immaturity of the German bourgeoisie originated from the class's long-standing apolitical nature, and that the crisis in Germany at the time was due precisely to the bourgeoisie's inability to take on the nation's power interest and represent its political future. Facilitated by an equal degree of political immaturity on the part of the proletariat class, Weber predicted that Germany would lapse into a vacuum. This prophecy was unhappily fulfilled. Some ten years after Weber's death, Hitler seized control of Germany, introduced the extremism of Fascist rule and brought the country close to irredeemable devastation. Using this as a yardstick, we may question the whereabouts of China's bourgeoisie or citizen class, and must ask whether the capitalist economy has created a new citizen consciousness or civil society. Maybe China has remained at a stage comparable to the time that Weber first diagnosed China as lacking "an independent and autonomous class of citizens", unable to find a "social force" comparable to the West that would promote the rationalisation of politics, economics, and society.[20]

[20] The Chinese government has recognised that globalisation also extends to non-government organizations (NGOs), and therefore began to encourage social organisations to exercise their strength and fill in the service gaps caused by state and market failure. However, after the Color Revolutions in Central Asia, China again tightened

Perhaps we can state the problem as follows. China's numerous cosmetic surgery procedures have helped it to acquire a capitalist "look" that does not appear too different from city life in other countries. Nevertheless, where the "inner spirit" is concerned, probably due to the oppression by Western imperialists in the past, intellectuals and the general public in China are still accustomed to adopting a confrontational stance toward the West. They have not even become a self-conscious and autonomous citizen class, let alone a civil society that can stand up to the state. This general mentality reflects vividly that on the spiritual level, China does not have the least intention of assimilating the values that attend capitalism, namely, political democracy and civil society. Intriguingly, Weber also admits that once Western capitalism has entered its "iron cage" era, the economic system will no longer needs "spirit," as its nutrients and religious roots will long since have withered. Hence, as China "transplants" the Western capitalist system, it will cease to need the economic ethic as a source of nourishment. As long as the personal or organisational interest has been set in motion, the market mechanism will run its course and attain the goals defined by the economic function.

This being the case, does the statement "specialists without spirit, sensualists without heart" predict the future outlook of Chinese capitalism? Starting with Weber's questions and after a series of investigations, the preliminary answer must be that China has not manifested an ethos at the economic ethic level that is commensurate with its transition to capitalism. All one can say is that China has once again demonstrated its trait of the "ethic of world adaptation", assimilating market mechanisms at the institutional level yet lacking the core qualities of modern citizenship at the level of action and behavior, including the fight for basic human rights such as the freedom of speech, freedom of association, and freedom of religion, and thus the right to run for political office, lobby on policies, and monitor the government. As Chinese society has been completely de-politicised, it would be totally unwarranted to wait, as Weber did, for the emergence of a politically mature citizen

---

its control over foreign foundations operating in the country. Scholar Yu Keping (2007) proposes the implementation of a loose-to-tight assessment and registration system and the introduction of a census to obtain basic information. This shows that despite the encompassing idea of promoting a harmonious society, stability and control remain the principles that guide the CCP in its dealings with civil organizations. China still lacks the basic political conditions to develop an autonomous civil society (Gries and Rosen 2004; Yu 2007).

class in China. Hence, what we are seeing is not the "China-isation" of modern, Western, and rational capitalism, but a "bird-cage capitalism" that is confined to the domain of economic exchange, unable to extend economic freedom to the sociopolitical arena.

This kind of restrained capitalism, in its inability to emancipate thought and spirit, demonstrates a de facto resemblance to the iron cage of which Weber warned. Its spiritual nihilism, which is manifested in its sole emphasis on money, has furthermore unveiled the state of alienation described by Karl Marx. When the tranquiliser of nationalism loses its effect, Yu Ying-shih's warning of "revolts and income inequality" will bother China time and again. Perhaps by then there will have been another wave of debate and ensuing change on the question of whether China should also assimilate the capitalist institutions of democratic politics and civil society. Only then will the historical question of "Where should China go?" be answered.

In sum, China has created a magnetic effect in the process of economic progress, absorbing the inflow of capital from around the world, which has resulted in the gradual integration of its production and consumption into the global economic system. Under these circumstances, the biggest risk facing China is that both its government and people, with their mass of resources and deficiency in thought and values, could easily follow the track of militarism in the style of pre-WWII Japan and Germany, or alternatively could attain hegemonic domination through a combination of nationalism and fascism. The rise of such a nation would definitely not benefit humankind, and hence we need the key to unlock the question of "Where should China go?" Although this essay has not found the key, it is a first step in that direction, and the author looks forward to opportunities to examine different theories in the future.

## V. *Conclusion*

Two thousand years ago, China's Confucian classic, the *Book of Rites*, in its "Chapter on Learning" (*Liji Xueji Pian*) documented a speech by Confucius, in which he proclaimed that, "For a person who is good at asking questions, it is like chopping a piece of hardwood, he will first start with the easy bits which are soft, then slowly moving to the harder bits. With time, the wood would disintegrate and fall out by itself. For a person who is not good at asking questions, he will use a method exactly opposite to the above. Likewise, for a person who is good at answering questions, it is like ringing a bell, ringing it softly will give out a soft noise whilst ringing it hard will give out a loud noise. The person who rings the bell must not be nervous and work at one's ease such that the ringing will have resonance and be a lasting one. For a person who is not good at answering questions, he will use a method exactly opposite to the above. All these are ways to increase one's knowledge."

This speech shows the importance of *problematique* in academic work. It also helps us to understand the nature of knowledge. Knowledge does not remain in stasis, but changes over time and with the appearance of new phenomena, in response to which a new generation of scholars will raise new questions and search for new answers. This constitutes the fundamental principle of knowledge growth and change. With the turn of the 21st century and against all indications of the tendency toward globalisation, we cannot deny that the movement of China from socialism to capitalism is a significant event that is likely to have a long-lasting impact on human history. At this juncture, if the social scientific community fails to respond to the shock of this experiential-fact with the right *problematique*, they can rightly be accused of being people who are not good at asking questions.

In the quest for an answer by following through with the *problematique*, Weber reminds us that the social sciences deal with "actors" who possess free will and are inclined to endow their actions with subjective meaning. Precisely because of this, social scientists not only need to explain why a phenomenon is historically so and not otherwise, but also need to arrive at an adequate meaning that makes sense of a phenomenon's web of meanings in the historical context. With Weber's expectation of the social sciences in mind, this essay ponders, from the angle of "cultural-meaning" (*Kulturbedeutung*), whether China has since its implementation of economic reform established a spirit or ethic that is compatible with Western capitalism, and has truly assimilated the ideas and institutions of modernity.

An investigation at the macro level reveals that China has made continuous progress in building the necessary accessories for the functioning of market mechanisms, such as institutionalising and perfecting its legal system and introducing technological innovations and knowledge advancement. Where external appearances are concerned, China has become a modern country. However, the ruling stratum of China remains antagonistic to democratic politics and civil society, and, since the collapse of the Soviet Union and Eastern Europe and the Color

Revolutions in Central Asia has tightened its grip on thought and speech. From this, it can be seen that the spirit of China's "traditionalism" will not be so easily shaken.

The Chinese are mostly a "docile people" (*Shunmin*) who do not inquire about politics after paying their taxes. With economic growth and the increase in purchasing power, China has become not only the world's factory but also a mass market for consumer goods. Capitalism in China implies freedom of consumption and the notion that money is everything, which bears no relationship with Weber's portrayal of Chinese asceticism, let alone efforts to imitate the Western citizen class' spirit of citizenship, in which China would seek to participate actively in public affairs after gaining economic power.

In an atmosphere of consumption and hedonism, capitalism in China merely means letting a small group of people get rich, and as such is unlikely to produce a spillover effect by which economic freedom is extended to political and social freedom. The average Chinese, unless coerced so much as to threaten their survival, will not revolt against the CCP. Put simply, although China has taken the capitalist path of economic development, it has retained traditional despotism as its spirit. China is engaged in a kind of "selective assimilation" of modernity and, in the mean time, traditional culture has been wielded as a tool for strengthening national identity and gratifying nationalistic confidence. China has not bred a new quality in the spiritual dimension that will allow her to raise human culture.

Needless to say, what I have discussed so far represents my current observations. The changes that have occurred in China since the Opium War have often exceeded expectations, so much so that they tally with what Hegel describes as "the cunning of reason." Capitalism has come calling to China numerous times, so why is it only under the rule of socialism was capitalism imported on a mass scale and appeared to have become a stable system? As has been mentioned, the CCP's ideology of anti-traditionalism successfully destroyed the socioeconomic structure that Weber referred to as "traditionalism," thus creating the opportunity to reconstruct an appropriate market mechanism.

Conversely, the CCP took over the pre-modern bureaucracy and rebuilt it into a party bureaucracy, obstructing the alliance of capitalism with political freedom and civil liberty. Such a result is hard to credit from the perspective of linear evolutionism, but its intrigue and reasonableness can be partially comprehended by the logic of historical dialecticism. Liu Xiaofeng asks why China did not accept the ideology of liberal capitalism, but rather turned to socialism in its emergence as a modern nation, and explains that it was due to the fading of Confucian ideology and the affinity between nationalist quests and ideas of equality that are enshrined in socialism. Together with an intense desire among the general public for the equalisation of wealth, the ideological choice is taking a clear direction (Liu 1996:104). Liu points out at the same time that "the idea of individual freedom had never anchored in the base-stratum of our society." Following his argument, that China still resists the substantive worth of individual freedom at the level of the spirit even after accepting the formality of capitalism is understandable as a means of effecting the "deconstructed-reorganization" of modern Western attributes.

From this perspective, contemporary China is not the perfect setting for the emergence of the spirit of capitalism. On the contrary, it is engaged in a kind of capitalism that has departed from asceticism, the spirit of citizens, and the spirit of individual freedom. This type of capitalism is embedded into the authoritarian structure of Chinese politics, and has become the cornerstone of the legitimate rule of the CCP. This is because the magical power of the capitalist market has helped China to emancipate its productive force, accumulate capital rapidly, overcome numerous obstacles to industrialisation, and move toward its emergence as a "great nation".

Undoubtedly, from the May Fourth Movement to the *River Elegy* (*He Shang*) fever and further on to the *Surge of Great Nations* (*Da Guo Jueqi*), the discourse of the Chinese intelligentsia has become more and more self-confident. It no longer suffers from anxieties about either Westernisation or being ousted from the ballgame. Instead, its concern has shifted to the search for the right posture for China to rise as a "great nation" so as to gain the recognition of the world. This sort of collective mentality invariably reminds us of Weber's warnings about Germany. It seems that the two countries, equally eager to attain the identity of a "great nation," have under divergent epochal conditions moved toward the same historical situation. His statement is worth thinking over, and can also be taken as the concluding words of this essay: "'Thousands of years had to pass before thou entered life, and thousands more years wait in silence for what you will do of this life of yours'. Whether an individual is able to, as Carlyle says, guide one's roles and actions with such historical vision I know not. Yet if a nation were to maintain a lasting place in history, it has to possess this historical breath of mind" (Weber 1997:115). I look forward to seeing China gain the ability to develop this sort of ethos one day, and hope that it does not degenerate into a spiritual wasteland that allows money and material desires to become its only religion.[21]

## *References*

Balzer, H. (2004). "State and Society in Transitions from Communism: China in Comparative Perspective." In *State and Society in 21st Century China*, edited by P. Gries and S. Rosen. New York: Routledge.

Beck, U., Giddens, A., and S. Lash. (1994). *Reflexive Modernization: Politics, Tradition, and Aesthetics in the Modern Social Order.* London: Polity Press.

Central News Agency 2007/4/25.

Chang, W. (1995). *Wenhua Yu Jingji: Weibo Shehuixue Yanjiu (Culture and Economy: A Study of Weberian Sociology)*. Taipei: Juliu.

Chart, P. (1992). "The Protestant Ethic Analogy in the Study of Chinese History", from the Website of David C. Lam Institute for East West Studies, Hong Kong Baptist University.

Cohen, J. (2002). *Protestantism and Capitalism: the Mechanisms of Influence*. Berlin: de Gruyter.

Cui, Y. (2005). "Weibo Wenti Yu Zhiye Lunli (The Weber Question and Occupational Ethic)," *Hebei Xuekan* 25 (4): 21–25.

Du, X. (1993). Zhongguo *Chuantong Lunli Yu Jindai Zibenzhuyi: Jian Ping Weibo "Zhongguo De Zongjiao" (China's Traditional Ethic and Contemporary Capitalism: with an additional comment on Weber's "The Religion of China")*. Shanghai: Shanghai Shehuikexue Yuan.

Fukuyama, F. (1993). *Zheng Xin* (Trust), translated by W. Li. Taipei: Lixue.

Gao, Z. (2003). "Shichang Jingji De Lunli Yu Jingshen Tansuo—Weibo Xinjiao Lunli Yanjiu De Shidai Jiedu," (An Exploration of the Ethic and Spirit of the Market Economy: a contemporary interpretation of Weber's research on the Protestant Ethic) *Hunan Wenli Xueyuan Xuebao (Shehuikexue Ban) (Journal of the Hunan College of Arts and Science [Social Science Edition])* 28 (6): 16–19.

Gries, P. and S. Rosen. (2004). *State and Society in 21st-century China: Crisis, Contention, and Legitimation*. New York: Routledge.

Hamilton, G. G. (1990). *Zhongguo Shehui Yu Jingji (The Economy and Society of China)*, translated by W. Chang, J. Chen, and B. Zhai. Taipei: Lianjing.

He, X. (2005). "Weibo Zhongguo Mingti Yu Dongya Zibenzhuyi De Fazhan (Weber's China Thesis and the Capitalist Development in East Asia)", *Dongnanya Yanjiu (Southeast Asian Research)* 1: 53–58.

Heelas, P., S. Lash and P. Morris. (1996). *Detraditionalization*. London: Blackwell.

Huang, J. and K. Wang, (eds.) (2005). *Shehuixue Shiye Xia De Hexie Shehui (The Harmonious Society from the Sociological Perspective)*. Beijing: Shehuikexue Wenxian.

Jian, H. (1988). *Weibo Lun Zhongguo* (Weber's Discussion of China). Taipei: Taiwan University.

Kaelber, L. (2002). "Max Weber's Protestant Ethic in the 21st Century," *International Journal of Politics, Culture and Society* 16 (1): 133–46.

[21] Many Western scholars have also observed that money and wealth are the new religions of China. As Balzer writes, "we need to ask if 'To be rich is glorious' inevitably translates into 'Greed is good'. Many China specialists are so caught up in what Charlotte Ikels termed 'the return of the God of Wealth' that they seem to think that wealth is *the* new religion, rather than one god among many" (Balzer 2004:250).

King, Y. (1978). *Cong Chuantong Dao Xiandai* (From Tradition to Modernity). Taipei: Wenhua Shibao.

——. (1983). "Rujia Lunli Yu Jingji Fazhan: Weibo Xueshuo Chong Tan (Confucian Ethic and Economic Development: Revisiting Weber's Scholarship)", *Lianhe Yuekan* 25: 70–79.

Ku, C. (1987). Traditionalismus und Rationalismus: Problem einer Unterscheidung am Beispiel der China-Studie Max Webers. Ph. D. dissertation. University of Heidelberg.

——. (1992). *Weibo Xueshuo Xin Tansuo (A New Exploration of Weber's Scholarship).* Taipei: Tangshan.

——. (1999). Shehuixue Lilun Yu Shehui Shijian (Sociological Theory and Social Praxis). Taipei: Yuancheng.

Lehmmann, Hartmut and Guenther Roth et al. (1993). *Weber's Protestant Ethic: Origins, Evidence, Contexts*, Cambridge: Cambridge University Press (Chinese translated version: *Weibo De Xinjiao Lunli: Youlai, Genju He Beijing*, translated by K. Yan. Shenyang: Liaoning Jiaoyu Chubanshe, 2001).

Levenson, J. R. (1958). *Confucian China and its Modern Fate: A Trilogy*. Berkeley: Berkeley University Press.

Li, H. (2004). *Zhongguo Danwei Shehui (China's Unit Society).* Shanghai: Shanghai Renmin Chubanshe.

Liu, X. (1996). *Xiandai Shehui Lilun Xulun (An Introduction to Theories on Modern Societies).* Hong Kong: Oxford University Press.

Luhmann, N. (1973). *Vertrauen*. Stuttgart: Mohr.

Peyrefitte, A. (1993). *Tingzhi De Diguo: Liang Ge Shijie De Zhuangji* (*L'empire Immobile*), translated by F. Mao et al. Beijing: Sanlian.

Pierotti, S. (2003). *The Protestant Ethic and the Spirit of Capitalism: Criticisms of Weber's Thesis*. http://www.ecs.gatech.edu/support/sandra/paper.html.

Pomeranz, K. (2000). *The Great Divergence: China, Europe, and the Making of the Modern World Economy.* Stanford: Princeton University Press.

Qi, Y. (2004). *Zibenzhuyi De Ling Yi Tiao Tui (The Other Leg of Capitalism).* Tianjin: Tianjin Shehuikexue Yuan.

Qiao, H. (2000). *Zheng Yi Mou Li: Jindai Xifang Jingji Lunli Sixiang Yanjiu (Proper Profit-Making: Study of Contemporary Western Thoughts on Economic Ethic).* Beijing: Shangwuyinshu Guan.

Qiu, C. (2005). Xinren Wenhua De Duanlie (Rupture in the Culture of Trust). Beijing: Shehuikexue Wenxian.

Schwentker, W. (2005). "The Spirit of Modernity: Max Weber's Protestant Ethic and Japanese Social Sciences," *Journal of Classical Sociology* 5: 73–92.

Song, L. (2005). "'Zhongguo Moshi' De Chenggong Yu Weilai (The Success and Future of the 'China Model')," In *Shehuixue Shiye Xia De Hexie Shehui (The Harmonious Society from the Sociological Perspective)*, edited by J. Huang and K. Wang. Beijing: Shehuikexue Wenxian.

Su, G. (1989). *Lixing Ji Qi Xianzhi* (Rationality and its Limits). Taipei: Guiguan.

Sun, C. (1987). "Chong Xinjiao Lunli Dao Rujia Lunli" (From Protestant Ethic to Confucian Ethic), In Yang C. and Tu N. (eds.) Rujia Lunli Yu Jingji Fazhan (Confucian Ethic and Economic Development), Taipei: Yuancheng.

Sun, L. (2003). *Duanlie: Ershi Shiji Jiushi Niandai Yi Lai De Zhongguo Shehui* (Rupture: the Chinese Society since the Nineties of the Twentieth Century). Beijing: Shehuikexue Wenxian.

Tian, C. (2006). "Weibo Lilun De Juxian Ji Qi Zai Zhongguo De Wuyong (Limitations to and Misappropriation of Weber's Theory in China)," *Wenshizhe* 295: 141–149.

Wang, S. and X. Liu (2002). "Xinren De Jichu (The Foundations of Trust)", *Shehui* Yanjiu, No. 3.

Wang, W. C. (2007). *Zhuanbian Zhong De Zhongguo Dalu Fazhi* (Transitions in Mainland China's Rule of Law). Hinzhu: Jiaoda.

Weber, M. (1951). *The Religion of China*, translated by H. Gerth. New York: The Free Press.
——. (1958). *The Religion of India: The Sociology of Hinduism and Buddhism*, translated by Gerth and Martindale. New York.
——. (1996). *Yindu De Zongjiao: Yindujiao Yu Fojiao II (The Religion of India: Hinduism and Buddhism)*, translated by L. Kang and H. Jian Taipei: Yuanliu.
——. (1997). *Minzu Guojia Yu Jingji Zhengce (Nation-State and Economic Policy)*, edited by Y. Gan. Hong Kong: Oxford University Press.
——. (2001). *The Protestant Ethic and Spirit of Capitalism*, translated by S. Kalberg, Roxbury Publishing.
——. (2002). *The Protestant Ethic and the "Spirit" of Capitalism and Other Writings*, edited and translated by P. Baehr, and G. C. Weels. London: Penguin Books.
Wong, S. (ed.) (1992). *Zhongguo Zongjiao Lunli Yu Xiandaihua* (China's Religious Ethic and Modernization). Taipei: Shangwuyinshuju.
Wong, R. B. (1997). *China Transformed: Historical Change and the Limits of European* Experience. Ithaca: Cornell University Press.
Xia, G. (2005). *Dongya Xiandaixing Yu Xifang Xiandaixing: Wenhua De Jiaodu (East Asian Modernity and Western Modernity: a cultural perspective)*. Guilin: Guangxi Shifan Daixue.
Xu, J. (2006). "Shichang Jingji Yu Chuantong Lunli De Chuangzaoxing Chonggou (The Creative Reconstruction of Market Economy and Traditional Ethic)," *Nanjing Zhengzhi Xueyuan Xuebao* 127: 40–43.
Yang, C. (1987). "Rujia Lunli Yu Weibo Mingti (Confucian Ethic and the Weber Thesis)", In C. S. Yang, and N. C. Tu (eds.), Rujia Lunli Yu Jingji Fazhan (Confucian Ethic and Economic Development), Taipei: Yuancheng.
Yang, C. and N. Tu (eds.) (1987). *Rujia Lunli Yu Jingji Fazhan* (Confucian Ethic and Economic Development). Taipei: Yuancheng.
Yu, M. (2004). "Weibo Rujiao Lunli Yu Zibenzhuyi Fazhan Lilun Jieshi (An Explanation of Weber's Confucian Ethic and Capitalist Development Theory)", *Zhongguo Shehuikexue Yuan Yanjiu Shengyuan Xuebao* 5: 83–86.
Yu, K. (2007). "Zhongguo Tese Gongmin Shehui De Xingqi (The Emergence of a Civil Society with Chinese Characteristics)," *21 Shiji Jingji Baodao* (Economic Report of the Twenty-First Century).
Yu, Y. (1987). *Zhongguo Jinshi Zongjiao Lunli Yu Shangren Jingshen* (Religious Ethics and the Spirit of Merchants in Late Imperial China). Taipei: Lienjing.
Zhai, X. (2005). "Zhongguoren Chuantong Hexie De Shehui Xinli Jichu Ji Qi Shanbian (The Social-Psychological Foundation and Transitions in the Chinese Tradition of Harmony)", In *Shehuixue Shiye Xia De Hexie Shehui (The Harmonious Society from the Sociological Perspective)*. Edited by Huang J. and Wang K. Beijing: Shehuikexue Wenxian.
——. (2005). *Quanqiuhua Shidai De Wenhua Rentong: Xifang Pubianzhuyi De Lishi Pipan (Cultural Identification in the Age of Globalization: A Historical Critique of Western Universalism)*. Beijing: Beijing Daxue Chubanshe.
Zhang, Y. (2003). "Qinjian, Lunli Yu Dongya Fazhan Bianxi (An Analysis of Hard Work and Frugality, Ethic, and East Asian Development)," *Huadong Shifan Daxue Xuebao (Zhexue Shehui Kexue Ban)* 35 (3): 54–59.
Zheng, Y. (2001). *Xinren Lun (On Trust)*. Beijing: Zhongguo Guangbo Dianshi Chubanshe.
Zheng, Y. and S. Peng. (2003). *Zhongguo Shehui Zhong De Xinren (Trust in the Chinese Society)*. Beijing: Zhongguo Chengshi Chubanshe.

# TAIWAN'S INDUSTRIALISATION: THE RISE OF A DEMAND-RESPONSIVE ECONOMY*

Gary G. Hamilton and Kao Cheng-shu

## *Introduction*

Over the past forty years, the world's most globally engaged economies have become increasingly demand-response economies. By demand-responsive economies, we mean that such economies are organised "backwards" from demand to production, instead of "forward" from production to demand. In making this claim, we are arguing that global retailers, generating intermediary demand in anticipation of final demand, have superseded manufacturers as the driving force that organises, directly through supply chain contracts and indirectly through their vast market power, whole sectors of the global economy.

On the surface, this change may not seem all that significant. Ever since Adam Smith, economists have recognised that factors relating to demand are prominent features of all advanced market economies. Without demand, so the dictum goes, supply withers. The timelessness of this maxim, however, masks the changes that have occurred in how supply and demand are configured over time. Conceptualised in the abstract, supply and demand are merely aggregations, respectively, of all sellers and all buyers relative to a good. Far from being static, in reality, at different times and places, supply and demand represent very differently organized groups of sellers and buyers. Since the writing of Chamberlin (1962 (1933)) and Robinson (1969 (1933)) on "monopolistic competition," economists have recognised that the organisation of sellers relative to buyers matters, but implications of monopolistic competition have seldom been applied to retailers, in large part because retailers have been seen as merely conduits between manufacturers and final consumers.[1]

---

* Reference to this article should be made as follows: Hamilton, Gary G. and Kao, Cheng-shu. 2007. "Taiwan's Industrialization: The Rise of a Demand-Responsive Economy".

[1] For an exception, see Spulber (1996, 1999).

More importantly, the implications of monopolistic competition have not been applied at the level of national economies. As we point out in this article, global retailers, or "big buyers" as Gary Gereffi (1994) calls them, are not benign intermediaries. They are big enough to influence the internal organisation of entire economies. Big buyers not only create demand, but they also organise suppliers and develop supplier markets to fill that demand. Through using advanced consumer research, point-of-sales information, supply-line management, and sophisticated information technology, retailers and merchandisers have restructured the relationship between buyers and suppliers, making the latter a price-sensitive organisational extension of the former. These forged links between the market-focused big buyers, on the one hand, and globally dispersed and largely faceless manufacturers, on the other, have had direct repercussions on economies around the world. In general, the more globally involved the capitalist economy, the more demand responsive that economy has become.

How do economies become demand-responsive, and what empirically and theoretically does that mean? This article gives a detailed answer to this question showing how the Taiwanese economy developed in response to orders given by global retailers and brand name merchandisers. In the first section, we use disaggregated trade data to demonstrate that the globalisation of supplier markets for U.S. based retailers and brand name merchandisers occurred first and most pervasively in East Asia, especially in Taiwan and South Korea, and to show the differential effects of these markets on structuring these Asian economies. The establishment of these suppliers in East Asia created what is known as "the Asian Miracle," the extraordinarily rapid and ongoing industrialisation that occurred from 1965 through the present day. A lot has been written about Asian economic development, but what is less known is that, in response to the retailers' orders, Asian economies developed in very different ways.[2]

In the main section of the paper, drawing on hundreds of interviews done over a period of over fifteen years, we show how these supplier markets in Taiwan actually developed and how many suppliers, in turn, responded to changing economic conditions by moving their businesses to Mainland China. These interviews allow us to specify how the

[2] For a related discussion of this literature, as well as an analysis of the rise of capitalism in East Asia, see Hamilton (2006).

Taiwan economy became organised "backwards" from the development of consumer markets in the U.S. to the development of supplier markets for final and intermediate goods in East Asia.

### *The Globalisation of Supplier Markets after World War II*[3]

Modern retailers are the "makers" of two types of markets, consumer markets and supplier markets. In the last half of the 20th century, both types of markets have grown tremendously, and have become increasingly global and increasingly rationalised over time. It is important to see these dynamics in a historical perspective because the emergent qualities of these market dynamics create a path dependent momentum that is difficult to alter short of a global economic catastrophe (Feenstra and Hamilton 2006).

### *U.S. Supplier Markets before 1965*

Our point of departure is 1965. Before 1965, consumer-goods suppliers for U.S. retailers were almost entirely U.S. firms. After 1965, these suppliers increasing came from outside the U.S. Before 1965, retailers had limited influence on large U.S. based manufacturers, but after 1965, retailers increasingly began to create and organise supplier market for the main consumer products they sold.

In 1965, the "retail revolution" that Bluestone and his colleagues (1981) identified was already well under way. At the end of World War II, U.S. manufacturers had emerged as the most prestigious in the world, and the consumer products they offered represented the most extensive lineup of such products anywhere. The European and the Japanese economies were just in the process of recovering from the effects of the war and some former manufacturing giants in those economies (e.g., Daimler Benz, Mitsubishi) had re-established their prominence at home. In the previous decade, in the 1950s, imports of consumer goods into the U.S. hovered around the levels they were at during the Great Depression. Most international trade from the U.S.

---

[3] For a more complete discussion of the transformation of U.S. retailing after World War II, see Feenstra and Hamilton (2006) and Hamilton, Petrovic and Feenstra (2006).

was outbound. Exports of automobiles as well as a considerable range of consumer goods began to "Americanise" consumer desires in Europe (de Grazia 2005) and other parts of the world.

In the midst of this parade of consumer goods, U.S. retailers, led by Sears, J. C. Penney's, and Macy's, began to expand their presence in U.S. consumer markets. During the long years of the Great Depression, fair trade laws made discount retailing illegal, and low demand had stymied the effort of retailers to expand throughout the U.S. But after the war, with economies improved and demand for consumer goods rising, department stores quickly began to expand their consumer markets.

Other events pushed this expansion forward. Changes in the 1955 tax code reforms allowed rapid depreciation of capital construction, and a shopping centre boom ensued as a direct consequence (Hanchett 1996). The Cold War need for national defense prompted the U.S. Congress, in 1956, to pass legislation creating the interstate highway system across the U.S., linking all major U.S. cities and creating ring roads around them. At the same time, the desire to own a family home led the parents of the baby boom generation to move to newly created suburbs surrounding most large U.S. cities. The number of shopping centres in the U.S. jumped from about 500 in 1955 to 7,600 in 1964, an expansion in shopping areas that accounted for about 30 percent of all retail sales in the U.S. in 1964. Only forty years later, in 2004, the number of shopping centres in the U.S. had reached nearly 50,000. As these new shopping centres developed, the same anchor stores and the same niche retailers began to appear in most places across the country, a development which led to the expansion and diversification of "chain stores."

Before 1965, the products fueling this rapid expansion in retailing came overwhelmingly from the U.S. manufacturers. As seen in Figure 1, imports into the U.S. remained very low from the time of the Great Depression through the 1960s, with a brief upsurge during World War II, and as stated above, most trade in manufactured goods after World War II until the late 1960s was U.S. exports. In 1965, the only Japanese import constituting over 10 percent of total U.S. consumption for a single product was an intermediate good, steel, which was imported to compensate for a decline in U.S. steel production brought on by a strike in the steel mills.

From 1965 onward, however, that picture of limited foreign imports would change rapidly and forever. As Figure 2 shows, starting in the

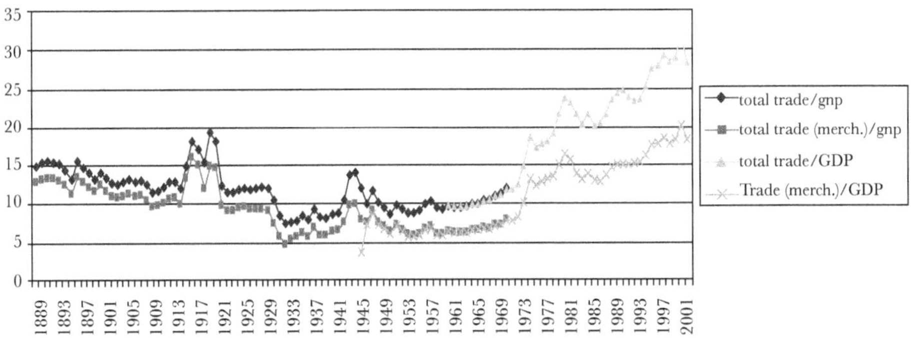


Figure 1: Trade in GNP, 1889–2000

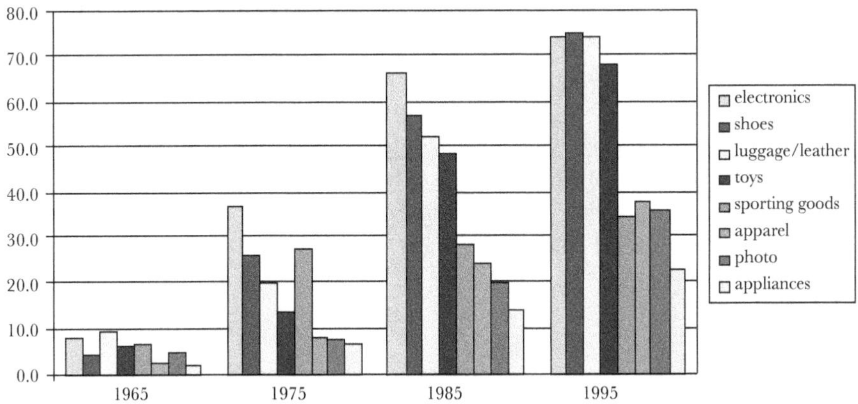


The share of imports in apparent consumption

Figure 2: Import Penetration in General Merchandise

late 1960s, imports of manufactured consumer goods began to rise rapidly and across all basic categories. The rate of import growth as a percentage of total consumption is surprising, but even more surprising is the increase of diversification of the products being imported. As we will explain in more detail below, one of the initial factors causing the globalisation of supplier markets is the use of store brands to get around fair trade laws. As retailers expanded in the late 1950s and 1960s, large department stores, such as Macy's and Sears, began to use private labels more extensively. Kenmore washers and Craftsman tools are two examples of Sears's in-house brands, but the use of in-house brands for clothing and shoes also became common place. This expansion of garment and footwear production quickly exceeded the capacity (and willingness) of U.S. manufacturers to provide these goods and led to the increasing use of Asian intermediaries (e.g., Japanese trading companies) to fill the orders.

### *The Growth of East Asian Suppliers after 1965*

Several aspects of these imports of consumer goods should be emphasised. First, most of the imports in every category came from newly industrialising countries (NICs) in East Asia. Even from the very first decade of growth, Taiwan, Hong Kong, South Korea, and Japan supplied most of the imported goods. Although the large enterprises in Japan and South Korea are well-known throughout the world, Taiwan, with by far the smallest economy of the three, supplied an extraordinary number of products in large quantities for the U.S. market. Figure 3 shows from which countries the consumer imports came. As is apparent, the Chinese areas (Taiwan and Hong Kong), supplied a large percentage of most types of consumer goods from the very first.

Now, just comparing Taiwan and South Korea, Figure 4 displays the number of imported items at the most disaggregated seven-digit TSUSA

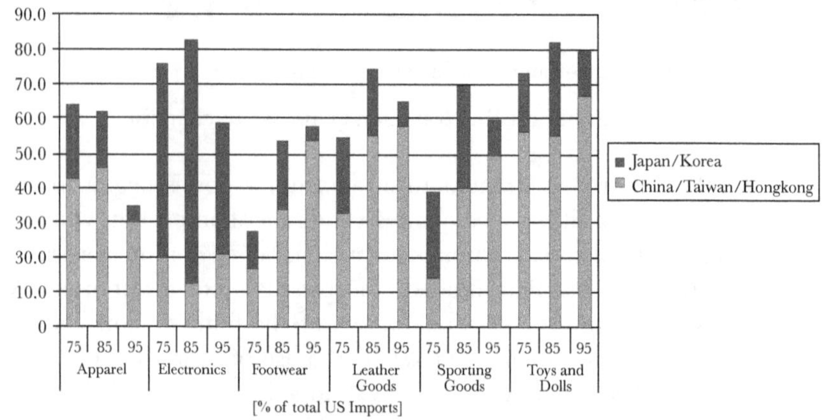


Figure 3: Import of General Merchandise from Asia

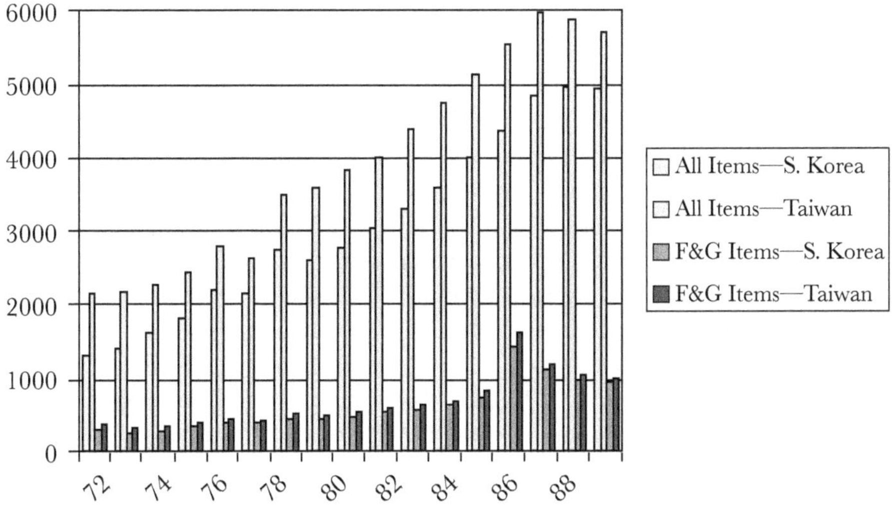


Source: NBER Trade Data

Figure 4: Number of Categories of Imports (TSUSA 7-Digit)
Total and Footwear and Garments Combined

codes during the time (1972–1988) that U.S. customs agents used this product classification. Over the entire period, Taiwan manufactured more, as well as a wider range of products than South Korea. Not counting exports of automobiles, the Taiwanese and South Korean economies combined to send more exports to the U.S. than Japan from the 1970s on.

Most writers miss the significance of these U.S.-bound exports. They typically emphasise the large volume and rapid growth of exports, which they explain through a "supply-side" narrative extolling the economic prowess of the exporting country. Using aggregated trade data, typically supplied by the exporting countries, they note the overall similarity in the exports, and as a consequence the overall similarity among the NICs. The similarity is indeed there—at the third digit TSUSA level, Feenstra and Hamilton (2006) show the "export landscape" for both South Korea and Taiwan using TSUSA data aggregated to three digits from 1972 to 1988. From these landscapes, it is apparent that most of the export value from these economies is primarily in just a handful of major categories and that, with a few exceptions, the export landscapes of the two countries look very similar. Moreover, the principal categories of exports from both South Korea and Taiwan are exactly those categories of consumer goods that fueled the retail revolution in the United States: garments, footwear, bicycles, toys, televisions, microwaves, computers, thousands of plastic household and office items, and a large array of electronic components that in turn became the building block of a vast and growing number of other products.

If we survey the main items of export throughout the period from 1972 to 1985, it becomes clear that products secured through contract manufacturing forms an extremely high percentage of the total exports. For instance, according to a report on the Korean garment industry, "Until 1988, approximately 95 percent of garment exports were produced under contract to foreign firms, rather than under Korean-owned labels" (Lee and Song 1994:148). According to Levy's analysis of the footwear industry in South Korea and Taiwan, "(I)n the initial phases of export expansion," Levy notes, "export business in both nations was based overwhelmingly on the fulfillment of orders placed by Japanese trading companies, and designed for the US market" (1988:46). Japanese trading companies were soon supplanted as Western firms began to place their orders directly. In both countries, Western brand name merchandisers, such as Nike and Reebok, controlled export footwear industry (Levy 1988, 1990). Also in his case study of the manufacture of personal computers in the two countries, Levy (1988) cites figures from the trade associations for electronic appliances that 84% of Korean-made personal computers and 72% of Taiwan-made computers were sold under non-local brand names. The world's largest exporter of bicycles during the 1980s and early 1990s, Taiwan's export industry until the late 1980s was largely OEM manufacturing (Cheng and Sato 1998). At one point in the late 1970s, Schwinn placed an order of 100 million bicycles with Giant, "which was then only a small factory" (p. 7).

Examining the lists of exported finished manufactured products in those early years of economic growth, it is difficult to find any major product category that was not dominated by contract manufacturing or any major retailers that were not involved in contract manufacturing in East Asia. Garments, household appliances, electronic products, toys, bicycles—the majority of all of these finished exports were sold under foreign-owned brand names and product labels. Many manufactured exports from both countries, but especially from Taiwan, were component parts, and other types of intermediate goods, such as textiles. A sizeable amount of other manufactured exports were inexpensive unbranded products, such as kitchen items and tools of various kinds, which were sold in a range of retail outlets, often in discount stores, such as K-Mart and Wal-Mart. As long as they were purchased from South Korean and Taiwanese firms in contracted batches for assembly or sale elsewhere, however, even the simplest and least expensive items were driven by intermediary demand.

From the perspective of America's total imports in the late 1960s and 1970s, those imports from East Asia represented only a modest but steadily increasing percentage, especially in comparison with growing imports of oil from the Middle East. But from the perspective of Asia's industrial expansion, these U.S. bound exports accounted for a huge percentage of the total output of these Asian economies and drove these economies forward into capitalism.

### *The Emergence of Divergent Economies*

The apparent similarities between U.S. imports from South Korea and Taiwan, however, mask the fundamental differences between these two Asian economies. As Feenstra and Hamilton (2006) have shown in some detail, these economies become progressively organised in response to big buyer orders. These emergent differences are obvious from an examination of the disaggregated seven-digit trade data. In the very early years when U.S. buyers were placing their first rounds of orders, buyers placed similar orders in different locations. For example, before 1975, garments exports were among the highest categories of exports from both countries, with garments providing about a third of the total value of Korea's exports to the United States and a quarter of Taiwan's. Among the 263 and 345 types of garments that South Korea and Taiwan, respectively, exported to the United States in 1972, the top five items provided 42% of the total value of garments from Korea and 39% from Taiwan. Three of the top five garment items are the same for both countries, namely specific types of sweaters, knit shirts, and trousers, all for women and girls.

From about 1975 on, however, the buyers began to grow more sophisticated in terms of both the consumer markets for their products and the supplier markets for the relative capabilities of different manufacturers. Within the next decade, 1975–1985, the South Korean and Taiwanese economies developed divergent specialties. The export segment of the Korean economy specialised in vertically integrated Fordist mass production systems. Led by *chaebol*, such business groups as Hyundai and Samsung rapidly expanded in response to big-buyer orders for large volumes of the same type of finished product. At the time that the large South Korean firms grew larger, the export segment of the Taiwanese economy became more intensively oriented toward the goods that networks of small, medium, and modestly large could produce.

The trade data give evidence of this divergence. Footwear was a large export for both South Korean and Taiwanese economies, but very early on, firms in the two economies specialised in a different system of shoe manufacturing that led big buyers to order different types of shoes from each country. Figure 5 shows these differences, and Brian Levy (1988: 47–8) who visited shoe factories in both locations in the early 1980s, describes the differences as follows:

> Neither Nike nor Reebok had the organizational capacity... to meet... surges in demand by subdividing... enormous orders among dozens of small, efficient producers. Instead both companies turned to the giant Korean footwear factories, which had inhouse operations in excess of forty production lines. Firms met (these) orders by expanding their capacity even further. (A consequence of these orders was) continued dependence of Korean footwear industry on a single footwear item—non-rubber athletic shoes—which accounted in 1985 for an overwhelming 71.3 percent of Korean footwear exports....

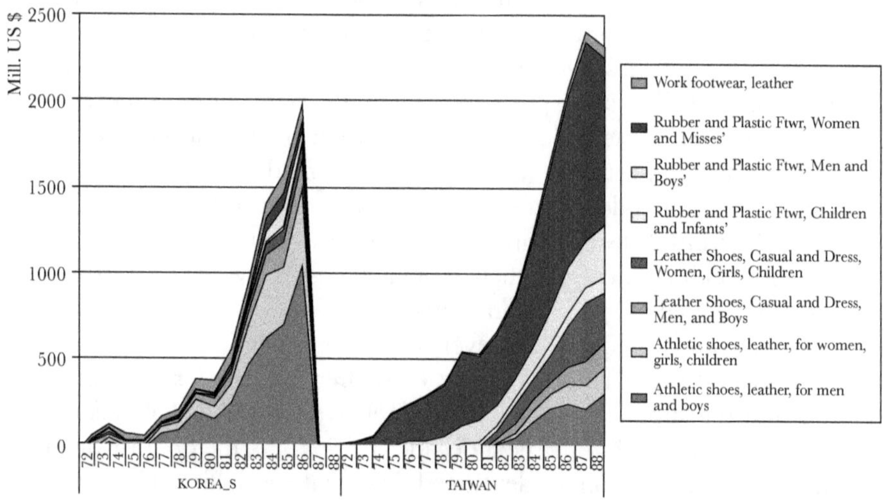


Source: NBER, HS U.S. Import data, 1972–2001

Figure 5: Footwear, 1972–88

> By contrast to Korea, footwear exports from Taiwan have become increasingly diversified over time...(The) small size (of Taiwanese firms) affords Taiwanese producers the flexibility necessary to fill rapidly shifting niches for small volume fashion items.

Divergence in the production between the two countries in rubber and plastic products is more dramatic. As Figure 6 shows, in 1972, when the data begin, both South Korea and Taiwan were exporting rubber and plastic raingear, but the large Korean firms quickly specialised in producing tires for vehicles, while small Taiwanese firms produced every manner of small plastic household products. The same is true for household appliances (Figure 7): Whereas Korean factories specialised in making microwave ovens, Taiwanese factories made small appliances, such as irons, toaster ovens, hair dryers and so forth.

In every industrial sector, the story is the same. Before 1985, Korean firms "mass produced," while Taiwanese firms "batch produced" goods, and both systems of production grew in response to orders. In effect, globalising retailers and brand name merchandisers patronised different supplier markets for different products. South Korean and Taiwanese manufacturers competed with each other in some of these supplier markets for specific goods, but for the most part, they specialised in different products.

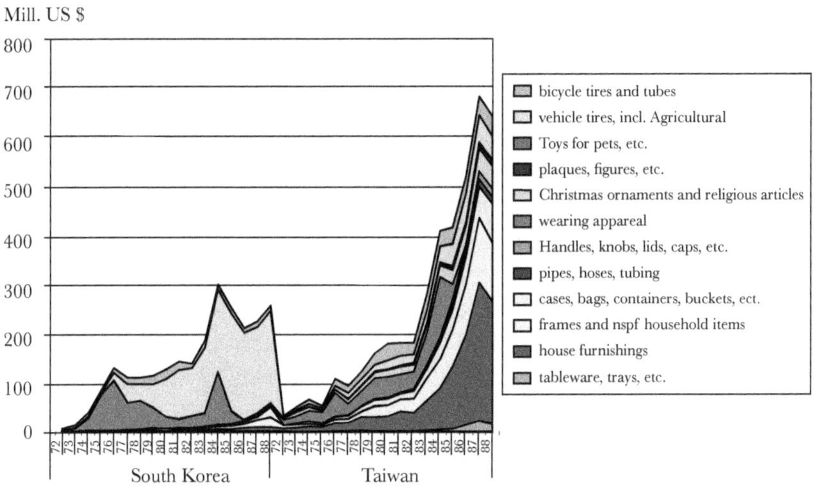


Source: NBER, HS U.S. Import Data

Figure 6: Rubber, Plastic Products, 1972–88

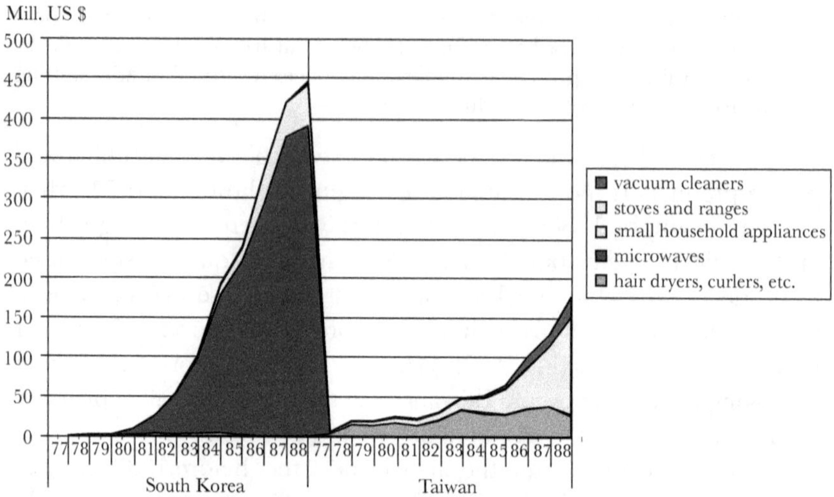


Source: NBER, HS U.S. Import data, 1972–2001

Figure 7: Household Appliances, 1972–1988

Now we will turn to the Taiwanese case in order to show the process by which these supplier markets emerged and by which the entire economy changes as a consequence.

### *Taiwan's Industrialisation: The Rise of a Demand-Responsive Economy*

It is hard to date the first moment when industrialisation began, and perhaps it is useless to do so. But it is certain that the new economic trend in Taiwan began when the first big buyers arrived. We do not know who these buyers were, because no one sufficiently noticed them to record their arrival. It is also certain that the initial intermediaries were not the Taiwanese themselves. In those early years, as far as the Taiwanese were concerned, Taiwan was a closed island, and they and their resources were locked inside. Martial law was enforced. The government strictly controlled both people and money. The Taiwanese, therefore, simply did not know the foreign markets for which they would soon be making products. And, of course, very few locals spoke any English at all. The historical context makes it clear that the foreigner buyers came to Taiwan before the Taiwanese went to the buyers in the U.S., Europe, and Japan, as they would do with increasing frequency in the 1980s.

### *Japanese Trading Companies*

It is very likely that the first buyers of Taiwan's products were Japanese trading companies. In our interviews from the late 1980s (Kao and Hamilton Forthcoming), factory owners across a wide range of industries recalled getting their start working with Japanese firms in one way or another. In the late 1960s, as American retailers began to use Japanese trading companies to fill orders for garments and footwear, these trading companies encouraged a range of Japanese firms to relocate to areas outside of Japan where cheaper labor could be found.[4] Drawing on their expertise in marketing, financing and information gathering, as Kojima and Ozawa noted the Japanese general trading companies "turned into overseas project organizers...and (played) a key role in helping Japanese manufacturers, and particularly small- and medium-sized enterprises, set up shop in labour-abundant developing countries to produce technologically mature, labour-intensive products by investing jointly and providing needed infrastructural services" (1984: 13). Two former Japanese colonies, Taiwan and South Korea, were the two places Japanese firms placed sizeable investments, first in Taiwan in the late 1960s and in South Korea in the early 1970s (Feenstra and Hamilton 2006:262–4).

Aside from our interviews and a few scattered references, however, it is difficult to find much on the role played by the Japanese trading companies in Taiwan's first period of rapid growth, from about 1965 to 1975. If they mention Japanese companies at all, most analysts (e.g., Gold 1986; Wade 1990) only refer to those notable cases of large Japanese manufacturing companies establishing joint ventures in the area of consumer electronics, such as Tatung's 1964 joint venture with Toshiba for producing television sets.[5] To most observers in the era,

[4] During the decades after the American occupation of Japan ended, Japanese business groups grew at a pace much faster than Japan's rapidly growing economy. In addition to selling finished products, the general trading companies for the main business groups imported intermediate goods needed by firms within the group. However, in the 1960s, as the main *keiretsu* firms grew more proficient in securing their own inputs and marketing their own products, many in Japan began to worry that the trading companies would lose their central role. This decline in local business "led to a belief that the trading companies would gradually become less and less useful and would eventually die out, a belief popularized in the so-called 'demise theory'" (Kojima and Ozawa p. 13). This belief prompted most trading companies to internationalise their operations.

[5] Constance Lever-Tracy (2000) argues that Japanese trading companies had only a limited role in the development of East Asian economies outside of Japan. However,

Japanese trading companies seem almost invisible, a presence about which little is known for sure. Our interviews, however, suggest that they served as the brokers that got Taiwan's industrialisation underway, a crucial but unheralded role.

Several factors lead us to the conclusion. The first reason is the language. In the 1960s, many ethnic Taiwanese older than 35 or so could speak some Japanese. They had learned Japanese during their compulsory primary school education in the colonial period. Moreover, Japanese at this time was not only the language of instruction, but also the language of international business, as well as the language of government. In the earliest years of growth, therefore, Japanese businesspeople and ethnic Taiwanese could speak to one another with some level of understanding and cultural familiarity.[6]

Second, the Japanese trading companies in the 1960s began to expand their operation outside of Japan. In the immediate post-war period, Japanese trading companies played an important role in rebuilding Japan's domestic economy. They coordinated and brokered exchanges among Japanese firms, especially firms in the same groups of firms that had constituted the pre-war *zaibatsu*. Having formed around family-owned holding companies, the *zaibatsu* were disbanded by the U.S. occupation government on the grounds of being illegitimate monopolists. After the American occupation ended, the firms constituting the former *zaibatsu* regrouped, but without the family-owned holding company at the top. In these reconstituted business groups, now called *keiretsu*, the general trading company, along with the main banks, served as one of the core firms that maintained the interrelatedness of group firms. By the 1960s, the general trading companies, called *sogoshosha*, served as the main import/export agents for firms in their respective business groups, and in addition began increasingly to serve as independent agents in establishing sources for goods for which they had received orders, but

her argument misses the important contribution that the Japanese trading companies made to create competent supplies in Taiwan and South Korea.

[6] The Kuomintang government, however, did not help in this matter. The government banned speaking Japanese in public, a law that was enforced after 1947. The mainland migrants to Taiwan, of course, viewed the Japanese with dislike and distrust. After all they had fought a war against Japan. Taiwanese residents, however, did not experience World War II in the same way. Although they were not without hard feelings toward the former colonisers, local Taiwanese could deal with the Japanese without animosity.

that were not supplied by member firms in the quantity, quality or price desired by the ordering firm.

It was their role as independent agents that was especially important for Taiwan. In the early 1960s, after over a decade of rapid economic growth, Japanese labor costs began to climb. For the years 1964–66, the average monthly cost of labor in Japanese textile factories was three times higher than in Taiwan's, at 69 U.S. dollars per month, as opposed to Taiwan's 23 U.S. dollars per month (Duan 1992). In the same period, the U.S. average wage in U.S. textile factories was 333 U.S. dollars per month. The rising wages in Japan encouraged the general trading companies to begin to look at locations outside of Japan as more profitable places to perform the tasks that they had perfected in Japan, skills at market-making, infrastructure creation, and financial backing. In the same deal, the general trading companies would make money in multiple ways. They would receive orders from American and Japanese retailers, and then would arrange production for the orders. In the early years, they had to create competent suppliers: they would broker deals leading to joint ventures between a Japanese company and a local company and, if needed, would supply or otherwise arrange for financing. Then they would import and sell the machine tools needed to establish the factory, train the Taiwanese how to use the machinery, supply the intermediate goods needed to make a product, and then coordinate the delivery of the goods to retail markets in Japan or more frequently in the U.S.

Third, during the late 1960s, Taiwan was the largest recipient of Japanese foreign investment (The Economist Intelligence Unit 1983). Records on foreign direct investments in Taiwan show that the absolute total of U.S. investments exceeded investments from Japan, but Japanese investments involved over three times as many individual investments than those from the U.S (Duan 1992:236). These figures point to a different investment strategy between the U.S. and Japanese businesses. On the U.S. side, a few large U.S. multinationals (e.g. RCA) set up stand-alone manufacturing plants in export processing zones producing consumer electronics, and on average these investments were much larger than FDI from Japan. In fact, in 1975, the nine of the ten largest companies in Taiwan by revenues were all American companies; the other one, Philips Electronics Industries, was a Dutch company (Chu and Amsden 2003:28). By contrast, guided by the general trading companies, Japanese companies usually established joint ventures with Taiwanese firms. Some of these Japanese companies themselves were modest sized companies; others were subsidiaries of the large Japanese business groups. In both cases, however, the firms established with Japanese direct foreign investment were smaller and economically more diverse than American firms. Typically, the Japanese firm controlled the technology and supervised the manufacturing process, and a Japanese trading company secured the order and then marketed the final product. In the 1960s, Hitachi, Matsushita (Panasonic), Sanyo Electric, Ricoh, Mitsubishi Electric, Casio, among many other Japanese firms, started operations in Taiwan.

Fourth, although the figures seem more like rough estimates than firm assessments, a number of analysts (Feenstra and Hamilton 2006; Fields 1995; Olson 1970; Wade 1990) state that Japanese general trading companies served as the broker for over half of Taiwan's exports from the late 1960s through most of the 1970s. If this figure is accurate, then we must conclude that the general trading companies were not just mere merchants, but rather were active agents in financing, supervising, and supplying the Taiwanese manufacturers. In effect, the Japanese trading companies initiated Taiwan's supplier markets.

This seminal role, however, did not last long, for very soon Western buyers and Taiwanese trading companies began to play active roles in establishing Taiwanese suppliers of goods ordered by Western retailers and brand name merchandisers. In the resulting mix, Japanese trading companies increasingly began to specialise in a narrow, but still important segment of the overall market economy, namely in supplying Taiwanese manufacturers with capital goods and intermediate inputs required in the manufacturing process: machine tools, the gear boxes for bicycles, and specialty metals and chemicals needed in a wide range of products. Starting in the 1950s, Japanese exports to Taiwan increased almost every year until the late 1990s (*Taiwan Statistical Data Book* 1997:194). If our interviews provide a sample of what was happening in the entire economy, it would seem that most of these Japanese exports were the result of orders placed by Taiwanese businesspeople through Japanese trading companies. Through the 1990s, these trading companies continued to source and supply the intermediate goods needed to manufacture Taiwanese exports.

In those initial years of economic growth, however, Japanese trading companies played all the crucial roles that got the Taiwanese businesspeople started. Moreover, they provided the Taiwanese with more than just access to distant markets, advanced technologies, and manufacturing know-how. Most importantly, they showed the Taiwanese how to make money from the global economy. They showed them how to participate as suppliers, how to be reliable and trustworthy partners to firms that ordered goods from them which they had little additional knowledge of.

*American Buyers and Local Trading Companies*

Japanese trading companies likely served as the first global brokers for the Taiwanese. Their very success with sourcing goods in Asia, however, soon did them out of business. Soon after the Japanese trading companies came to Taiwan, the American buyers arrived as well. They established buying offices in Taipei, Seoul, and Hong Kong. Sears opened their Taiwan buying office in 1967, K-mart and J. C. Penney's in 1971, and Associated Merchandising Corporation (buyers for Dayton Hudson, Federated Department Stores and Target) and Mast Industries (buyers for The Limited) in 1973 (Gereffi and Pan 1994). By eliminating the middle man, American buyers could reduce their costs, but more importantly they could begin to work with the Taiwanese manufacturers, could help them be better suppliers, and as they became better suppliers, the Western buyers began to order greater quantities of a much wider range of goods.

Here the U.S. trade statistics are revealing. As shown above in Figure 4, in the very first year they were collected, 1972, the 7-digit US custom data show that Taiwan was already exporting products to the United States in over 2100 categories. By 1985, the number had risen to over 8400 categories. This increase represents an extraordinary growth in the variety of products Taiwan made for export to the U.S.

Most of the value of these exports, however, was quite concentrated, with nearly 30% of the total value in only the top ten product categories and nearly 80% of the total value in the top hundred categories. The top twenty exports in 1972 were dominated by consumer electronics and items of clothing, most of which are likely the result of multinational manufacturing and joint ventures.[7] However, once outside the top twenty or so items, then one begins to find a wide variety of

[7] Among the top ten exports were two types of TVs, one type of radio, one type of integrated circuit for an unspecified final product, one type of Christmas tree lights and one type of mahogany plywood, as well as three types of clothing (acrylic sweaters, knit shirts, and trousers made from synthetic material) and one category of footwear (vinyl shoes), all for women and girls. The consumer electronic products were likely

products that were almost certainly ordered by U.S. retailers and made in Taiwanese-owned factories. Among the next twenty items of export are types of umbrellas, luggage, bicycles, toys, household utensils, handbags, Christmas tree lights, and curtains. Going further down the list of products the array of products is dazzling: types of handbags, sewing machines, loudspeakers, religious articles made of plastic, inflatable rubber toys, guitars, belt buckles, gloves, clocks, headwear, badminton sets, baseballs, bicycle tires, tennis rackets—all these along with many different kinds of garments and shoes.

The custom records show that, from 1972 to 1985, these second-tier products were shipped in greater and greater quantities and accounted for more and more of the total value. This shift occurred at the same time as Taiwanese manufacturers took increasing shares of the export production in consumer electronics made in Taiwan.[8] By the time our interviews start in 1987, Taiwanese businesses, rather than foreign-owned firms, dominated every sector of the Taiwan export economy.

As we interviewed factory owners from the late 1980s on, the question at the back of our minds was how did this particular factory come to be making that particular product. And, every time, the answer to that question was that they had the order from a buyer. Without the order, they said, they would not make whatever they were making. They explained that the capital invested in the factory and in the inputs used to make the goods had come out of their own pockets, or out the pockets of a small group of family and friends who were the primary investors; therefore, they would not risk making something that had not already been ordered. When we probed where the order can from, they typically told us that American buyers had ordered the products, and as proof, they would show us the U.S. brand names on the products that they were shipping.

But at this point the obscurity would start. How were the orders actually arranged? Part of the obscurity was due to our failure to ask the crucial questions. In the 1980s and early 1990s we, along with most other observers, focused more on how Taiwan businesspeople put together their production networks than on how they obtain their

made in factories wholly or partially owned by Americans or Japanese, but the other products likely came from factories owned by Taiwanese.

[8] It was not until 1990, however, that most multi-national manufacturers had withdrawn from Taiwan (Chu and Amsden 2003:37).

orders. We knew they had the orders, we knew they depended on having the orders, and so we did not query them on the intricacies of how the ordering system worked. However, part of the obscurity also came from the fact that the orders had come from a variety of sources. Some came directly from the retailers or brand name merchandisers, others were handled by Japanese trading companies, and yet others were arranged by local trading groups.

Knowing the importance of local trading companies, we interviewed several dozen different trading companies. We learned that in the years of our interviews, mostly in the early 1990s, the owners of trading companies had to work hard to get the orders. They would take their case of samples to the U.S. or Europe, and go from retailer to retailer looking for orders. These kinds of trading companies were colloquially referred to as "suitcase companies" (*pibao gongsi*). But suitcase companies only became commonplace after the Taiwanese were able to travel overseas freely and after the foreign exchange markets were open, and this did not occur until the mid 1980s. The question that we did not ask was how the ordering system worked during the crucial decade between 1965 and 1975.

During that crucial decade, we also knew that the government did not provide much, if any, assistance. In the early 1990s, a lot of export manufacturers obtained contracts by showing their wares at trade fairs and at fixed stalls at the Taipei World Trade Center. But the Taipei World Trade Center was not opened until 1988. Before that, the China External Trade Development Council handled most of the official matters involving trade. The Council was established in 1970, but was continually short staffed and under-funded. Allowed only thirteen employees, the first general secretary of the Council, Wu Kuan-hsiung, recalled being so frustrated with the lack of government support that he quit after a few years and went to Singapore. As early as 1973, he had recommended the government build a trade centre, but the plan was put off year after year. The government, he complained, liked industry, but not commerce or trade.

Putting together bits and pieces of information from our interviews and from other sources, we think it is likely that the American buyers and the local trading companies began to collaborate in the early 1970s and built a momentum that continued through the 1980s. One fact stands out for this period: local trading companies grew in number at a pace even faster than the Taiwanese economy in the same period. In 1973, official records show that there were 2,777 trading companies in operations in Taiwan,[9] but by 1985, that number of trading companies has risen to 55,000. One out of every ten registered companies was a trading company. The trading companies were uniformly small, averaging less than ten employees each. Knowing the trading companies from our interviews in the early 1990s, we surmise that nearly every category of export products was represented by many local trading companies competing for orders. Although small, the local trading companies took on a multitude of roles, chief among which was to work both sides of the demand/supply equation. Their offices were usually in Taipei, near the buying offices established by American retailers. They worked to identify products that will be saleable to the big buyers and then worked to obtain orders for those products, thereby generating demand. Then the owners of the trading companies would help to arrange production networks to fill the order, thereby generating supply. They were more than simply matchmakers, they were instrumental in creating competent suppliers for American buyers. Local trading companies helped to create a market of suppliers willing to bid on and to make nearly any product imaginable.

Another fact equally stands out about these local trading companies. Once a market of suppliers existed, once the trade fairs and the World Trade Center were in operation, there no longer existed the same role for the local trading companies. Their basic role had been completed. From the late 1980s on, local trading companies began to diminish in number.

### *Imitation and Innovation*

Although we did not ask many questions about the process of obtaining orders, we did ask again and again how factory owners were able to make the products for which they had the orders. Many of the products were extraordinarily complex or required very complex manufacturing procedures. It always seemed remarkable to us that the Taiwanese manufacturers, often with very limited education, would be able to figure out how to make the products that they were, in fact, making. For instance, the Chairman of Thunder Tiger, a firm making airplanes for the hobbyist market, had only an elementary school

---

[9] This number is, of course, sizeable in its own right, especially as compared to Korea in the same period (Feenstra and Hamilton 2006:268–72).

education, and yet, among his many accomplishments, he figured out how to manufacture miniature drone jet airplanes. Chairman Tseng, the manufacturers of plastic lawn chair furniture, who at the time of our interview had huge contracts from both Wal-Mart and K-mart, had only an equivalent of a junior high education, and yet he invented a one-step manufacturing process to change raw plastic into finished products. Their stories are not unusual. In fact, most factory owners in Taiwan's first wave of industrialisation not only did not have advanced degrees, but also had no training in manufacturing in general or in making their specific product in particular.

The question that we asked repeatedly was how did they learn to make the products. The answer that we received was always some form of imitation and innovation based on an existing product. This process of imitation and innovation is usually a very difficult and complex process. The term often given to this process is "reverse engineering" which makes the process sound simple, but there is nothing easy or automatic about copying someone else's design. In the case of OEM production, the big buyers would often bring the samples, sometimes amounting to nothing more than just an idea designed on paper with them to Taiwan, and ask the manufacturers, or more likely the owners of trading companies, "Can you make it for such and such a price?". Then, before they could obtain the order, they would have to deliver a prototype, just to show that they could do it. The turnaround time on such a query was often very short, because frequently the buyers would just sit in their hotels waiting for the prototype to appear. With a very short lead time, the Taiwanese manufacturers would have to produce their prototype.

This process of innovating based on an existing product design is a skill that Taiwan manufacturers learned how to perfect. In the first decade of rapid growth, many of the OEM products were relatively simple and were ordered in fairly small batches. Taiwanese manufacturers learned how to produce these products in a variety of ways, some from their experience in working in other factories, some on instructions provided by the Japanese trading companies and suppliers of machine tools, and some from the big buyers themselves. However, once in business, they learned quickly from others in their production network. In this context, learning was both singular and collaborative.

It was singular in the sense that one firm typically took the lead to produce the prototype. The owner and key employees of this firm would design and make a prototype. At this stage, very few people might be involved, but those people would have to have a lot of knowledge about the product, and would have to go to some lengths to acquire this knowledge. Factory owners frequently told us that they would obtain this knowledge by going to trade shows, by finding samples of similar products and taking them apart, by closely reading trade journals where new developments are announced, and by pursuing others who have knowledge about the product or materials the products are made of. Wherever they obtained this knowledge, they would then actively try to innovate on the design to come up with something special that would give their goods a distinctive feel.

Learning was also collaborative in the sense that the process of production was a function of the network and not simply the firm. Therefore, learning how to produce a given prototype required considerable cooperation among a group of independent manufacturers. These manufacturers would have to work together very closely on coordinating all aspects of production. In the course of this collaboration, the division of labour among manufacturers had to be cost effective, because any inefficiencies would cut into their collective profits. The network of producers, therefore, would constantly learn how to produce products with higher quality while achieving lower costs and how to work together seamlessly. This process of manufacturing also led to improvements in product design.

In another location, we show how this combination of individual imitation by and cooperation among businesspeople is anchored in distinctively Chinese patterns of social organisation (Kao and Hamilton 2006). We refer to these patterns as an adaptation of "round-table etiquette" applied to economic activity, with the result that Taiwanese businesspeople could quickly take advantage of money-making opportunities that began to appear in the 1970s. The constant interaction between the product and the process of production, as well as between the firm and the networks of which the firms are a part, created in Taiwan's first wave of industrialisation a particularly dynamic approach to manufacturing. Some examples from our interviews will illustrate these various levels of interaction.

### *Kai Hsiang: Making Jacks*

The first time we interviewed Ling Wen-chuen, the general manager of Kai Hsiang, a hydraulic jack manufacturing firm in Chiayi, was in 1990. Although we would revisit him many times during the next fifteen years, that first visit left a lasting impression. At the time, he was a youthful 34-year old and was completely at ease with having us in his factory. A very jovial man, he kept us there for the better part of the day, which ended with a banquet that he hosted for the entire research team, a total of twelve people. A close family friend of one of the Tunghai graduate students, Ling welcomed us warmly and answered all of our questions in detail.

In 1990, Kai Hsiang was the second largest of the six major jack factories in Chiayi. It employed about 200 people in the main factory and worked with a large network of subcontractors consisting of over 100 small firms. Kai Hsiang was one of a number of businesses owned by the Ling Wen-chuen's parents, and his role as general manager was given added weight by the fact that it was a family business, technically owned by his father, but in reality collectively owned by the entire family.

The family businesses began with Ling Wen-chuen's grandfather, who owed a pharmacy in Chiayi. Having a taste for business, but not wanting to take over the family store, Ling's father, Ling Suen-yi, looked around for other opportunities. In the early 1960s, responding to the growing export markets in Japan for agricultural products (Feenstra and Hamilton 2006:200–10), farmers in the southern Taiwan had begun to invest heavily in growing a range of animals commercially, including pigs, chickens, fish, and shrimp. Sensing an opening, Ling Suen-yi started a factory producing feed for chicken and fish. As a part of this business, he had to import grains such as corn to make the feed, and he had to go round the island of Taiwan to market the animal meal to feed shops. Through his contacts in the feed business, Ling Suen-yi heard, in the early 1970s, about a Japanese luggage company that wanted to locate a contract manufacturer to make some low-end luggage. The Japanese were willing to invest some capital such a company. Ling Suen-yi quickly took them up on the offer, and investing some of his own money in the factory as well, he started making luggage. While Ling Suen-yi worked full-time to establish his luggage factory, his wife took over the agribusiness. Through working with the Japanese company, he was able to upgrade the quality of his luggage and land some additional OEM contracts.

In 1980, running a successful luggage export business, Ling Suen-yi was approached by a friend of a friend. This person owned a jack factory, which he wanted to sell. The factory was not doing well, and the person wanted to sell the factory to the Ling family at an attractive price. A few years earlier another jack factory had opened in Chiayi called Hsinfu. The owner of Hsinfu and Ling Suen-yi were friends, and, sensing an opportunity, Ling Suen-yi hoped to collaborate with Hsinfu to produce a wider range and larger quantity of hydraulic jacks. The year before they bought the jack factory, the person we interviewed, the son, Ling Wen-chuen, had just graduated from National Taiwan University in Taipei, with a BSc degree in Forestry. In the year after his graduation, he had worked for his father in the luggage company, learning sales and marketing and making use of the English that he had learned in college. When Ling Suen-yi bought the jack factory in 1981 for 20 million NT dollars, his son Ling Wen-chuen, immediately became the general manager.

In the late 1970s, in addition to Kai Hsiang and Hsinfu, four other jack assembly factories started operation in Chiayi. Although each one was independent and in competition with the other firms and although each had a network of dedicated subcontractors, they also shared some subcontractors who made specialised parts. As a function of being part of an extensive network of assembly factories and overlapping parts suppliers, the entire agglomeration of firms, although internally competitive, shared substantial knowledge about how to manufacture products with hydraulic components. As general manager of Kai Hsiang, Ling Wen-chuen made good use of this information to improve the production facilities in his factory.

The agglomeration of jack factories in Chiayi created a large demand for steel of a certain size and quality. Not far from Chiayi, near Kaohsiung, is the state-owned steel mill, China Steel, as well as several large privately-owned steel mills. At first, the jack factories ordered steel from some of these factories, but they soon switched their orders to a newly established local steel mill. This firm has been established in the late 1970s by a local man who had worked as an apprentice in one of the Kaohsiung mills. As the jack factories began to receive substantial orders, this person was encouraged to open a mini-mill dedicated to serving the specific needs of the jack manufacturers in Chiayi.

In the first years of operation, Kai Hsiang was a subcontract manufacturer for Hsingfu, which was then on its way to becoming the world's largest producer of hydraulic jacks. Ling Wen-chuen told us that in the first year of operation, they made 200 million NT$ in total revenues, with profit margins running about 6 percent. After two years, they were able to turn a profit. As a subcontract assembly firm for Hsinfu, however, Kai Hsiang's production depended on Hsinfu's ability to get OEM orders. Although the firm was quite successful, Ling Wen-chuen wanted to expand his business. Using his English language skills, he went to Taipei, and eventually to the U.S., to meet American buyers. When we asked him how he knew what firms to go to, he said that that was not a problem. What he had done was to go to the subcontract firm in Chiayi that was making the brand name-labelled cardboard boxes used to package the finished jacks and to see which American companies were ordering jacks. He then went to those companies, and as a result, he was able get substantial OEM orders on his own. These orders allowed him to expand his network of subcontractors. Within six years after buying the jack factory, by 1987, Kai Hsiang became the second largest jack assembly firm in Chiayi.

Our first interview with Ling Wen-chuen was in 1990. Within five years of that first interview, most of the jack assembly firms in Chiayi, including Kai Hsiang, had moved operations to Mainland China. The Ling Family luggage business continues in full operation, with one large factory in Mainland China and the small factory in Chiayi, where the high-end luggage continues to be made. The factory making animal feed ended operations at about the time that the farmers in southern Taiwan began to quit raising animals and seafood due to pollution and other causes. No longer running their agribusiness, Ling Suen-yi's wife opened a stock brokerage firm. The Ling Family jokingly called their businesses "nomadic" (*youmu*), because they never stopped searching for new opportunities to make money.

### *Yeh-Bao: Making Bicycles*

Located about 40 kilometers north and west of Taichung City, Ta Chia is one of many small villages lining the coast and skirting the river flood plains along Highway 1. Well removed from the main North/South freeways, Ta Chia before the 1970s was noted only for making small products woven from grass: hats, floor and bed mats, and slippers. Only eleven years later, by 1981, Ta Chia had become the centre of Taiwan's export bicycle industry, and by that time Taiwan had become the world's largest bicycle exporter (Cheng and Sato 1998:8). At the peak of the industry in Taiwan, in 1986, the number of bicycles exported reached more than ten million (Cheng and Sato 1998). Giant, Taiwan's best known bicycle company, is located in Ta Chia. It is the largest of many bicycle assembly firms in the region. Yeh-Bao is another firm in Ta Chia, but its owner, Lin Shun-san, built his business by specialising only in the manufacture of bicycle frames.

Chairman Lin started his first business in 1975. At that time, he had recently graduated from a nearby technical school with a specialty in telecommunications and had received the equivalent of a high school degree. Not knowing what to do, he returned to his hometown, Ta Chia, to look for opportunities. In the early 1970s, as Ta Chia was just becoming the centre of Taiwan's bicycle production, there were many opportunities in the region to enter the industry in one capacity or another. With only very little capital and acting on the advice of a friend, Lin and his wife decided to start a company making plastic saddle bags that attach to the rear fender of low-end bicycles. They called their company, Jun-ye (successful enterprise), and depending on the workload, employed between ten and twenty people, all from the local village. Their orders for the saddle bags came from other firms in Ta Chia. These bags would be attached to the bicycles in the final stages of assembly, just before the bicycles were packaged and shipped to the OEM buyers.

Building on his personal connections within the local community of bicycle assemblers and part suppliers, Chairman Lin, in 1978, got an opportunity to establish a new firm to make one of the technologically most difficult parts to manufacture, the frame. He called his firm Yeh-Bao (wild treasure) in Chinese and A-PRO in English. At the beginning they used low-end metals, mainly aluminum and stainless steel, to construct the frame. The first couple of years, he recalled, were extremely difficult because he had to work out the production technique for making the frame solid and unbreakable. To accomplish this task, precision welding is absolutely crucial, because so much pressure is placed on critical points on a bicycle, particularly the metal fork holding the front wheel. "Can you imagine," he said, "a 200 pound American guy riding on a ten pound bicycle at a speed of 30 miles an hour. Oh boy, the frame has to hold together. You know an automobile has four wheels, but a bicycle only has two."

Because competition at the low end was so tough, Chairman Lin decided he had to upgrade his position in the network of firms around Ta Chia. He borrowed money from his friends and bought new equipment in order to improve the quality of his frames. He also began to use new metals, such as carbon graphite, titanium, as well as higher grades of aluminum and steel. Then he hired the best welders he could find, paying then double and sometimes treble the going local wage for welders. When he first bought the specialty metals from a Japanese company, the Japanese company sent representatives to teach him and his welders the best techniques to cut and weld the frames. But Chairman Lin complained to us that Japanese companies never explain everything. They kept some of the core technology to themselves. Therefore, as they began to work with the new metals, Lin and his employees had to work out many of the problems on their own, and they had to test and retest the durability of their frames. Chairman Lin, however, continued to buy the high-end materials from Japan (e.g. titanium and carbon graphite) and to rely on Japanese manufacturers for key component parts, such as the Shimano gear boxes.

Once they had perfected the manufacturing process, Chairman Lin began to participate in international bicycle fairs, usually held in Cologne, Germany and New York, and he started to obtain OEM orders, especially from Europe. Quickly his own business improved. He had successfully upgraded his firm's position in the manufacturing network, just as the entire network had also upgraded itself as an OEM producer for major European and American retailers of bicycles. As Yeh-Bao grew in size, the firm was able to handle larger and more differentiated orders. Chairman Lin's strategy matched the strategy of the entire network of firms, namely to make differentiated products for mass produced low-end and middle range bicycles, and batch produced high end models, this along with a lot of bicycle accessories.

By 1992, when we interviewed Chairman Lin for the first time, he had established six independent factories in Taiwan, each making different component parts. The very first firm, Jun-ye, was still in operation, then managed by Lin's wife and making sophisticated bicycle accessories. Yeh-Bao was the largest of the six firms. Chairman Lin was the owner and boss (*laoban*) of each of these factories. We asked him, since he was making so many different bicycle parts, why not vertically integrate and make the entire bicycle himself, or at least become a downstream assembler. He answered decisively that that would not be a wise move. "If you try to vertically integrate in Ta Chia," he said, "then everyone will be your competitor. If you keep your firms separate, then you will be everyone's supplier." He said there were other reasons not to integrate as well. If you make a small number of products, you do not have to make a huge capital investment in any one of them. Modest investments, he said, give better returns with lower risks. Finally, he noted that Taiwan's tax code also favor having multiple companies rather than one big firm. Continually starting small firms means that you can deduct startup costs, which would not be available if one began a new operation within an existing firm. Also, multiple firms create multiple lines of credit. One big company only has one credit line. And finally different sizes of firms are subject to different tax rates. Although all these reasons are important, he reflected, the main reason not to vertically integrate is the risk of going it alone, of trying to make money without help from others.

Chairman Lin thought it was much better for him to make himself indispensable within the overall network of firms. The bicycle industry is continually changing, he said; it is a "fashion industry". A network of firms is much more flexible in changing with the trends than is one big vertically integrated firm. "It used to be that the big firms in South Korean would make huge quantities of bicycles", but the Taiwanese producers were able to follow the trends so much faster that the "Koreans got out of the bicycle business".

### *Pao Chen: Making Shoes*

Among Taiwanese firms, Pao Chen is a legend. In the late 1990s, Pao Chen, along with its subsidiary Yu Yuan, became the largest shoe manufacturer in the world, making nearly a quarter of all athletic shoes in the world. Also among private sector Chinese firms, Pao Chen is one of the largest employers, with over 250,000 employees worldwide and with over 80,000 employees in one of its Mainland Chinese factories alone. Like other Taiwanese firms, however, Pao Chen started small.

When we first interviewed Pao Chen's owner, Tsai Chi-ray, in 1988, it was a considerably smaller firm of about 500 employees, operating five assembly lines producing shoes,[10] but by Taiwan's standards of the day, even then it was relatively large. Our first interview with Pao Chen occurred just at the time when the company was beginning surreptitiously, to move part of its operations to China. Secrecy was required because the Taiwan's government absolutely forbade everyone from making investments in Mainland, but after the 1985 Plaza Accord,

[10] It is almost certain that the Tsai brothers owned other shoe companies in the region. At the time, the general pattern was to own multiple companies and be part of multiple networks, instead of creating one big firm to vertically integrate the operations.

which caused Taiwan's currency to appreciate, contract manufacturers in Taiwan had increasing difficulty in meeting the buyer's price points and still earn a profit. At our interview in 1988, we did not learn about their plans to move to China. Instead, we marvelled at their operations in Taiwan.

In 1969, Tsai Chi-ray, along with his three younger brothers, started Pao Chen in their hometown of Yuanlin, in those years, a modest sized town in Changhwa County south of Changhwa City. Reasonably prosperous in the 1960s, Yuanlin was noted for its agricultural products, particularly mushrooms, asparagus, preserved fruits, as well as its food processing plants that canned, bottled and otherwise processed these food products for export as well as for domestic consumption. A graduate of a local teacher's college and then a teacher in the local junior high school, Tsai Chi-ray wanted to take advantage of the new economic opportunities that he saw appear in his hometown in the late 1960s. He borrowed 500,000 NT$ (equivalent to $12,500 US dollars) from close family members so that he and his three younger brothers could start a factory.

With ten employees, in addition to the four brothers, Pao Chen began making the kind of plastic slippers known colloquially in the United States as "flip-flops." At the time the Tsai brothers opened their firm, a number of other factories in the area had also started making the same style of plastic shoes. Some of Tsai family members had had previous experience making slippers out of woven grass, which they obtained from Ta Chia. Now they began to use that experience to make these new kinds of shoes. The flip-flop had been designed by an American firm in imitation of a style of Italian-made leather shoes for women. The flip-flops initially sold well in the American market, but the price per unit was very low. American buyers for the main retail outlets, especially K-mart, Sears, and Wal-Mart, then only a regional discounter, began to place orders in Taiwan. The raw plastic material used to make the flip-flops was readily available in Taiwan from Nanya Plastics, a subsidiary of Formosa Plastics. Working through a local trading company, the Tsai brothers were able to land a contract for a quantity of these plastic shoes. At the same time this was occurring, the U.S. demand for flip-flops surged, which led in turn to much bigger orders. The U.S. buyers for the retail chains then began to come directly to the suppliers, Pao Chen included, and began to work closely with them to increase both the quantity and the quality of the products. Chairman Tsai recalled being especially impressed with the buyers from Wal-Mart, with whom they gradually developed a close relationship.

In the early 1970s, Pao Chen began to receive some direct orders from the main retail buyers. In response to these orders, Pao Chen increased the size of its factory and began to develop its own subcontracting network. At this time the market for non-leather shoes in the United States began to diversify. Pao Chen's breakthrough came when the company got some large orders for a new type of shoe, a canvas covered plastic shoe, variously called "sneakers" or "tennis shoes". The construction was fairly easy and the unit price was very low. Working with their production network, however, Pao Chen was able to keep their production costs low, produce these shoes in large quantities, and still have everyone make a profit. At the same time that Pao Chen's orders for sneakers began to come in, two related developments pushed Taiwan shoe manufacturers in new directions. First, the technology used in making shoes changed dramatically when Mitsubishi's general trading company, CITC, transferred Japanese technologies for making shoes to Taiwanese suppliers. CITC was one of the primary intermediaries between a range of specialised retailers of sporting goods and Taiwanese shoe manufacturers. In Japan at the time, a new type of shoe was being developed, a highly functional and durable shoe that would become known as the "athletic shoe". These shoes required new machinery, advanced plastic materials, and high quality sewing and lamination techniques. Making these shoes was very labor intensive. Taking advantage of Taiwan's cheaper labor costs and batch production techniques, CITC taught Taiwanese suppliers the new shoe-making technologies and also sold them the machines and the materials to make the shoes.

The German shoe manufacturer, Adidas, had been trying to develop a similar type of shoe with technologies similar to those developed by the Japanese. Keeping in step with their Japanese competitors, Adidas in 1971, decided to try contract manufacturing in Taiwan as well, and signed an agreement with Hwagang, a shoe company located in northern Taiwan. In the following year, 1972, Reebok came to Taiwan, as did the Japanese company Mizuno. These companies signed contracts with a number of shoe manufacturers, among them Chinglu, a firm located in the same county as Pao Chen. Although they had only been in business for about five years, all these contracts for athletic shoes made Taiwanese shoe manufacturers one of the main global suppliers for this new type of athletic shoe.

The extraordinarily rapid growth of the Taiwan's shoe manufacturers created huge demand for specialised inputs and for the machinery to make shoes, much of which were initially supplied by the Japanese trading companies. By the mid-1970s, local firms began to emerge that supplied both the inputs and the machinery. This follows the general rule in demand-responsive economies: orders for final products come first, markets for intermediate inputs for those products come later, which encourages niche suppliers for intermediate inputs to emerge.

The second important development in Taiwan's shoe industry was the arrival of Nike and a surging global demand for athletic shoes that was in part created by Nike. In the early 1970s, Kihachiro Onitsuka, the owner of Asics Tiger, cooperated with the American company called Blue Ribbon Sports, which later became Nike, to manufacture a shoe designed by Phillip Knight. Knight's story is well known: he saw that there was no shoe designed for running and other athletic endeavors. He designed the shoe and contracted Asics Tiger to make it. In only a few years after their introduction, Nike captured a huge share of the newly developed market in athletic shoes in the U.S. At first this market seemed to be a niche market that filled, as well as created demand from the new popularity for jogging and aerobics. The niche expanded, as more and more athletic type shoes were worn for all occasions. At the beginning, Asics Tiger made Nike shoes, but with competition from Adidas and Reebok, Knight decided to move his contract manufacturing out of Japan. He split his orders between footwear manufacturers in South Korea and Taiwan, with Korean companies making mass-produced shoes for low-end markets and Taiwanese companies making the batch-produced specialty shoes. In Taiwan, Nike's lead firm was Fung-Tai, also located in Taichung County, about 30 minutes north of Yuanlin.

From 1966 to 1985, the global export of sport shoes from Asia grew 1200 times. Most of these shoes were produced in only two countries, Taiwan and South Korea. By 1985, Taiwan and South Korea produced 50% of all shoes imported into the US. By this time, American shoes manufacturers had gone into a decline from which they would never recover. Because of the sudden demand in the U.S. for these new types of shoes, the large retailers and trade name merchandisers did a lot of research on how to put the shoes together to get maximum performance. In the early years, recalled Tsai Chi-ray, when Pao Chen made flip-flop and sneakers for the big box retailers, price was the most important issue. Later, when Pao Chen began to cooperate with the brand name merchandisers, the ability to use advanced technology was more important than price. What all these brand name companies most needed were manufacturers who could transform these R&D models into a manufactured commodity that yielded a good profit for all concerned. The secret of the Taiwan manufacturers was the know-how to do this.

As Pao Chen continued to make sneakers for the big box retailers, they started to invest heavily in new equipment needed to produce athletic shoes, equipment sold to them by CITC. By 1977, they also set up their own internal research division (*neibu yanjiu xiaozu*) to further develop materials to make shoes. They began to do some subcontracting work for other Taiwanese firms that had primary orders for athletic shoes.

In 1979, they received their first order from Adidas through a local trading company arm of Hwagang. At the time Hwagang handled all of Adidas's local sales (the sales agent), did a large portion of Adidas's contract manufacturing, and arranged for subcontracts to do the remainder. The arrangement was very successful for Pao Chen. In 1982, Pao Chen became the primary OEM manufacturer for New Balance, and gained a good reputation for the quality of their shoes. The quality of their production attracted Reebok, which signed an agreement with Pao Chen in 1988. Then in 1989, Nike signed on as well.[11]

By the time Pao Chen received its first big contract from Nike, Pao Chen was then transferring much of its manufacturing capacity to China. The golden period for Taiwan's shoe production was just ending, and the great rush to China was just beginning. In retrospect, we can see that, in 1989, the golden period for Pao Chen was just about to begin.

### *Demand-Responsive Manufacturing*

Between the late 1960s and 1985, Taiwanese manufacturers developed into sophisticated suppliers of consumer goods for global markets. In the beginning of the period, they had very little experience in any kind of manufacturing and very limited knowledge of the consumer goods that they would soon be making for overseas markets. At the end of the

[11] Nike's agreement with Pao Chen came after Nike had made a near disastrous attempt to contract production from Chinese firms in China. In 1980s Nike located a manufacturer in China to make a large portion of their shoes, but the effort failed due to poor quality manufacturing and the lack of supporting suppliers. Then Nike returned their operations to Taiwan, and started to work with Pao Chen.

period, they had advanced expertise in the process of manufacturing for OEM buyers and equally advanced knowledge of the products that they were making. In slightly over fifteen years, Taiwanese manufacturers, the Taiwanese economy, and the global economy had become tightly interconnected and transformed.

After 1985, in the wake of the Plaza Accord that raised the value of Taiwan's currency about forty percent relative to the U.S. dollar, Taiwan manufacturers had increasing difficulty meeting the price points set by U.S. retailers and brand name merchandisers. In the next decade, from 1985 to 1995, waves of Taiwanese SMEs began to move to Mainland China, and once in China, the lead firms having the major contracts reorganised their production networks to better fit the needs of overseas buyers. These reorganisations by Taiwanese manufacturers greatly increased their capacity to make products on demand from overseas buyers. From this reorganisation emerged a new set of Taiwanese-owned business groups that rank among the world's most successful enterprises. Three such enterprise groups—Pao Chen, the world's largest manufacturer of footwear; Hon Hai, the world's largest contract manufacturer for consumer electronics; and Quanta, the world's largest manufacturer of laptop computers—are barely known outside of East Asia, but are among the largest exporting firms from Mainland China. In fact, of the top twenty exporters from China, ten are owned by Taiwanese.

The modular organisation designed for flexible production grew out of the demand-responsive production systems that developed in Taiwan during the first fifteen years of rapid growth, from 1970 to 1985. Each of these case studies above illustrates this process of transformation.

- The manufacturing of each product came to rely on production networks that broke down the production process into distinct steps that standardized the product, the component parts, and the roles of the participants (Kao and Hamilton 2006).
- All varieties of contract manufacturing (e.g., OEM, ODM, OBM) grew out of a progressively reorganising economy in which individual firms were parts of larger economic units. As the orders for products increased, this form of manufacturing became highly sophisticated and highly responsive to buyer demand. This form of manufacturing is not a second class or substandard form of production, which some analysts make it out to be. The literature often describes the goal of OEM producers as needing to upgrade, but our interviews show that even in this first wave of industrialisation, demand-responsive manufacturing, as a definable process, began to take shape and was progressively rationalised over time.

- Demand-responsive manufacturing was the result of self-conscious organising on the part of Taiwanese manufacturers. It was done intentionally, in part because of the limited resources they possessed and because of the social organisation that they were accustomed to.
- Our interviews show that from the outset, Taiwanese manufacturers operated on three principles. The first principle of contract manufacturing is to make money for your buyer. If they don't make money, they will not be back. This understanding led Taiwanese manufacturers to organise by taking the buyer's perspective into account and, in fact, by making it their own perspective. The second principle of OEM production is to work for the return contract. Meet the buyer's expectations in quality, quantity, and price point the first time. If the buyers come back, then they will have made money and will feel like they could make more. The third principle of OEM is to make money for yourself. How you achieve these three principles is through taking calculated risks. However, if you don't make money for yourself you will not be able to survive. Maybe you will not make money with the first few contracts, but if you make yourself indispensable to your buyers, you will make lots of money over the long haul.
- How do you organise to make money for your buyers? As we said, you do that by organising from the perspective of the buyer. Organise backward from the product itself and from the order for that product. You have the specifications for the product, and you know how many they want. Do not try to develop a totally new product. Simply try to reproduce an existing product with high quality, at low cost, and in the desired quantity. The production unit you organise is in direct response to the product and the orders. Different ways to organise production evolve over time, but in the early years it was always a production network.
- How do you organise to make money for yourself? First, establish a foothold in the production networks. Learn by doing. Make incremental changes to improve what you are doing, cut down the production process, and accept low margins in the short run in hopes of receiving larger margins going forward. Be a network player and accept the network agreements about the profit margin. When the opportunity arises, fill the niches that appear in the production process or develop new niches that others will find useful.
- Second, try to get multiple orders for the same product from different sources. Multiple orders will allow you to develop a strategy of product differentiation, based on standardised parts for all models.
- Third, modularise the production across the producing units. Standardise each step in the production to make the manufacturing process transparent to all those engaged in making the product. Adopt external standards for the products, as specified by the buyer, and adopt internal standards for the process of production, as developed and specified by the network of independent manufacturers.

## *Conclusion*

Taiwanese entrepreneurs developed and perfected a model of how to manufacture for foreign buyers. The model they developed contains a number of elements that led to a comprehensive reorganisation of the Taiwanese economy, making Taiwanese economy into a demand-responsive economy. This economy had the following features: the economy organised around products that big buyers ordered and services related to those products. For each product, sets of competing core firms emerged. These core firms assembled and sometimes made key parts and then subcontracted components to other firms. This production strategy led to the development of clusters of firms and to internal markets for intermediate goods and services. These flexible networks supplying final and intermediate goods and services would expand when demand was great and would contract when demand was low. Typically, the product concentration led to a geographical concentration as well, because the production system relied on a just-in-time delivery of parts to the assembly location. The Taiwanese learned these techniques from the Japanese and perfected them in Taiwan.

As overseas demand for products increased, product differentiation also increased. Product differentiation created concentric rings of manufacturing networks, networks that intersected across numbers of core manufacturers. These intersecting rings contained many niches for expansion and development of additional products and for supporting services. Buyer demand also led to rigid cost controls that fed back across all supporting sectors, which in turn created the continuing need to rationalise production and upgrade products relative to big-buyer orders. As Taiwan's entire economy became oriented to export production in response to buyer orders, Taiwan's economy also became subject to economic trends in the U.S. Economic downturns and rising retail concentration in the U.S. began to drive fluctuation in the Taiwanese economy, later prompting many Taiwanese businesspeople to move all or a portion of their manufacturing to Mainland China. In Mainland China, they reorganised their businesses in response to rapid increases in retailer orders. The Taiwanese, along with Hong Kong, businesspeople played a crucial role in creating export-oriented capitalism in China.

This brings us to our final point. It is our belief that the debates about the causes of East Asian industrialisation need substantive revision. The current explanations are "supply-side narratives" that entirely ignore the role of intermediaries and the demand, as well as the demand responsiveness, they helped to produce. Global retailers and the reorganisation of the global economy that retailers have helped create have changed the way Asian economies fit into a global economic order. To miss these features of capitalist development is to miss some of the most important aspects of global capitalism today.

## *References*


Bluestone, B., Hanna, P., Kuhn, S., and Moore, L. (1981). *The Retail Revolution: Market Transformation, Investment, and labor in the Modern Department Store.* Boston: Auburn House Publishing Company.

Chamberlin, E. H. (1962/1933). *The Theory of Monopolistic Competition: A Reorientation of the Theory of Value.* 8th edition. Cambridge, Mass.: Harvard University Press.

Cheng, L. L. and Yukihito Sato. (1998). "The Bicycle Industries in Taiwan and Japan: A Preliminary Study Toward Comparison between Taiwanese and Japanese Industrial Development," *Joint Research Program Series*, No. 124. Tokyo: Institute of Developing Economies.

Chu, W. W. and A. Amsden. (2003). *Chao yue hou jin fa zhan: Taiwan de chan ye sheng ji ce luë.* Taipei: Lian Jing.

de Grazia, Victoria. (2005). *Irresistible Empire: American's Advance through Twentieth-Century Europe.* Cambridge, Mass.: Harvard University Press.

Duan, Chengpu (1992). *Taiwan zhan hou jing ji.* Taipei: Ren jian chu ban she.

Economist Intelligence Unit. (1983). *Japanese Overseas Investment.* London, U.K.: The Unit.

Feenstra, R. C. and G. G. Hamilton. (2006). *Emergent Economies, Divergent Paths: Economic Organization and International Trade in South Korea and Taiwan.* Cambridge: Cambridge University Press.

Fields, K. J. (1995). *Enterprise and the State in Korea and Taiwan.* Ithaca, New York: Cornell University Press.

Gereffi, G. (1994). "The International Economy and Economic Development." Pp. 206–233 in *The Handbook of Economic Sociology*, edited by Neil Smelser and Richard Swedberg. Princeton: Princeton University Press.

Gereffi, G. and Pan, M. L. (1994). "The Globalization of Taiwan's Garment Industry." Pp. 126–146 in *Global Production: The Apparel Industry in the Pacific Rim*, edited by Edna Bonacich, Lucie Cheng, Norma Chinchilla, Nora Hamilton, and Paul Ong. Philadelphia: Temple University Press.

Gold, T. B. (1986). *State and Society in the Taiwan Miracle.* Armonk, New York: M. E. Sharpe.

Hamilton, G. G. (2006). *Commerce and Capitalism in Chinese Societies.* London: Routledge.

Hamilton, G. G. and C. S. Kao. (Forthcoming). "Making Money: How the Global Economy Works from an Asian Point of View."

Hamilton, G. G., M. Petrovic, and R. C. Feenstra. (2006). "Remaking the Global Economy: U.S. Retailers and Asian Manufacturers." Pp. 146–184 in *Commerce and Capitalism in Chinese Societies*, edited by Gary G. Hamilton. London: Routledge.

Hanchett, T. W. (1996). "U.S. Tax Policy and the Shopping-Center Boom of the 1950s and 1960s," *American Historical Review* 101, October: 1082–1110.

Kao, C. S. and G. G. Hamilton. (2000). "Reflexive Manufacturing: Taiwan's Integration in the Global Economy," *International Studies Review* 3(1), June, 1–19.

——. (2006). "The Round Table: A Reconsideration of Chinese Business Networks," in *Paradigms and Perspectives on Hong Kong Studies*, edited by Wong Siu-lun. Hong Kong: University of Hong Kong Press.

Kojima, K. and T. Ozawa. (1984). *Japan's General Trading Companies: Merchants of Economic Development.* Paris: Organisation for Economic Co-operation and Development.

Lee, S. H. and H. K. Song. (1994). "The Korean Garment Industry: From Authoritarian Patriarchism to Industrial Paternalism." Pp. 147–161 in *Global Production: The Apparel Industry in the Pacific Rim*, edited by Edna Bonacich, Lucie Cheng, Norma Chinchilla, Nora Hamilton, and Paul Ong. Philadelphia: Temple University Press.

Lever-Tracy, C. (2000). "The Irrelevance of Japan." Pp. 183–204 in *Chinese Business and the Asian Crisis*, edited by David Ip, Constance Lever-Tracy and Noel Tracy. Hampshire, U.K. Gower Publishing Limited.

Levy, B. (1988). "Korean and Taiwanese Firms as International Competitors: The Challenges Ahead," *Columbia Journal of World Business* (Spring): 43–51.

——. (1991). "Transactions Costs, the Size of Firms, and Industrial Policy: Lessons from a Comparative Case Study of the Footwear Industry in Korea and Taiwan," *Journal of Development Economics* 34: 151–178.

Olson, L. (1970). *Japan in Postwar Asia.* New York: Praeger Publisher.

Robinson, J. (1969/1933). *The Economics of Imperfect Competition.* 2nd edition. London: Macmillan.

Spulber, D. F. (1996). "Market Microstructure and Intermediation," *Journal of Economic Perspectives* 10, 3 (Summer): 135–152.

——. (1999). *Market Microstructure: Intermediaries and the Theory of the Firm.* Cambridge: Cambridge University Press.

*Taiwan Statistical Data Book.* (1997). Taipei: Council for Economic Planning and Development.

Wade, R. (1990). *Governing the Market: Economic Theory and the Role of Government in East Asian Industrialization.* Princeton: Princeton University Press.

# *TAISHANG*: A DIFFERENT KIND OF ETHNIC CHINESE BUSINESS IN SOUTHEAST ASIA*

Hsin-Huang Michael Hsiao, Kung I-Chun and Wang Hong-zen

## I. *Introduction*

Taiwanese transnational capital emerged in the mid-1980s, and its importance is now widely recognised by Taiwanese scholars in various disciplines. There has been an increasing interest to investigate the nature of this newly emerging transnational capital, which is considered to be different from the Western or Japanese ones. Studies of Taiwanese businesses (*taishang*) in Southeast Asia have concentrated on the domains of overseas investment patterns (Chen 1994, 1998; Lin 2001), industrial relations (Kung 2002; Wang 2002), and ethnic relations and overseas Chinese networks (Hsiao and Kung 1998; Tseng 1999). Some scholars have noted that, to *taishang*, Southeast Asia is not only a geographical area, but also a cultural entity, and thus their investment behavior as a whole is embedded in the social contexts of the region. As latecomers to transnational capital in Southeast Asia, the *taishang* demonstrates some distinguishing features.

This paper argues that the *taishang* phenomenon in Southeast Asia should be understood first in terms of its capital formation and special characteristics, and second in terms of the influences of the political economy of the host countries. This paper tackles the issue of how the *taishang* have globalised their capital and business strategies to maintain their competitiveness in the world economy. It also explains how the *taishang* have reorganised their industrial production networks and how they manage labour relations in Southeast Asia.

The information that feeds this paper is primarily drawn from interview data collected in various research projects conducted by the three

* Reference to this article should be made as follows: Hsiao, Hsin-Huang Michael, Kung, I-Chun and Wang, Hong-zen 2007. "*Taishang*: A Different Kind of Ethnic Chinese Business in Southeast Asia".

authors over the past decade. These projects include 1) "*Taishang* in Southeast Asia: Networks and Ethnicities," a three-year project sponsored by the National Science Council between 1999 and 2002, which involved fieldwork in Malaysia, Indonesia, Thailand, Vietnam, and China; 2) "Exit: Cross-border Investment and the Local Embeddedness of *Taishang* in Asia Pacific", sponsored by the National Science Council in 2002; 3) "Market and State Together? Changing Labor Relations in Taiwanese Companies in Southeast Asia", financed by the Academia Sinica in 2001; 4) "Transnational Capital, International Migration and Ethnic Division of Labor: Labor Regimes in Vietnam's *Taishang* Factories"; and 5) "A New Paradigm or an Old Trick? Effect of Private Codes of Conduct on Industrial Relations in Vietnam", supported by the National Science Council in 2001 and 2003–2004, respectively. The fieldwork interviews were conducted with Taiwanese Business Associations, as well as *taishang* employers and managers in various Southeast Asian countries. The informants were selected from the membership list of the Taiwanese Chamber of Commerce in Malaysia, Vietnam, Thailand, Indonesia, and China, and from the Taiwan Directory of Overseas Firms published by the Ministry of Economic Affairs.

## II. *Reorganising* Taishang *Production Networks in Southeast Asia*

### *Production Networks Enclave*

Investment by Taiwanese companies (*taishang*) in Southeast Asia has grown significantly since the late 1980s, a phenomenon that has been attributed by many economists primarily to the changing economic environment in Taiwan. The abrupt appreciation of the Taiwanese currency in the late 1980s caused problems for many export-oriented and labour-intensive local industries. In 1987, the New Taiwan dollar rose 22.4 per cent (from NT$36.00 to NT$28.95) against the U.S. dollar. This led to the increase in the average monthly wage in the manufacturing sector from US$353 in 1985 to US$821 in 1990 and then to US$1,086 in 1992, which undermined the competitiveness of labour-intensive small-medium enterprises. Inevitably, foreign direct investment (FDI) emerged as an alternative for such businesses. Since then, from being a meager investor in Southeast Asia before 1986, the *taishang* have emerged as the largest investors in the region. Between 1959 and 2006, Taiwanese companies ranked third in terms of investment in approved projects among foreign investors in Malaysia, third in Thailand, sixth in Indonesia, seventh in the Philippines, and third in Vietnam (Table 1). Before 1990, overseas investment from Taiwan was concentrated in Southeast Asia, but as the political tensions between Taiwan and China eased at the beginning of the 1990s, and as China began to open up its economy and market, huge amounts of Taiwanese capital began to flow into China since 1991 (IDIC 2002). Most of this investment has gone into the manufacturing industry, which is the most competitive sector in Taiwan's economy. As the official surveys of the Taiwanese government have repeatedly shown, the most important reason for moving factories abroad is the need to secure cheap labour.

When Taiwanese enterprises move into Southeast Asia, one of the strategies that allowed them to remain competitive was to persuade suppliers in the same production network in Taiwan to move to the region as well, which means that seemingly new production networks in Southeast Asia have, in fact, been transplanted from original production networks in Taiwan (Jou and Chen 2002). How the transplanted pattern of production network works depends on the size and business strategy of the enterprises and the business environment in the destination country. Nevertheless, an important asset of these newly established production networks is their "Taiwaneseness", or the fact that they are mainly composed of enterprises of Taiwanese origin. Taiwanese businesses tend to work with other Taiwanese companies, to form an "enclave network" that is founded on past experiences in Taiwan and Taiwanese cultural affinity. From the perspective of social embeddedness, these reconstructed overseas production networks are more or less ethnically closed. These networks serve to reduce transaction costs and the risks associated with an imperfect market mechanism, insufficient information, and the different legal and social systems in foreign countries.

Not only do *taishang* rarely cooperate with indigenous Southeast Asian business to establish a production network, it is also very rare to find cooperation between *taishang* and local ethnic Chinese capital. If there is any, such cooperation usually takes place at the initial stages of investment when a *taishang* firm needs to understand local socio-economic conditions. In addition, when *taishang* companies want to evade strict regulations on foreign investment, such as caps on the percentage of total shares that they can own and land purchase restrictions, they use the names of local ethnic Chinese as "fake owners". However, these private agreements are very risky, and it sometimes happens that a *taishang* company or property registered in the name of a local Chinese

Table 1: Taiwanese Investment in Southeast Asian Countries (from 1959 to March 2007) (Unit: US$million)

| | Thailand | | Malaysia | | The Philippines | | Indonesia | | Singapore | | Vietnam | | Cambodia | |
|---|---|---|---|---|---|---|---|---|---|---|---|---|---|---|
| Year | Cases | Amount | Cases | Amount | Cases | Amount | Cases | Amount | Cases | Amount | Cases | Amount | Cases | Amount |
| 1959–89 | 642 | 2,097.25 | 477 | 1,257.05 | 348 | 349.41 | 75 | 1,381.38 | 35 | 22.72 | 2 | 4.69 | 0 | 0 |
| 1990 | 144 | 782.70 | 270 | 2,347.83 | 158 | 140.70 | 94 | 618.30 | 10 | 47.60 | 8 | 135.80 | 0 | 0 |
| 1991 | 69 | 583.50 | 182 | 1,326.17 | 109 | 12.00 | 58 | 1,057.80 | 13 | 12.50 | 13 | 224.19 | 0 | 0 |
| 1992 | 44 | 289.90 | 137 | 574.70 | 27 | 9.10 | 23 | 563.30 | 11 | 8.79 | 15 | 615.80 | 0 | 0 |
| 1993 | 61 | 215.40 | 86 | 331.18 | 21 | 5.40 | 20 | 358.90 | 12 | 69.47 | 30 | 757.66 | 0 | 0 |
| 1994 | 88 | 477.50 | 100 | 1,122.76 | 42 | 199.15 | 48 | 2,484.03 | 19 | 171.19 | 55 | 575.48 | 2 | 15.87 |
| 1995 | 102 | 1,803.90 | 123 | 567.80 | 34 | 13.60 | 89 | 567.40 | 20 | 31.65 | 45 | 913.34 | 14 | 10.03 |
| 1996 | 66 | 2,785.20 | 79 | 310.40 | 22 | 117.11 | 111 | 534.60 | 54 | 165.00 | 47 | 478.62 | 34 | 163.73 |
| 1997 | 62 | 414.30 | 63 | 480.40 | 16 | 80.56 | 101 | 3,419.40 | 27 | 230.32 | 54 | 249.56 | 62 | 44.04 |
| 1998 | 69 | 253.60 | 74 | 263.40 | 19 | 30.48 | 91 | 165.20 | 56 | 158.18 | 62 | 258.15 | 25 | 138.51 |
| 1999 | 86 | 211.10 | 66 | 70.26 | 18 | 19.15 | 92 | 1,486.10 | 19 | 324.52 | 80 | 201.33 | 15 | 55.39 |
| 2000 | 120 | 437.41 | 92 | 241.07 | 10 | 5.42 | 82 | 134.54 | 40 | 219.53 | 135 | 403.33 | 15 | 18.85 |
| 2001 | 50 | 158.69 | 88 | 296.58 | 9 | 11.99 | 69 | 83.85 | 26 | 378.30 | 140 | 1,004.92 | 8 | 56.97 |
| 2002 | 41 | 62.93 | 64 | 66.29 | 22 | 236.35 | 50 | 83.18 | 27 | 25.76 | 198 | 511.82 | 4 | 6.82 |
| 2003 | 57 | 338.83 | 57 | 163.69 | 17 | 47.11 | 49 | 117.54 | 15 | 26.40 | 190 | 540.67 | 1 | 1.00 |
| 2004 | 53 | 268.53 | 78 | 109.09 | 11 | 29.52 | 41 | 68.87 | 18 | 751.78 | 171 | 562.53 | 6 | 4.60 |
| 2005 | 63 | 417.66 | 71 | 113.64 | N.A. | 25.30 | 43 | 133.39 | 16 | 97.68 | 187 | 570.59 | 4 | 4.19 |
| 2006 | 63 | 284.30 | 70 | 110.48 | N.A. | 38.05 | 27 | 218.62 | 18 | 806.30 | 125 | 241.61 | 1 | 16.44 |
| 2007 (1–3) | 13 | 78.68 | 10 | 11.61 | N.A. | N.A. | 9 | 10.36 | 1 | 0.49 | 18 | 101.80 | 1 | 5.99 |
| Total | 1,893 | 11,961.38 | 2,187 | 9,764.40 | 883 | 1,370.40 | 1,172 | 13,486.76 | 437 | 3,548.18 | 1,575 | 8,351.89 | 192 | 542.43 |
| Ranking | 3 | | 3 | | 7 | | 5 | | N.A. | | 3 | | 3 | |

Source: ROC. Ministry of Economic Affairs. Department of Investment Services. "Statistics of Investments to ASEAN" [available in Chinese only] <http://www.dois.moea.gov.tw/asp/relation3.asp> Accessed on 6 Aug., 2007.

person is appropriated. As time goes by, the "fake" cooperation model disappears as true cooperation among the *taishang* gains significance. Therefore, when we talk about ethnic Chinese cultural affinity, we must distinguish between the different kinds of business networks that are formed between new *taishang* and old ethnic Chinese business, which, despite conventional beliefs, are quite limited (cf. Gomes and Hsiao, 2004).

There are two major reasons why it is difficult for *taishang* and local ethnic Chinese companies to establish business networks in Southeast Asia. First, their differing historical development paths have led them to adopt different business models. The *taishang* is more familiar with industrial capitalism, which has been the development strategy adopted in post-war Taiwan. The production of the *taishang* is mainly export-oriented, and emphasises innovation, human resources, and new skills. In contrast, local Chinese businesspeople in Southeast Asia mostly specialise in businesses that can be liquidated quickly, such as finance, trade or services, so that they can move out swiftly whenever political risks arise (Chen and Liu 1998:107; Tseng 1999:9). Second, the development policies of the Southeast Asian states, which emphasise attracting foreign capital for industrialisation, have produced a dual economy in which foreign capital, with its abundant capital and high level of technology, dominates the export sector, whereas indigenous businesses, with less capital and lower level of technology, remain in the domestic market. This is especially prominent in Malaysia. Malaysian Chinese and indigenous companies usually have only weak links with foreign capital due to the differences in product quality, ways of doing business, and purchasing power, and are therefore only seldom incorporated into the production networks of foreign businesses. As a result, *taishang* companies find no synergy or benefit from networking with local Chinese businesses in Southeast Asia.

### *Enlarging Taiwanese Business*

When a *taishang* company starts to invest in a Southeast Asian country, it often quickly realises that it is difficult to find a local business partner that can provide high-quality and low-price products that are delivered on time, and thus it internalises production within the group of Taiwanese suppliers that were previously its subcontractors in Taiwan. The enlargement of the scale of operations is the most important feature of the *taishang* in Southeast Asia, and is the major mechanism by which they continue to accumulate capital. Coming as they do from a semi-peripheral country, the position of the *taishang* in the global commodity chain constrains their overseas investment strategies, timing, and choice of location. However, when buyers in the core countries press the *taishang* to reduce costs, *taishang* is obliged to use overseas investment as a strategy to ward off such pressure due to the increasing cost of domestic labour and land in Taiwan. This is different from the situation with Western overseas investment, which is the result of long-term planning backed by abundant financial capital and human resources (Jou and Chen 2002).

The overseas investment strategy of the *taishang* has been termed a "passive and defensive globalisation" strategy by Taiwanese scholars (Chen 1998; Chen and Chen 1998). To compete globally, the small- and medium-sized enterprises (SMEs) in Taiwan that produce labour-intensive products need to reduce their costs, and increasing the economies of scale to reduce unit costs is an important strategy that allows them to maintain a competitive edge. Amsden and Chu (2003) contend that the core competitiveness of Taiwanese enterprises lies in their ability to swiftly expand their production capacity to a large scale, such that they can beat their competitors and consolidate their dominant position in the global commodity chain. It is cross-border investment that allows Taiwanese SMEs to increase their production scale so rapidly. In this way, a company that in Taiwan hires no more than a hundred workers can expand to employ more than a thousand workers abroad.

For Taiwanese SMEs, their overseas investment experience in Southeast Asia often turns out to be the first step toward globalising their business. Sharing industrial zones with international brand name companies buys them a place in foreign production networks in which they supply components and intermediary goods to U.S. and Japanese transnationals. In the process, they learn new business models and practices that were absent from their domestic production experience, which enhances their production skills and ability to conduct business globally.

Experiencing business enlargement and globalization in Southeast Asia helped the *taishang* to set up business in China in the later stage of Taiwan's overseas investment in the early 1990s. One of the main factors that attracts foreign capital to China is the country's unlimited supply of cheap labour, and the mass employment of China's domestic migrant workers in *taishang* factories has helped the *taishang* to achieve even better economies of scale. Indeed, with the help of subsidiaries in Southeast Asia and China, many *taishang* companies have become the world's largest producers of specific products, such as notebook computers, motherboards, and mobile phones (Jou and Chen 2002; Lin 2001).

Until the 1980s, Taiwan mainly supplied original equipment manufacturing (OEM) industries, but has since then gradually moved to the upper scale of the global commodity chain. Many scholars have pointed out that OEM not only involves the division of labour between core and peripheral countries, but also serves as a channel through which new skills are acquired. Suppliers in the commodity chain acquire technology and managerial skills from the buyers in the core countries (Chao 1998; Cheng 1999; Cheng and Hsu 2002; Lin 2001), a trend that we also witnessed in our fieldwork research. It takes six months to two years for Taiwanese subcontractors to be accredited by buyers. During this period, engineers are stationed by the buyers in the factory to transfer the relevant skills, examine the product quality, labour processes, and factory management until the accreditation certificate is issued. The spillover effect of gaining recognition from one big buyer is that other buyers will also recognise the certificate, which allows the Taiwanese subcontractors to expand their business opportunities. For example, after one *taishang* was accredited by DELL, other buyers recognised the certificate and subsequently adopted the company as a supplier. Therefore, through cross-border investment and subcontracting for core companies, the *taishang* have successfully organised the economic and human resources of the host countries to promote their own productivity, extend their production scale and potential buyer pool, and consolidate their position in the global commodity chain. The *taishang* can thus be said to be acting as a semi-peripheral middleman between core and peripheral economic resources.

Table 2 presents the historical development of Taiwanese overseas investment, and clearly shows the significant move between the 1960s and the 1990s from the operation of single production bases in Taiwan to triangle manufacturing in several different countries. The marketing and R&D functions of the *taishang* are still based in their headquarters in Taiwan, but the major production bases are now in China, along with some R&D, with many of the subsidiaries in Southeast Asia running independent marketing, R&D, and production functions. It can be seen that this triangle is mutually supportive, and no area is left to rely on one specific market or product.

Table 2: Regional Division of Labor in Taiwanese Transnational Companies since the 1960s

| Region \ Year | 1960~ | Mid-1980s~ | 1992~ |
|---|---|---|---|
| Taiwan | Securing orders<br>Manufacturing | Operational HQ<br>Securing orders<br>R&D<br>Overseas production coordination | Operational HQ<br>Securing orders<br>R&D<br>Overseas production coordination |
| Southeast Asia | — | Manufacturing | Starting to secure orders<br>Small-scale R&D<br>Production lines partly moved out |
| China | — | — | Mass production<br>R&D |
| The United States and Europe | — | — | Warehouses for global logistics |
| Development Stage | OEM | ODM | Global logistics management |

Source: Compiled from fieldwork data collected by the authors.

The products that Taiwanese suppliers make for Western buyers are mostly labour- intensive involving medium-level technology, such as apparel, footwear, or information technology products. It is often suggested that this kind of subcontracting and the manufacturing of products that are based on low labour costs will inevitably be taken over by other countries with even lower labour costs. As one interviewee described, "It is not difficult at all to produce a keyboard. You just have to take it apart and understand its internal structure. There are very few barriers to this industry". However, latecomers will find it hard to surmount the systematic barrier that is built up by the synergy of R&D, production procedures, economies of scale, and service provision. The *taishang* understand this competitive advantage well. Such a systematic barrier began to form in the 1960s when Taiwan was incorporated by the First World into the global production chain. The production scale of the *taishang* progressed from small to medium, and nowadays can be described as large, and their production capacity has become indispensable to the functioning of the global production chain. Taiwan's semi-peripheral economy is now linked with core economies such as the United States, Europe, and Japan, a position that cannot be easily replicated by other countries.

Another competitive advantage of the *taishang* is that, because of their production scale, latecomers are not able to compete to secure orders from Western buyers. It is almost impossible for a newly established company to produce millions of keyboards or sporting shoes per month. One *taishang* owner candidly stated that, "To enter this market, you need a large scale production capacity and high quality to be able to survive. It is very difficult to have such scale, such a system, and such quality when one enters the market". Economies of scale are also important for the vertical integration of different companies into an industry. For example, mass production enables footwear producers to support upstream suppliers to develop and supply cheaper and better quality components, which in turn helps footwear producers to strengthen their competitiveness in terms of price, quality, and delivery.

There are two commonly held viewpoints on Taiwan's economic future. The first is that, because of the new international division of labour, overseas Taiwanese investment is driven by low labour costs, and thus in the future Taiwanese capital will move to lower cost destinations, just as it has done in Southeast Asia and China. Contrarily, the second thesis postulates that China's economic development will soon allow it to replace Taiwan in the global economy. Both views can be questioned on the following grounds. First, labour costs are not the only factor influencing the overseas investment decisions of Taiwanese companies, and thus Taiwanese capital will not necessarily withdraw from Southeast Asia and transfer to China or other regions. Second, it will be difficult for China to replace Taiwan's role in the global production chain. By coordinating different production sites in China and Southeast Asia and through their capacity to reproduce an efficient and market-responsive production network anywhere, the *taishang* will be able to maintain their established business networks with their long-term buyers in the core countries, a position that Chinese firms are unlikely to be able to replicate in the foreseeable future. Thus, production networks based on cultural affinity with ethnic Chinese human resources and a large production capacity have ensured the competitiveness of the *taishang* in the world market in the last two decades.

Another important point to note is that enlargement brings about not only a change in industrial network structures, but also a change in internal managerial structures. Before transnationalisation, Taiwanese companies in Taiwan were usually small- or medium-sized, each with a staff of just a few dozen workers.[1] Upon their move into Southeast Asia and the mass employment of workers, these companies have found it necessary to hire more managerial staff to manage and restructure production lines, which are now very different from those back home in Taiwan. The internal organisational structure of the *taishang* companies is no longer characterised by simple boss-worker relationships, but involves more middle layers. In addition, the employment of workers of different ethnicities from the host country in the same factory has forced the *taishang* to adopt new management styles and approaches.

## III. *Restructuring* Taishang *Production Relations in Southeast Asia*

### *Mobilisation of the Ethnic Chinese Managerial Class*

Another unique feature that distinguishes the *taishang* from other transnational businesses from the core countries is that all the owners speak Mandarin or a Minnanese language, which helps them to build links with overseas ethnic Chinese communities in many of the host countries in Southeast Asia. The data that we collected shows that the ethnic Chinese play an important role in the initial stages of *taishang* business establishment in the region. As most *taishang* cannot speak fluent English or the local language, they have to rely on local ethnic Chinese and their relatives, friends, or customers to mediate their initial investment, handle official documents, and even to help manage the company. For example, *taishang* companies may need to engage with local civil servants to buy land, apply for a license to build a factory, or obtain approval for operations; these would be impossible without the help offered by the local ethnic Chinese, as they would be unable to communicate with the relevant bureaucrats and officials. To mobilise ethnic Chinese human resources, many *taishang* also recruit employees from other countries in the region, such as China, Malaysia, or Singapore (Wang 2007). Ethnic Chinese of different origins usually occupy different positions in Taiwanese companies in Southeast Asia, earn different wages, and are subject to different forms of discipline from the management (Kung and Wang 2006).

---

[1] A "large company" in the manufacturing sector, according to the definition of the Taiwanese government, is one that hires more than 200 workers.

Southeast Asian ethnic Chinese can be considered a kind of social resource that helps to link the *taishang* with individual Southeast Asian markets. However, this does not mean that all overseas Chinese are included in this mobilisation. Many scholars point out that an important characteristic of ethnic Chinese businesses in Southeast Asia is their networking activity. The *taishang* initially joined these Southeast Asian ethnic Chinese networks following their mass investment in the region in the mid-1980s, but have since then gradually built up their own types of economic networks. The centre of such networks is the industrial capital of the *taishang*, which they have used to mobilise the local ethnic Chinese networks to achieve their economic goals. In addition to providing them with employment and establishing cooperative relationships with them, the *taishang* have also mobilised local ethnic Chinese managers to work for them in other Asian countries. For example, the Taiwanese company Hualong has a subsidiary in Malaysia, and when it began to invest in Vietnam, it recruited Malaysian Chinese to work in Vietnam instead of sending Taiwanese managers directly from Taiwan. These *taishang*-centered networks were virtually constructed around various globalised production sites in different countries, and thus differ from the traditional trade-based Chinese networks in Southeast Asia.

*Taishang* factories in Southeast Asia usually employ an ethnically diverse labour force. In Malaysia, for example, the three major ethnic groups—the Malays, ethnic Chinese, and ethnic Indians—habitually work together, and since the labour shortages that have occurred since 1990 have been joined by migrant workers from Bangladesh and Indonesia (Kung 2002). The situation is the same in the *taishang* factories in Vietnam, where Vietnamese workers are supervised by managers from China, rather than Taiwan or Vietnam (Wang and Hsiao 2002). In this multicultural working environment, both the hierarchy of power and the division of labour are different from the norm.

Table 3 clearly demonstrates that the employees who occupy the top positions in *taishang* business are mainly Taiwanese, although in some cases in Malaysia, they are local ethnic Chinese. It is important to point out that the ethnic Chinese that occupy these important positions are not just any local Chinese, but are those who have studied in Taiwan as "*Qiaosheng*" (overseas Chinese students). In contrast, most of the PRC Chinese who work for the *taishang* are hired as factory heads or middle-level managers. Apparently, the *taishang* prefer to recruit local ethnic Chinese with Taiwanese connections rather than PRC Chinese into the upper management echelons.

Table 3: Ethnic Division of Labour in Taishang Companies in Malaysia and Vietnam by Ethnic Group

| Positions in Factory | *Malaysia* | *Vietnam* |
|---|---|---|
| Owner and Top Managers | Taiwanese, with some local ethnic Chinese with "Taiwanese connections" | Taiwanese |
| Administrative Managers | Local ethnic Chinese with "Taiwanese connections" | Local ethnic Chinese, PRC Chinese professionals |
| Low-ranking Managers, Technicians orSupervisors | Local ethnic Chinese | PRC Chinese professionals, a few Vietnamese |
| Blue-collar workers | Mainly migrant workers, some Malays | Mainly Vietnamese, some local ethnic Chinese |

Source: Research data collected by the authors.

Other ethnic Chinese who work in administrative functions normally occupy middle- to lower-level management positions in accounting, finance, or purchasing. They are usually supervised by Taiwanese senior managers, who are not necessarily familiar with how the production lines really work. As the *taishang* need interpreters to communicate with the local workers, these local ethnic Chinese administrators become indispensable to the functioning of the production facility, and come to occupy better positions in the company than other local staff members. Again, the *taishang* prefer to hire local ethnic Chinese who have studied in Taiwan for these positions if possible. One *taishang* told us:

> The way of thinking of students who have graduated from the American or European schools is very different from ours, and the barrier does not only lie in the language. The difference may have resulted from cultural differences.... There are more than twenty engineers in the technical department, and all of them graduated from Taiwanese colleges. There were once some MBA engineers who had graduated from the UK and the USA, but they stayed here only for a short period of time. In contrast, most of the engineers who are graduates of Taiwanese universities work in our company for a long time.

Experience of living in Taiwan and familiarity with Taiwanese society and culture are the key factors that explain the popularity of Taiwanese-trained local ethnic Chinese among the *taishang* in Malaysia. Most of the local ethnic Chinese engineers employed by the *taishang* have lived in Taiwan for more than four years, and can easily acclimatise themselves to the work ethic that is expected, namely, to work hard and take few holidays. The importance of this first-hand knowledge learned from living in Taiwan contradicts what is postulated by the human capital theory, which depicts a person's ability as deriving only from education and skills.

If the local *taishang* cannot find suitably Taiwan-connected managers, then PRC Chinese may be an alternative, especially as they cost less. The *taishang* have thus generated a large ethnic Chinese skilled labour market in Asia. Employing staff from the PRC to work as middle-level managers has become a common human resources management practice among the *taishang* in Southeast Asia, given the lower salary cost of these workers compared to Taiwanese expatriates and their language proficiency. PRC Chinese are attracted to work overseas by the higher incomes offered by the *taishang* companies, and are recruited through three channels: internal corporate transfers, social networks, and placement agencies (Wang 2007).

Finally, the major objective of the *taishang* in Southeast Asia is to build a production facility within as short a period of time as possible to meet their buyers' demands for lower prices and better quality. The *taishang* utilise all possible means to mobilise both local and foreign resources to achieve this objective, and in this situation the employment of local ethnic Chinese professionals is highly desirable. The hiring of ethnic Chinese by the *taishang* can thus be viewed as a way of mobilising ethnic resources.

### *Authoritarian Labour Control*

Southeast Asia is a multi-ethnic society, and most *taishang* employ workers from various ethnic groups. It is this distinct situation that gives rise to another characteristic of the transnational *taishang* companies: their use of an authoritarian management style to control their labour. The *taishang* prefers to employ workers who will accept subordination, such as Bangladeshi migrant workers in Malaysia or female migrant workers in Vietnam and China. To keep industrial relations in check on the shop floor, the *taishang* usually employs rather coercive means of disciplining workers of different origins. However, this should not be mistaken as an extreme measure as depicted in the hegemonic model described by Burawoy (1985).

The labour control practices that are imposed by the *taishang* on migrant workers in Malaysia cannot be applied to local Malay workers. For example, Bangladeshi migrant workers usually have to work for more than twelve hours a day, and sixteen hours is not unheard of. They live in the factory compound, and their daily activities are under strict surveillance. If these workers cannot finish the work that is required of them in the allotted time, then the *taishang* managers will demand that they stay back to finish it. In contrast, *taishang* or Malaysian Chinese managers must choose their words carefully when talking to or persuading local Malays or ethnic Chinese to work. Managing Bangladeshi workers "is much easier; you just push them. Just press and press. When I set them a target to achieve, well, they have to reach the goal, no matter how difficult it is". According to one of the *taishang* managers that we interviewed, such workers have to work from eight in the morning to eleven at night for the entire year, and they cannot ask for sick leave. Another *taishang* boss stated even more explicitly: "I told them, 'give me two thousand pieces tomorrow. If not, I will cancel your residence permit status and send you back'. I don't need to remind them to work overtime. It's enough to scare them to work hard.".

Other than threatening to send the workers back home, the *taishang* also manipulate the wage structureto control migrant workers. One *taishang* owner described this vividly:

> The wage is structured into five parts: basic wage, full attendance bonus, efficiency bonus, night shift bonus and overtime work wage. Do you know how low their basic wage is? Only ten-something Ringgit! If they do work hard overtime, they can earn about thirteen hundreds or more. If they do not follow, they will get no overtime work, and their monthly wage will be about four hundred only. How could they survive with such little money to pay their living cost, and the debt they owe at home for overseas work? I don't fire them, nor will I send them back. After one or two months, they will come to me and ask for more work. Then, they will show their obedience to me (Kung and Wang 2006).

In Vietnam, *taishang* footwear factories employ a large number of female workers, as was the case in Taiwan, South Korea and Hong Kong in the 1960s and 1970s. A clear division of labour on gender lines is practiced where the sewing, gluing, and quality control work are carried out mainly by female workers, whereas the packaging, loading, and raw materials production are undertaken by male workers. The male labour force constitutes only a small fraction of the entire workforce in the factory.

The standard explanation offered by the *taishang* for the "feminisation" of the labour force is that the Vietnamese society is a matriarchal society; Vietnamese women have to take care of the family, and are therefore able to put up with the working pressure that is imposed on them, whereas Vietnamese men are "lazy, useless, and not able to work under stress". However, if we look at the labour process in these *taishang* factories, we find the reason to be otherwise. Female workers are preferred by the *taishang* in Vietnam because they are more submissive than men to the company labour control mechanisms. Working hours in Taiwanese factories are normally long, sometimes up to twelve hours a day.[2] We also found in one of the factories where we conducted interviews that workers are only allowed to go to the washroom only three times a day; they must take a card whenever they use the washroom, and only three cards are issued on a production line at any one time.

Engaged as they are in labour-intensive industries, the *taishang* try to extract maximum labour value by imposing an authoritarian management style. The enforcement of labour control in Vietnam is imposed through a clear ethnic division of labour: the top managers are Taiwanese; the professionals hired from China occupy the middle-level management positions, and the Vietnamese work on the shop floor (see Table 3). Many *taishang* invested in the footwear industry in China in the early 1990s, thereby creating a pool of low- to middle-level managers in China trained in the *taishang* way. When the Taiwanese footwear industry shifted its investment to Vietnam in the mid-1990s, these managers were later mobilised to work in Vietnam. The widely reported management practices of the military were that the *taishang* employed in China, was therefore transplanted by the PRC Chinese managers to Vietnam. During our research, we often heard complaints from Vietnamese workers that PRC Chinese supervisors or shop floor managers shout at them or scold them. We also heard of a case where a Taiwanese top manager transferred from China asked his PRC Chinese managers to get up at 4:30 am to go jogging and made them line up under the scorching sun before lunch, which eventually resulted in a strike. Some Taiwanese top managers admitted that although they have refrained from using authoritarian management control in Vietnam,

[2] Compared to the working conditions in the Zhujiang delta in southern China, the working hours in Vietnam are significantly shorter. For further comparisons between Taiwanese factories in China and Taiwan, see Chan and Wang (2005).

they still cannot stop protests by Vietnamese workers. One *taishang* manager stated:

> It is too much of a luxury and too early to talk about [labour] human rights in Vietnam. [Sighs]. You have seen our factory, and if you go to their home you can't imagine what it looks like. It is very ironic. We Taiwanese have already gone through this stage in the past and understand what it was. The key point right now is how to make everyone rich. Strong human rights [for workers] will not make a nation wealthy. They protect workers too much, and they [workers] demand their rights too much. A country with US$370 GDP per capita wants to have the same human rights as in a country with US$10,000 GDP per capita; that is not reasonable. In Vietnam, you can't even touch Vietnamese workers, let alone abuse them.

The manager of a large *taishang* sports shoes company even commented that his industry basically rests on a patriarchal form of management. Many Taiwanese managers learned to make shoes through an apprenticeship, and the only form of management that they have ever learned in Taiwan is to scold. Indeed, they equate "management" with "scolding". When this authoritarian management style is confronted with the resistance from Vietnamese workers, and male workers especially, this is countervailed by the management's accusations against these Vietnamese men for their laziness and their lack of interest in working hard. It is for these reasons that the conforming and docile female workers are much preferred by the *taishang* for their operations in Vietnam, and this has nothing to do with the "matriarchal society" rationale. The construction of the Vietnamese society as a matriarchal society is, in fact, a "patriarchal discourse" on the part of the *taishang* to enforce and maintain their labour regime.[3]

## IV. *Concluding Remarks*

The *Taishang*, as a modern capitalist development in Asia, are Taiwanese businesses that have been investing globally since the mid-1980s. Global economic change since the mid-1980s, especially after the Plaza Agreement, has forced Taiwanese companies to seek other means by which

[3] For a discussion of management practices and discourses on Vietnamese society, see Wang (2004).

their accumulation of capital can be continued. Southeast Asia and the next big investment destination—China—have become strategic regions for the *taishang* in pressing ahead with their global production plan. The United States is no longer the most important trading partner: it is Southeast Asia and China that have emerged as the most significant areas for the *taishang*.

In tracing the history of the overseas investment of the *taishang*, it becomes clear that most started out as SMEs, which contradicts the commonly held belief that SMEs have insufficient capital, human resources, or management capacity to proceed with overseas investment. This "rational economic model" apparently does not apply to the *taishang* SMEs after the mid-1980s, which took on the mantle of overseas investment until the larger *taishang* became involved in the early 1990s. This succession pattern of overseas investment is quite different from the course of U.S. or Japanese overseas investment (Hsiao and Kung 1998).

The rise of the *taishang* is, of course, a product of global capitalist development. As latecomers to transnational business from a semi-peripheral state, the position of the *taishang* in the global division of labour is certainly different from that of transnational companies from the core states, and their paths to globalisation are different. In this paper, we discussed the historical process of *taishang* investment and analysed the characteristics of the *taishang*'s reorganisation of industrial production networks to allow expansion and the massive up-scaling of production. The *taishang* also represent a form of transnational capital with a distinct cultural trait, given their cultural affinity with Chinese human resources, which has helped them to mobilise ethnic Chinese human resources all over Asia to support their production networks in various countries. An additional characteristic of the *taishang* network is the coordination of a host of Taiwanese firms to generate the final product, which has led to the creation of Taiwanese production network enclaves that seldom cooperate with local Chinese business. These characteristics set the *taishang* outside the discussions of overseas Chinese business networks in the literature.

This paper also demonstrated that the mobilisation of ethnic Chinese human resources and the practice of authoritarian labour control have helped the *Taishang* to consolidate and sustain their competitiveness in the contemporary world production system. The *taishang* have undoubtedly emerged as distinct ethnic Chinese transnational business entities in the modern capitalist world.

Finally, it is essential to emphasize again that the development of Taiwan's semi-peripheral economy has resulted from the combination of economic, social, and human resources from Taiwan, Southeast Asia, and China. It is cross-boundary and truly global in nature. The ability to respond quickly to market demand, efficient and flexible production, and unique production networks all helped the *taishang* to remain competitive in the volatile world market. The *taishang*'s role in the global production chain cannot be easily displaced by business networks from other countries, as this distinct business structure is embedded in a very complex socio-economic context.

## *References*

Amsden, A. H. and W. W. Chu. (2003). *Beyond Late Development: Taiwan's Upgrading Policies*. Cambridge, Mass.: MIT Press.

Burawoy, M. (1985). *The Politics of Production: Factory Regimes under Capitalism and Socialism*. London: Verso.

Chan, A. and H. Z. Wang. (2005). "The Impact of the State on Workers' Conditions—Comparing Taiwanese Factories in China and Vietnam." *Pacific Affairs* 77(4) 629–646.

Chao, Y. W. (1998). "The Positive Effect of OEM on Taiwanese Electronic Firms." *Sun Yat-Sen Management Review* 6(4): 1113–1136 (in Chinese).

Chen, T. J. (1994). "FDI by Small and Medium-Sized Enterprises form Taiwan: A Survey of Parent Firms." Paper presented at the Workshop on Taiwan's Small and Medium-Sized Firms' Direct Investment in Southeast Asia at the Chung-Hua Institute for Economic Research, Taipei, Nov. 18–19.

——. (1998). *Taiwanese Firms in Southeast Asia: Networking Across Borders*. Northampton, Mass.: Edward Elgar.

Chen, H. and T. J. Chen. (1998). "Network Linkage and Location Choice in Foreign Direct Investment." *Journal of International Business Studies* 29(3): 445–468.

Chen, H. and M. C. Liu. (1998). "Noneconomic Elements of Taiwan's Foreign Direct Investment." Pp. 97–119 in *Taiwanese Firms in Southeast Asia: Networking Across Borders*, edited by Tain-Jy Chen. Northampton, Mass.: Edward Elgar Publishing.

Chen, Y. C. (1997). *Investment and Regional Development of Newly Industrial Country: The Political Economy of Taiwanese Business in Malaysia* (in Chinese). M.A. thesis for the Graduate Institute of Building and Planning, National Taiwan University.

Cheng, L. L. (1999). "The Invisible Elbow: The Semiperiphery and the Restructuring of International Footwear Market." *Taiwan: A Radical Quarterly in Social Studies* 35: 1–46 (in Chinese).

Cheng , L. L. and J. Y. Hsu. (2002). "Revisiting Economic Development in Post-War Taiwan: The Dynamic Process of Geographical Industrialization." *Regional Studies* 36(8): 897–908.

Cumings, B. (1984). "The Origins and Development of the Northeast Asian Political Economy: Industrial Sectors, Product Cycles, and Political Consequences." *International Organization* 38(1): 1–40.

Gomes, T. and H. H. M. Hsiao. (eds.). (2004). *Chinese Business in Southeast Asia: Contesting Cultural Explanations, Researching Entrepreneurship*, London: RoutledgeCurzon.

——. (eds.) (2004). *Chinese Enterprise, Transnationalism and Identity*, London: Routledge-Curzon.

Hsiao, H. H. M. and I. C. Kung. (1998). *The Business Networks between Taiwanese Business and Southeast Asian Chinese.* PROSEA Occasional Paper No. 18, Taipei: Program for Southeast Asian Area Studies, Academia Sinica (in Chinese).

IDIC. (2002). "*Taishang* zai dalu touzi gaikuang" (Taiwanese Investment in China). Access at http://www.idic.gov.tw/html/c3409.html.

Jou, S. C. and D. S. Chen. (2002). "Latecomer's Globalization: Taiwan's Experiences in FDI and Reproduction of Territorial Production Networks in Southeast Asia." Pp. 33–94 in *Taiwanese Business in Southeast Asia: Network, Identity and Globalization*, edited by Hsin-Hung Michael Hsiao, Hong-zen Wang and I-Chun Kung. Taipei: Asia-Pacific Research Program, Academia Sinica (in Chinese).

Kung, I. C. (2006). "Mobilizing Chinese in Asia: Reshaping Ethnic Chinese Transnational Network through Taiwan Capital." Paper presented at the Annual Conference on Taiwan's Southeast Asian Area Studies, National Cheng Kung University, Apr. 24–25.

Kung, I. C. and H. Z. Wang. (2006). "Socially Constructed Ethnic Division of Labor: Labor Control in Taiwan-owned Firms in Malaysia and Vietnam." *International Sociology* 21(4): 580–601.

Lin, C. P. (2002). "Corporate Transformation and Spatial Interaction Process of Taiwan Business' Foreign Direct Investment: A Case Study of Taiwan Electronic Firms in Penang, Malaysia." Pp. 137–96 in *Taiwanese Business in Southeast Asia: Network, Identity and Globalization*, edited by Hsin-Hung Michael Hsiao, Hong-Zen Wang and I-Chun Kung. Taipei: Asia-Pacific Research Program, Academia Sinica (in Chinese).

Shu, M. L. (2000). *Proceedings of the Conference on Taiwanese Enterprises in Southeast Asia: Experiences in Singapore, Malaysia, Indonesia, and the Philippines*, Taipei: National Taiwan University (in Chinese).

——. (2001). *Proceedings of the Conference on Taiwanese Enterprises in Southeast Asia: Experiences in Vietnam and Thailand*, Taipei: National Taiwan University (in Chinese).

Tseng, T. F. (1999). "Foreign Capital and Ethnic Relations: Taiwanese Business in Indonesia." Paper presented at the Conference on Foreign Investment of Taiwanese Business: Perspectives of Economic Sociology, Department of Sociology, National Taiwan University, Sept. 9 (in Chinese).

Wang, H. Z. (2004). "Othering Discourses, Business Practices and Local Resistance: Case Studies from Taiwanese Factories in Vietnam." *Taiwan Journal of Southeast Asian Studies* 1(2): 37–64.

——. (2007). "PRC Skilled Labor on the Move: Mobilizing Ethnic Resources by Taiwanese Business in Asia." *Asian Survey* (forthcoming).

Wang, H. Z. and M. H.-H. Hsiao. (2002). "Social Capital or Human Capital? Chinese Professionals in Overseas Taiwan Company." *Journal of Contemporary Asia* 32(3): pp. 346–362.

# ENTREPRENEURSHIP AND RISK: THE BECOMING OF THE KOO BUSINESS DYNASTY*

Ho Tsai-Man C.[1] and Sun Wenbin[2]

## I. *Introduction*

The Koos are a family of great wealth and power in Taiwan who have been thriving for four generations, challenging the conventional wisdom that family fortunes never last more than three generations. Studying this family provides us a unique opportunity to probe into the source of its dynamism. The metamorphosis from a family business into a business conglomerate echoes the theme of this collection—the development of Chinese capitalism.

This paper examines several critical advances that have transformed the family business and have allowed family members to exhibit their entrepreneurial talents. Compared with the other four big families in Taiwan, the rise of the Koo family has been controversial and, is often ascribed to their powerful political network (Szu-Ma 1998; Tu 1992; Yanaihara 2003).[3] Previous studies on the relationships between the Koos and the government have shed light on the socio-political background that has shaped the development of Taiwanese enterprises, but have not revealed the dynamic interaction between government and

* Reference to this article should be made as follows: Ho, Tsai-man C. and Sun, Wenbin. 2007. "Entrepreneurship and Risk: The Becoming of the Koo Business Dynasty".

[1] We gratefully acknowledge financial support from the Hong Kong Research Grants Council (RGC) (HKU7264/05H) for the research project entitled "Entrepreneurial Families: the Rong, Gu and Ho Tung Business Dynasties".

[2] Please send correspondence to: Ho Tsai-Man C. at <tsaimanh@hku.hk>.

[3] There are five prominent families renowned and familiar to most people in Taiwan. They are 1) the Lin family of Ban-Chiao, who rose in the Qing Dynasty and owned more than 40 enterprises, including those in sugar, land, trust, and camphor industries; 2) the Chen family of Kaohsiung, who rose to power through ownership of a large sugar company during the late Qing Dynasty; 3) the Lins of Wu-Feng, who also rose in the Qing Dynasty and belonged to the landlord class; 4) the Yen family of Keelung, whose prosperity began in the Japanese colonial period through their endeavors in the mining industry; and lastly, the Koo family of Lukang, whose prosperity also began in the Japanese ruling period and who concentrated their activities in land reclamation and the sugar industry.

business. For instance, a favorable political contact does not necessarily lead to successful business operations, and there are always challenges and uncertainties when the political regime changes. Political networks may partly explain the rise of the Koos, but do not cover all of the factors that have supported the family's sustained prosperity over four generations.

By closely examining the expansion of the Koo family, a pattern of innovation gradually comes to light—each generation of the Koo family has taken the lead or changed customary practice, often when key economic institutions in Taiwan were in transition or property rights obscure. It is these innovative advances—the very essence of entrepreneurship—upon which this paper focuses. The remainder of this paper is organised as follows. The first section discusses the sources of entrepreneurship, and explores the dynamic relationships among the government, entrepreneurs, and society in relation to entrepreneurial activities.

Much of the text is then devoted to examining the relationships between the government's role in securing property rights and the rise of the Koos. The third section focuses on issues related to innovation and risk, and in the fourth part the discussion turns to the question of how each generation of the Koos has enhanced the legitimacy of their innovations to eliminate risk factors.

## II. *Literature Review: Sources of Entrepreneurship, Legitimacy, and Risk*

Is entrepreneurship a matter of individual capability, or a socially grounded construction? What is the source of entrepreneurship? Thornton (1999) classifies the studies of entrepreneurship in the literature into two schools: those that take the supply-side perspective and those that take the demand-side perspective. According to her framework, the former school focuses on the individual traits of an entrepreneur, whereas the latter emphasises the push-pull factors of the social and political environments. This duality is reflected in most studies of entrepreneurship. Jones and Wadhwani (2006) highlight that although the older generation of entrepreneurial studies placed too much stress on the deterministic role of history and the social environment, newer scholarship has focused exclusively on entrepreneurial behaviour and has largely ignored the broader context in which entrepreneurial actors operate. They echo Schumpeter's plea for an exchange between history and theory in studying entrepreneurship.

In Schumpeter's conception, an entrepreneur is someone who promotes innovation. Schumpeter contends that the essence of entrepreneurial activity lies not only in pulling together a business in established ways, but also in creating "new combinations". Successful new combinations disrupt the market equilibrium and are a source of "entrepreneurial profits". Entrepreneurial behaviour thus seeks to accomplish something different, and needs a set of abilities completely different from what is required to sustain the flow of an existing business (Schumpeter 1950). Entrepreneurship means the disruption of the economic status quo, and Goss (2005) identifies from Schumpeter's work three types of factors that inhibit the expression of entrepreneurial action. The first relates to the nature of the innovation: because it is new, it will be more difficult for one to plan and understand when compared to well-established and customary activities. The second refers to the inertia in the businessperson. The third is the fear of social sanction that is heaped upon destructors and deviants, or, as Schumpeter puts it,

> "the reaction of the social environment against one who wishes to do something new. This reaction may manifest itself first of all in the existence of legal or political impediments. But neglecting this, any deviating conduct by a member of a social group is condemned, though in greatly varying degrees according as the social group is used to such conduct or not" (1934:86).

Thus, the ability to lead and influence others stems from social processes. Schumpeter's conception of entrepreneurship is about social control "resting upon the constraints of convention, routine, habit, and social sanction" (Goss 2005:207). Such social control regulates behaviour and limits the extent to which individuals will be prepared to engage in "deviant" innovative action.

Two features inherent in entrepreneurship deserve more attention: newness and deviance. Being new refers not only to the implementation of a new way of running a business, but also to the formation of a new order that seeks legitimacy. Some scholars argue that the degree of approval or disapproval of a certain entrepreneurial act influences the act's further development (Gerschenkron 1962, 1966; Marris and Somerset 1971). These scholars assume the gaining of legitimacy to be an external factor in the commencement of a new entrepreneurial venture, but the deviant nature of entrepreneurial ventures, as has been noted, begs for such legitimacy.

It must be asked at this point, who possesses the right to legitimise entrepreneurial behaviour? For Schumpeter, the answer lies in the legal and political spheres: it is these areas in which entrepreneurs attempt to win legitimacy. Having said this, the legal and political reality may also be a double-edged sword. For instance, the political reality may not necessarily be negative for the development of entrepreneurship. As Campbell and Lindberg emphasise, the government not only has the power to allocate key resources, but also has a huge capacity to manipulate property rights. This means that it has the capacity to shape various institutional organisations in the economy, and can create pressure for change and constrain the selection process (Campbell and Lindberg 1990).

Where property rights are enforced, the rules determine the conditions of ownership and control of the means of production. According to Campbell and Lindberg (1990), the state's role in securing property rights is linked to new forms of economic organisation. The state can manipulate property rights to influence the selection process in many ways. Where state actors assist to directly select a certain type of governance regime, the effect of the state as an institutional structure is indirect and unintentional, because it sets the range of governance options from which private actors can choose (Campbell and Lindberg 1990). One of the most important ways in which the government influences the selection process is through its capacity to ratify or undermine new business patterns. In the previous literature on entrepreneurship, the influence of the government on values and cognitive systems is emphasised (Aldrich 1999; Aldrich and Staber 1988; Gerschenkron 1962, 1966; Lounsbury and Glynn 2001; Wilken 1979). Inspired by Campbell and Lindberg's arguments, we suggest that the government's role is not only to legitimise innovative action, but also to facilitate new markets, primarily through the redefinition of property rights.

The uncertainties that are generated when property rights are in transition offer both opportunities and risks. Not everyone is able to identify the opportunities, even if they result from government-led institutional changes. Because opportunities do not appear in a pre-packaged form (Venkataraman 1997), the process of opportunity identification is far from trivial. With any new innovation, entrepreneurs may fail to identify the opportunities or may identify the wrong opportunities. The discovery of opportunities is therefore an important part of the domain of entrepreneurship research (Shane 2000). It has been found that the individual capability of entrepreneurs stems not only from their individual personalities, but also from their network positions. Burt's (2000) seminal work on structural holes suggests that entrepreneurship can be conceptualised as a means of connecting two networks. In tracing the story of the Koo family, we explore how entrepreneurs locate themselves between two networks or institutional holes, the very place where room is available for the generation of benefits.

While governments initiate institutional change, they take a passive role in response to new combinations. Entrepreneurs need political connections to enable their innovations to be secured through property rights, but the real risk for entrepreneurs is incurring the disapproval of the legal system. Mezias and Boyle's analysis of the U.S. film industry underlines how uncertainties in the legal environment affect the initiation of new actions (2002). Once the re-delimitation of property rights fails, the risks that follow may jeopardise the survival of an enterprise.

This study of the Koo family dynasty not only extends the research implications of entrepreneurship, but also highlights the importance of mixing business acumen and political acumen in the Chinese society of Taiwan. We identify that a particular player in each generation of the Koo family has come forward to fulfill the entrepreneurial role, and in the meantime has had to struggle with the redefinition of property rights. It is hoped that this article answers Schumpeter's call for more historical work on the interaction between institutional forms and entrepreneurial activity (Schumpeter 1990:414).

## III. *The Role of the Government in Generating Markets and the Rise of Entrepreneurship*

In the eyes of Yanaihara, it was by playing up to the Japanese in power that Koo Hsien-jung turned himself from a merchant into an industrial capitalist. The rise of the Koo family has largely been attributed to various monopolistic rights granted by the Japanese colonial government. For instance, Koo Hsien-jung was appointed as the chief executive officer of a wholesale salt distributor (Yanaihara 1956:14). Here, we encounter the question about the social conditions of Taiwan, which was just about to be absorbed into the Japanese capitalistic system at that time. Entrepreneurship may be a universal feature of all societies, but, as Blaug asserts, certain institutional settings help to release the entrepreneurial spirit (2000:86). For Blaug, such institutional settings relate specifically to capitalism, yet we can also find links between entrepreneurship and institutional transition.

Land reclamation most probably explains the rapid accumulation of wealth among the first generation of the Koos. Koo Hsien-jung's land development corporation bought up croplands that were equipped with irrigation functions, which were then rented out to tenants. Following the Kuomintang's Land Reform from 1953 to 1954, the Koo family ended up with over 40,000 *chia* (one chia equals 2.39 acres, or 1.03 hectares) of land scattered all over Taiwan, making the family the biggest landholder in Taiwan (DeGlopper 1995:114). Land was the most vital asset in which Koo Hsien-jung invested, and is what made him a financial capitalist and what led his heir, Koo Chen-fu (KCF hereafter), to transform himself from a landlord into an industrial capitalist under the ruling Nationalist Party (hereafter the KMT) regime. Nevertheless, the sources of the Koo family's prosperity need to be examined in the broader context of Taiwan's social transformation.

### *The Japanese Land-tenure Reform*

Before Japanese rule, property rights and land use in Taiwan were in chaos. In 1895, China signed the Shimonoseki Treaty, which in ceding Taiwan to Japan had led Taiwan down the path of a different social system. The fourth governor-general, General Kodama Gentaro, assumed office in 1898; most of the policy making and government supervision that had formerly been conducted in Tokyo was placed under his command. Kodama delegated jurisdiction over domestic affairs to his chief of civil administration, Goto Shinpei. This enabled the Taiwanese governor-general to operate from a more consolidated base, and allowed Goto considerable leeway in shaping plans and policies for the island colony during Kodama's tenure (Lamley 1999:209). Because Japan itself was under heavy financial pressure after the war, the Japanese colonial government sought to maintain Taiwan's fiscal autonomy so as not to create a further burden for itself. In this way, Goto launched a variety of projects that laid the foundation for the extensive economic development and modernisation of Taiwan.

Goto's goal was to make Taiwan an agricultural appendage of Japan (Lamley 1999). Nitobe Inazo, who had been sent earlier from Japan to research forestry and subtropical agriculture, drew up a long-range programme for the development of commercial agriculture (Azuma 2000). According to his plan, more land was to be placed under cultivation and irrigation projects were to be initiated so as to increase rice and sugarcane production on the central and southern coastal plains. However, these projects could not be carried out because of the confusion over ownership. Concerned about both revenues and the development of the agricultural industry, the Japanese colonial government decided to engage in land-tenure reform after an extensive investigation of existing land use and ownership that began in 1898 and ended in 1901. As a result of this investigation, a larger amount of untaxed "hidden land" was registered in 1903, and more landowners were placed on the tax roll when the liability for tax was shifted from the "large-rentholder households" (*da zu hu*), whose claim to the land was redeemed in marketable bonds, to the "small rentholders" (*xiao zu hu*), the actual farmers. By so doing, the colonial government transferred agrarian ownership from the nominal landowners to the people who actually tilled the soil and worked in the fields.

Taiwanese people at that time had very little knowledge of the nature of bonds and the modern banking system. Most of the large rentholders did not know what to do with the redeemed bonds because, to their understanding, bonds could not be used to purchase commodities and the interest rate was too low. In fact, the colonial government tried hard to educate people about the value of these bonds. The government sent staff out to buy back the redeemed bonds and encouraged those willing to set up business to use the bonds to do so. The entrepreneurism of Koo Hsien-jung was demonstrated in his confidence during the period of property rights transition. While the short-lived Russo-Japanese War further damaged most people's trust in government bonds, Koo Hsien-jung bought up a large amount of these redeemed bonds. In fact, among the five eminent families, the Koos were the only family who has set up a company collecting the bonds of large rentholders.

According to a study by Tu (1992), the First World War boosted the Japanese economy; this precipitated the economic growth of Taiwan, exports from which experienced a continuous increase over the period from 1916 to 1920. The soaring price of rice was transferred to ground rents, which made huge fortunes for landlords. The second source of wealth accumulation came from merchant activities. Again, the best example of this is Koo Hsien-jung, who made himself an enormous profit out of speculation in the sugar trade between 1918 and 1919. Furthermore, the amendment to the land tenure laws in 1919 allowed the Koos to move their capital from land rents to newly developed businesses, giving them the opportunity to invest in modern industries and financial banking.

In 1897, the Taiwan Bank Act came into force, with three purposes. The first was to develop Taiwan's industrial and commercial activities and to make Taiwan a supportive node for Japan's extension into the trade and financial activities of the South Pacific. The second was to pursue economic independence for Taiwan, and the third was to clean up the chaos of the monetary system and to put Taiwan's currency in order. To introduce a banking system in the modern sense, the Japanese colonial government established the first bank—the Taiwan Bank—to provide capital flow and mortgages to those who were engaged in the development of industries and the public infrastructure. The 20th Anniversary Special Historical Review of the Taiwan Bank gives a description of the social context in which the bank was established: "a decent bank was really needed in Taiwan. The inadequacy of capital flow meant that people suffered seriously from underground usury. In addition, the currency system was extremely chaotic. The Taiwan Bank therefore took on the responsibility of stabilising the financial order here in Taiwan" (Taiwan Bank 1919:14–15, authors' translation).

Just how advanced Taiwan's banking system was at that time and how others perceived the new financial organisation is pertinent here. Information from the Chang Hwa Bank (1996) records that during the colonial period, Taiwanese depositors outnumbered the Japanese in terms of households, but in terms of the total amount of savings, that of the Taiwanese was far lower when compared to the Japanese. Even fifteen years after the Chang Hwa bank had been established, many Taiwanese still kept themselves at a distance from the modern banking system. Recognising people's distrust of the use of banknotes, Koo Hsien-jung minted a huge sum of silver dollars for people to exchange at any time to quell the scepticism toward the "new invention". Encouraged by the Japanese colonial government, Koo Hsien-jung used the redeemed bonds he collected from large rentholder households as shares (or investment), and thus became the general manager and a member of the supervisory board of the Chang Hwa Bank.

Koo Hsien-jung might be said to have advanced his economic capital by cooperating with the Japanese colonial government. It should be noted, however, that his actions on the front line of his business demonstrate how entrepreneurship was manifested in that era, during which property rights and institutions were redefined and reconstructed.

### *The KMT Land Reform*

Before 1949, there were no securities transactions in Taiwan. In 1953, the KMT government took specific steps to ensure the transfer of agricultural capital into the industrial sector, initiating a land reform programme called "Land to the Tiller". Under the programme, landlords were partially compensated for their land; they were given 70% of bonds in kind and 30% in shares of the four leading public corporations, namely the Taiwan Cement Company, the Taiwan Paper Company, the Taiwan Agriculture and Forestry Company, and the Taiwan Industry and Mining Company. It was hoped that this would enable the government to transfer public corporations to private ownership, force land capital into industry, and stimulate the interest of the otherwise conservative landlords in industrial activities.

It has been taken for granted that it was KCF's cooperation with the KMT over the land-reform programme that made him the head of the Taiwan Cement Corp. Again, the event should be examined against the backdrop of the society at that time, which did not recognise the significance of this transformation of property rights. The shares of the four major companies were issued in March 1954, and by the end of that year, their market price on the stock exchange remained only 40% to 50% of their face value.

The stock market was totally alien to Taiwan's landlords and the general public in the early 1950s. They knew very little about security investments, and were doubtful about the value that could be redeemed in exchange for land. The operation of a modern corporation and the concept of separating ownership and management were also new to the public and the landlords (Peng 2003). Moreover, inflation rates remained high for quite some time, and the relatively higher interest rates for mercantile business compared to the industrial sector made industrial investment even less appealing. Given the rising price of land and commodities, many landlords were more than willing to dispose of their shares at any price to any stock collector to expand their usury activities.

Having inherited a large amount of land, KCF could have stuck to the role of a merchant capitalist, like many others in Taiwan. Nonetheless, he decided to cooperate with the government's policy of land reform. Unlike others, KCF understood the implications of capital securitisation. How did he identify the significance of the opportunities that were generated by this institutional reform? Campbell and Lindberg (1990) are right to highlight the government's role in influencing the selection process. However, although the institutional change in this case was government-led, very few people were able to grasp the ensuing opportunities. Although a government may encourage innovation, not all members of the society, including economic actors, will necessarily be ready for the emergence of a new field. However, the network positions of actors may help them to identify the opportunities (Burt 2000), thereby shaping the selection process. In other words, the capability to spot opportunities can be constructed intentionally or unintentionally on the basis of the experiences that an individual derives from separate networks and social institutions.

The knowledge and networks acquired by KCF worked exactly in this way. Koo Hsien-jung died before World War II, and left a sizeable inheritance to KCF. He did not take up his tasks right away, but assigned the management of the business to his younger brother. KCF went to Japan to continue his graduate studies and to work in Dai-Nippon Seitou, the Japanese company that had bought out Koo Hsien-jung's sugar business in the Japanese colonial period. KCF started as a cashier in the company, and underwent training in several positions. Compared with the other major families of Taiwan, KCF's choice and behaviour was pioneering for his era, but all of the subsequent heirs of the Koo family have since followed suit. His nephew, Jeffrey Koo Sr., a third-generation heir of Koo Hsien-jung, was educated in Japan until he was thirteen, obtained his bachelor degree in Taiwan, and completed his graduate studies in New York.

To ensure the continuance of the Koos' family business, KCF and Jeffrey Koo Sr. put a premium on management training for the next generation. Many of the family members studied in Japan for a period of time, and the four principal heirs (two sons from each side of the family) hold MBAs from the elite Wharton School at the University of Pennsylvania, of which the Koos are major benefactors. It is estimated that between 15 and 20 members of the Koo family and executives in the Koo group have passed through Wharton's MBA and advanced-management programmes. The training includes the fast-tracking of the family members through two to three years of internships in multinational companies that are friendly to the family.

Owing to the Koo family's experiences in the Chang Hwa Bank and his early training in Dai-Nippon Seitou, KCF was familiar with the structure of the Japanese Kabushiki Kaisha and with the operation of a joint stock corporation. This helped KCF identify and maximise opportunities. Such a central position and ability gives an actor an advantage over others in terms of accessing novel sources of knowledge. As a result, while others disposed of their stock securities, KCF collected them, which allowed him to become the biggest shareholder in the Taiwan Cement Corporation and later the president of the company.

The entrepreneurship of Koo Hsien-jung and KCF had something in common: their accumulation and transformation of capital started when property rights were redefined by the government. As the public was unfamiliar with the new institutions and the associated actions, the Koos became positively involved and extended their business boundaries. Their judgement and insight in identifying opportunities can be attributed to their experiences and their network positions.

This trait of entrepreneurship was also passed down to the third and forth generations. In the 1960s, Taiwan's stock market was characterised by small retail investors, and could thus be easily manipulated by a few large stockholders. Their manipulation of the equity market resulted in repeated episodes of market booms and busts, and eventually the authorities sought to stabilise the capital market by amending the regulations and allowing security companies to be set up within the private sector.

The China Securities Investment Corporation (the predecessor of the Chinatrust Commercial Bank) was founded by the Koo family in 1966. Jeffrey Koo, Sr. joined the company in the following year. At that time, the Taiwan's stock exchange had only twenty categories of listed companies, each of which comprised very few firms. The scale of operation constrained the development of the underwriting business (Huang and Huang 2005:179). In light of the above, Jeffrey Koo Sr. suggested that the government should allow the security companies to act as underwriters and, in particular, that listed companies should be asked to issue 20% of their "right issues" for public placing through securities investment companies. This would also help to decentralise the share structure of the listed companies, making it more difficult for individual minority controllers to manoeuvre; the release of the table stakes would also help the market to prosper. Reflecting on these years, Jeffrey Koo Sr. stated that, "at that time, no one knew anything about the underwriting business. We taught the government how to regulate us, and meanwhile, instructed other securities investment companies and investors how to play the game. That situation was again just like the beginning of the credit card market in Taiwan" (Lai 2003:275). The Chinatrust Commercial Bank was indeed the first and the biggest credit card issuer on the island. In 1992, Taiwan opened up the financial market, and the China Securities Investment Corporation was the first of its counterparts to be successfully converted into a commercial bank.

### IV. *Risk and Innovation*

Each of the three generations of the Koo family has been imbued with the venturing spirit that has been exercised in the social context of the state's property rights actions. However, in most cases, only one man or a few men could see a new possibility and overcome the resistance and difficulties that entrepreneurial action is confronted with outside of the ruts of established practice (Schumpeter 1990:413). At the end of his article on the study of entrepreneurship, Schumpeter raises several questions concerning the economic, cultural, and political conditions that produce, shape, favor or inhibit entrepreneurial activity, and states that "though the entrepreneurial function cannot be transmitted by inheritance—except, possibly, by biological inheritance?" (1990:419). It is very difficult to tell whether or not entrepreneurship could be transmitted by such inheritance, but to keep the family in business usually demands something new in the generational transition.

The challenges do not stop when the entrepreneurial function has been carried out. Risk trails innovation, and not every new economic action will be legitimised and sanctioned by the government and society. The emergence of entrepreneurship is usually related to processes of institutional redefinition, and to discuss the legitimacy of entrepreneurial behaviour is to talk about possible opposition from the government, economic actors, or the society as a whole. After all, the government plays an important role in clarifying indefinite property rights.

When the Democratic Progressive Party (hereafter the DPP) took power from the ruling KMT in 2000, it launched a series of policies to reform the financial system and encourage the merging of financial groups. The fourth generation of the Koo family, headed by Jeffrey Koo Jr., the elder son of Jeffrey Koo Sr. and the leader of the Chinatrust Financial Holding (Chinatrust), formed a team and initiated an acquiring plan immediately. He made a bold attempt to acquire the state-controlled Mega Financial (Zhao Feng Jin Kong) in mid-2005 as part of the government's plans to promote banking consolidation and to half the number of financial holding firms to seven. Chinatrust bought up 3% of Mega's shares from the stock market via its subsidiaries, including the Chinatrust Commercial Bank. Later, the Hong Kong branch of Chinatrust Bank bought US$390 million worth of structured notes from a Hong Kong securities firm and demanded that the latter link the notes to Mega shares, thereby securing a further 3.9% of Mega's shares.

In February 2006, the Financial Supervisory Commission (thereafter, the FSC) approved the request of the Chinatrust Financial Holding to acquire a 10% stake in Mega.[4] Chinatrust's Hong Kong branch then sold the structured notes to Red Fire Development Ltd., which redeemed the notes in mid-February, prompting the Hong Kong securities firm to sell out the linked Mega shares to cash in US$30 million of profits. Chinatrust secured 70% of the Mega shares sold by the Hong Kong securities firm, and on June 23 gained four seats on the board of directors of Mega. This caused serious concern in the government, which had tried to secure its own dominance of Mega Financial.

One month after the election of the board of directors of Mega, the FSC exposed the dubious practices of Chinatrust, and Red Fire was suspected of being a front company that was actually controlled by the Koo family. The FSC demanded management changes, and Chinatrust was fined NT$10 million (around US$305,500) for irregularities connected to its controversial investment in Mega Financial. Later, the FSC declared that although Chinatrust's practice of acquiring shares via "fake" overseas capital was not illegal, it violated the "law-abiding spirit" (*Taipei Times*, Oct 19 2006, p. 1). Following the declaration, the FSC halted the bank's plan to open overseas branches and to engage in fundraising ventures, which led to the resignation of Jeffrey Koo Jr. Afterwards, the French brokerage firm BNP Paribas Securities, and later Moody's Investors Services downgraded the rating of Chinatrust. Taipei prosecutors then placed Koo Jr. on the most-wanted list and set a 25-year limit.

Although Taiwan's judicial system has deemed Koo's practice to be inappropriate, analysts in foreign investment companies have taken it as a normal way of conducting business. The device of structured notes is a new invention that relates to synthetic funds that are purchased by investors, and is used as a financial tool to provide customised equity returns or exposure by hedging positions. From the viewpoint of returns, Chinatrust's practice has not only secured their bid for target companies, but has also earned large profits for its shareholders. Some experts are therefore astonished by the FSC's poor knowledge of the device of financial derivatives (*Economic Daily News* June 29, 2006), and

[4] The FSC, one of the five independent agencies of the Executive Yuan in Taiwan, was established in 2004 with the objective of consolidating the supervision of the banking, securities, and insurance sectors, and to act as a single regulator.

Koo Jr. himself stated publicly, "I believe our actions [in conducting the investment] were honorable and honest, and we will fully cooperate with investigations. I believe that the impartiality of the judiciary and the results [of the probe] will help clear our name" (*Taipei Times*, Oct 19, 2006, p. 1).

The aforementioned case raises the issue that to develop innovation into social action demands collective sanction; otherwise, entrepreneurs are not able to execute entrepreneurial functions. It is the government that is tasked with the specific mission to establish property rights actions, as Campbell and Lindberg contend. Property rights are not only about defining the relationship between an individual and a commodity, but also express the relationship among people. One person's ownership and control usually corresponds to another's absence of ownership and control. Because property rights specify the relations among people, they also define the institutional basis of power relations in the processes of production, exchange, and accumulation (Campbell and Lindberg 1990:635). To enhance the legitimacy of an innovation, the innovator is obliged to struggle with any actor, including the government, that has the power to manipulate property rights. The following section discusses how the Koo family has dealt with the various political regimes in their attempts to win legitimacy.

## V. *Sources of Legitimacy: Relationships with the Government*

The extent to which the first three generations of the Koos have engaged with Taiwan's turbulent changes is impressive. Members of the family have sought to reduce the risk and enhance the legitimacy of their entrepreneurial endeavours in part through the cultivation of social networks and in part by engaging in political lobbying. However, as we have seen in the foregoing, there is no guarantee of success for either strategy, especially during the transition of regimes.

It has been stated that Koo Hsien-jung was granted monopoly businesses by which he prospered, but it must be questioned why these monopolies were given to him. The Japanese army arrived in 1895, the Chinese troops fled, and looting broke out everywhere in Taiwan. To restore social order, Koo Hsien-jung and some other members of the gentry opened the gates and guided the Japanese into Taipei city (Lamley 1999). Intriguingly, among them, only Koo Hsien-jung managed to embark upon this incident the beginning of a new and profitable career as a mediator between the Japanese invaders and the Taiwanese populace.

Koo Hsien-jung worked closely with the Japanese and became involved in both foreign and domestic affairs. Domestically, he suggested to Goto that he should adopt the *baojia* system (an administrative system organised on the basis of households) to guard the city against armed men who could be described either as "bandits" or "loyal anti-Japanese resistance fighters". He was later nominated head of the Taipei Security Bureau (*bao liang ju*). In terms of foreign affairs, when the Russo-Japanese War broke out in 1904, Koo Hsien-jung sent his own junk out on patrol and gained valuable intelligence for the Japanese government. In 1921, he was selected as a council member of the Taiwan Governor's Office, and in 1934 was chosen as the first Taiwanese to be a congressman in the house of the Diet. It was said that the honour was bestowed to give him a legitimate position from which he could represent the Japanese government in political activities. In carrying out the role, he travelled often to China, Japan, and throughout Taiwan, and visited several important political figures, such as Wang Ching-Wei and Tuan Chi-jui, and even helped Chiang Kai-shek in a struggle with a rebel.

During the colonial regime, the monopoly business had earned the Koo family legitimacy, but as the regime changed, these good connections turned into a negative asset. KCF found himself entangled in a political crisis when the regime was in transition from the hands of the Japanese to the KMT's. When Japan was defeated, some Japanese military personnel attempted to cooperate with those in Taiwan who sought independence. A newly established organisation, the Taiwan Social Security Maintenance Organisation (Taiwan *Zhi An Wei Chi Hui*), asked the colonial Governor General Andou Rikiti to declare independence. KCF immediately came under suspicion and was imprisoned by the KMT government for one to two years. It was only through marriage network and the legacy of his father's assistance to Chiang Kai-shek that KCF survived the political crises and eventually returned to Taiwan after a period of exile in Hong Kong. He later regained the confidence of the KMT government and successfully reclaimed his assets, enabling him to keep the family business going.

For decades, KCF was one of Taiwan's most venerated public figures despite the fact that he never held public office. As a confidant of former President Lee Teng-hui, he was the chairman of the quasi-official Straits Exchange Foundation since 1990, and also represented Taiwan on many international occasions, including many of the APEC summits. He rubbed shoulders with the likes of Chinese former president Jiang Zemin and U.S. former president Bill Clinton. His nephew, Jeffrey Koo Sr., also served as a travelling envoy for Taiwan and a senior advisor to successive Taiwanese presidents. When Japan severed their diplomatic ties with Taiwan, the KMT government relied very much on KCF's relationships with the Japanese, and in particular the networks extended from the Dai-Nippon Seitou[5] to continue the interaction between the two regions. The personal involvement in foreign affairs of these members of the Koo family mirrors the special conditions to which Taiwan has been subject on the international stage.

As the Koos have done so much for successive governments, it must be asked what the latter have given in return. The government repeatedly lent a hand in the Koos' competition with other members of the board of directors for control of, for example, Taiwan Cement. As a joint stock company, the board of Taiwan Cement has long been dominated by three families, of which the Koos are one. Whenever it comes to deciding the incumbent of the controlling position of the president, the Koos have always gained the upper hand and triumphed over their competitors with the support of the government's vote. The Koos are also capable of exerting extraordinary power over public companies, even whey they own only a minority of the shares. However, this relationship between the government and the Koos has changed since the KMT's authoritarian regime was challenged at the same time when the power of other capitalists has grown. The government's support for the Koo family is no longer a given: the government's vote is now placed with those who have the largest portion of shares. Business competence has become the stake for gaining control.

*Involvement in property rights actions: Lobbying*

Although the legitimacy of new actions can be secured by the legal system, the elimination of political risk is also crucial. For instance, after the

[5] The company of Dai-Nippon Seitou was where KCF spent his years as an intern. The director of the company at the time was Fujiiyama Aiichiro, who later became the Secretary of State for Foreign and Commonwealth Affairs when Nobusuke Kishi was the 57th Prime Minister of Japan from 1958 to 1960. Nobusuke's brother, Sato Eisaku, was Prime Minister from 1964 to 1972, and it was during Sato's term that KCF obtained from Emperor Hirohito the Order of Sacred Treasure and the Medal with Blue Ribbon for his contribution to the public.

Second World War, the KMT government took over Japanese-controlled properties and turned them into state-owned companies. The Lin family, one of the five most eminent families in Taiwan, successfully asserted their ownership of real estate in downtown Taipei that was previously leased to the Japanese colonial government (Szu-Ma 1998:114). This shows that the legal system not only safeguards personal property, but also regulates the role of the government.

The changes in the delimitation of property rights are partly attributed to the evolution of economic logic on the one hand, and social variables on the other. In terms of the delimitation of property rights, an actor must gain political support in every aspect, because the new economic action needs a legal status. Nonetheless, such reformation may not be successful every time, and failure will lead to the abortion of new actions. The obstacles may come from non-economic sectors, such as internal conflicts within the political sphere. For example, from 1964 to 1985, Taiwan's money supply increased fifty-fold, and the existing financial system could no longer function. A huge amount of savings were transferred into underground financial activities. Lawmaker Tsai Chen Chow, his brothers, together with Jeffrey Koo Sr. from the Chinatrust as the representative of the industrial sector, gained positions on a bill draft committee through which they attempted to challenge financial policies, proposing that investment trust companies should be allowed to proceed with the business of short-term financing. However, because of a power struggle within the KMT, their first attempt to achieve this in the 1980s failed (Wang 1996:114–9).

Becoming a policy maker or engaging in lobbying is compatible with the entrepreneur's interests. The Wu family, owners of the Shin Kong Group (*Xin Guang Wu Jia*), and the Tsai family, owners of the Cathay Group, had respectively family members who worked directly in the Legislative Yuan as lawmakers.[6] Unlike them, the Koo family's influence on policy has been more indirect. KCF and Jeffrey Koo Sr. were members of the Chinese National Association of Industry and Commerce (CNAIC), which was established in 1952 and comprised leading business elites. In the past, the CNAIC carried out an important

[6] Cathay's Tsai Chen Chow was the first supplementary legislator representing the KMT. Shin Kong's Wu Tong Sheng represented the KMT as supplementary legislator in the second term, and represented the Taiwan Solidarity Union (Tai Lian) as legislator in the fifth term.

lobbying function. KCF was chairman for more than 30 years, and his nephew, Jeffrey Koo Sr., succeeded him in this position for 8 years.

During the KMT's authoritarian period, the CNAIC and the General Chamber of Commerce worked very closely with the ruling party. They either endorsed policies or lobbied for bills, and functioned as an extension of the KMT's control over the economic sector. The head and chief secretary of the associations mostly came from the KMT's party organisation. In fact, Koo Cheng-fu, Lin Ting-Sheng of the Tatung Company, as well as Kao Ching Yuen of the Uni-President Enterprises Corporation were members of the KMT's Central Standing Committee for a long period of time. As directors of these associations, they acted as bridges connecting the political and the business worlds. The advantage of this was that they entered the core of policy making, and at the very least were able to make suggestions to the government.

During the eight years when Jeffrey Koo Sr. was chairman of the CNAIC, the relationships between these three associations and the government went through subtle changes. Each of the political leaders inside the KMT party had their own business networks, and became affiliated with various interest groups. When the DPP took the reins in 2000, the power struggle became even more intense. The rise of the National Association of Small and Medium Enterprises, favored by President Chen Shui-bian, weakened the function of the three associations. More business representatives from other associations or interest groups have later been co-opted into the government, further diluting the influence exerted by the three aforementioned associations.

The function of the formal lobbying channels has also changed. After KCF passed away, the Taiwanese government is relying less on the Koo family's networks in its foreign affairs. Thus, although each generation of the family has shown their venturing spirit and their excellence in grasping the opportunities afforded by the changes in the rules, it is their interaction with the government that has determined whether or not the risks pay off.

## VI. *Conclusion*

The uncertainties generated by institutional change can be both risks and assets in the development of entrepreneurship. Although the risks experienced by the fourth generation of the Koo family with the present DPP government may not threaten the viability of the greater Koo

Group, they do demonstrate the challenges that face each heir of the family enterprise in sustaining the business over generations. Preserving the status quo may not be sufficient to overcome the increasing pressure of market competition. After all, as Schumpeter puts it, the cycles of economic activity require only habit and routine, and generate conservative tendencies that eventually lead to a decrease in profits.

By delineating the story of the Koo family, this paper asserts that entrepreneurship is a necessary factor if businesses are to last over generations. It has been discovered that the various instances of entrepreneurship among the Koo family correlate closely with their network positions and the government's actions in relation to property rights, and it is shown how each family innovator identified the opportunities in the face of public scepticism toward novel developments. Each of the family heirs has used different means to defend their innovations. The effects of good political connections are historically embedded, and the first three generations of the Koo family in particular had assumed special roles in Taiwan's foreign affairs. The family has attempted to take part in the definition and transformation of property rights, and in so doing has attempted to construct more favorable conditions for the family business. This paper provides a basis for further comparisons in different societies to determine the links among institutional change, the initiation of entrepreneurship in business dynasties, and the way in which such dynasties gain legitimacy for their innovations.

## *References*


Aldrich, H. (1999). *Organizations Evolving.* Thousand Oaks, CA: Sage Publications.

Aldrich, H. and Udo Staber. (1988). "Organizing Business Interests: Patterns of Trade Association Foundings, Transformations, and Deaths." Pp. 111–129 in *Ecological Models of Organizations*, edited by Glenn Carroll. New York: Ballinger.

Azuma, Y. (2000). *The General Economic History of Taiwan.* Taipei: Hai Xia Xue Shu (in Chinese).

Blaug, M. (2000). "Entrepreneurship Before and After Schumpeter." Pp. 76–88 in *Entrepreneurship: The Social Science View*, edited by Richard Swedberg. UK: Oxford University Press.

Burt, R. (2000). "The Network Entrepreneur." Pp. 281–309 in *Entrepreneurship: The Social Science View*, edited by Richard Swedberg. UK: Oxford University Press.

Campbell, J. L. and L. N. Lindberg (1990). "Property Rights and the Organization of Economic Activity by the State". *American Sociological Review*, 55 (October): 634–647.

Chang Hwa Commercial Bank. Editorial Board. (1996). *Chang Hwa Bank's 90 Years History*. Taichung: Chang Hwa Bank (in Chinese).

Ching, S. (1999). *The Legend of Koo Hsien-jung.* Taipei: ChienWei (in Chinese).

Cole, A. H. (1959). *Business Enterprise in Its Social Setting.* Cambridge: Harvard University.

DeGlopper, D. (1995). *Lukang, Commerce and Community in a Chinese City*. NY: State University of New York.

*Economic Daily News*. (2006). "Structured Notes, Entrepreneur's Most Favored Secret Weapons." June 29 (in Chinese).

Gerschenkron, A. (1962). *Economic Backwardness in Historical Perspective*. Cambridge: Harvard University.

——. (1966). "The Modernization of Entrepreneurship." In *Modernization: The Dynamics of Growth*, edited by M. Weiner. NY: Basic Books.

Goss, D. (2005). "Schumpeter's Legacy? Interaction and Emotions in the Sociology of Entrepreneurship." *Entrepreneurship: Theory and Practice*, 29(2): 205–18.

Hsieh, K. H. (1999). *Tainanband: The Rise of a Taiwan Native Business Group*. Taipei: Yuanliou (in Chinese).

——. (2002). *Chen Fong-Yuan (1893–1982)*. Taipei: Asian Culture (in Chinese).

Hsu, H. H. (2005). "The Prosperity and Decline of the New and Old Families." *Wealth Magazine*, 2, 222–242 (in Chinese).

Hsu, P. Y. (1996). *The Reminiscences of Hsu Ping and Hsu Po-yen*. Taipei: Institute of Modern History, Academia Sinica (in Japanese, abstracts in Chinese).

Huang, T. T. and Huang Z. Y. (2005). *The Life of Koo Chen-Fu* (authorized by the Koo Foundation). Taipei: Lien-Ching (in Chinese).

Jones, G. and R. Wadhwani. (2006). "Schumpeter's Plea: Historical Methods in the Study of Entrepreneurship." *Academy of Management Best Paper Proceedings Series* (forthcoming).

Ka, C. M. (1993). *The Contradictory Relationship Between Rice and Sugar: Development and Dependency in Colonial Taiwan, 1895–1945*. Taipei: Socio Publishing (in Chinese).

Lai, N. (2003). "Nowadays, Taiwan has no Financier: Jeffrey Koo's Thirty-eight Financial Years." *Wealth Magazine*, 6, 274–280 (in Chinese).

Lamley, H. (1999). "Taiwan Under Japanese Rule, 1895–1945: The Vicissitudes of Colonialism." Pp. 201–260 in *Taiwan: A New History*, edited by Murray Rubinstein. NY: East Gate Books.

Liu, G. C. (1995). *Economical Analysis of Post-War Taiwan*. Ren jian chu ban she (in Chinese).

Lounsbury, M. and M. Glynn. (2001). "Cultural Entrepreneurship: Stories, Legitimacy, and the Acquisition of Resources." *Strategic Management Journal* 22: 545–564.

Marris, P. and A. Somerset. (1971). *The African Entrepreneur: a Study of Entrepreneurship and Development in Kenya*. New York: Africana.

Mezias, S. J. and E. Boyle. (2002). Organizational Dynamics of Creative Destruction. *Entrepreneurship and the Emergence of Industries.* NY: Palgrave MacMillan.

Ozaki, H. (ed.). (1939). *The Biography of Koo Hsien-jung*. Taipei: Editorial Board for the Biography of Koo Hsien-jung (in Japanese).

Peng, K.C. (2003) *Taiwan Securities Market for the Past Half Century*. Taipei: Good Morning Press.

Schumpeter, J. (1934/1961). *The Theory of Economic Development: An Inquiry into Profits, Capital, Credit, Interest, and the Business Cycle*, translated from German by Redvers Opie. Cambridge: Harvard University

——. (1950). *Capitalism, Socialism, and Democracy.* London: Allen & Unwin.

——. (1990). "Comments on a Plan for the Study of Entrepreneurship," in *Joseph A. Schumpeter*, edited by Richard Swedberg. UK: Princeton University Press.

Shane, S. (2000). "Prior Knowledge and the Discovery of Entrepreneurial Opportunities." *Organization Science* 11(4): 448–469.

Szu-Ma, H. C. (1998). *The Koos of the Koos Group: the Rich and Powerful Families in Taiwan.* Taipei Metropolis: Taiwan Interminds Publishing Inc. (in Chinese).

——. (2000). *Taiwan's Rich and Powerful Families: The Old Monies.* Taipei Metropolis: Taiwan Interminds Publishing Inc. (in Chinese).

*Taipei Times*. (2006). "Agents Seize Documents in Raid on Chinatrust's Offices," Oct 19, p. 1.

Taiwan Bank. (1919). *The 20th Anniversary Special Historical Review of the Taiwan Bank (Taiwan Yinhang Ershi Zhounian Shi Tekan)*. Taipei: Taiwan Bank (in Chinese).

Thornton, P. (1999). "The Sociology of Entrepreneurship." *Annual Review of Sociology* 25:19–46.

Tu, Z. Y. (1992). *Taiwan under Japanese Imperialism*. Taipei: Ren jian chu ban she (in Chinese).

Venkataraman, S. (1997). "The Distinctive Domain of Entrepreneurship Research: An Editor's Perspective." In *Advances in Entrepreneurship, Firm Emergence, and Growth*, edited by J. Katz and R. Brockhaus. Greenwich: JAI Press.

Wang, J. H. (1996). *Who Rules Taiwan?* Taipei: Juliu (in Chinese).

Wilken, P. (1979). *Entrepreneurship: A Comparative and Historical Study*. NJ: Ablex Publishing Corporation.

Yanaihara, T. (2003/1956). *Taiwan under Imperialism*, translated by Zhao Hsien Wen. Taipei: Hai Hxia Press (in Chinese).

Ye, D. P. (1997). *The History of Lukang*. Chung Hua: Zuo Yang (in Chinese).

Ye, J. C. (2002). *The Development of Taiwan's Modern Financial System*. Taipei: Morning Star Press (in Chinese).

# ARTICLES

# FAMILY RESOURCES AND EDUCATIONAL STRATIFICATION: THE CASE OF HONG KONG, 1981–2001*

Wu Xiaogang[1]

Education plays an important role in modern societies, both as an avenue of social mobility and as a tool for social reproduction. On the one hand, formal schooling can help children from disadvantaged backgrounds to change their fates; on the other hand, the schooling that individuals receive depends on the advantages/disadvantages that their parents confer on them throughout childhood (Ishida, Muller and Ridge 1995). In other words, access to educational opportunities is unequally distributed among different social groups. The increasing importance of education, together with long-term growth in enrolment in a school system in the process of economic development, has led some scholars to claim that individuals' educational achievement has become more and more independent of their family backgrounds (Boudon 1974; Treiman 1970). However, linear regression analyses of educational attainment reveal that the effects of family backgrounds have been stable over time in many industrialized countries (e.g. Featherman and Hauser 1978). To explain this phenomenon, Mare (1980) proposed a logit model of school transitions/progressions on family backgrounds and demonstrated that the expansion of education and the distribution of educational opportunities are two separate processes: the former may not necessarily lead to a more equal access to education among different social groups.

Comparative studies of educational attainment in 13 industrialized societies have confirmed the following general patterns of educational

---

* Reference to this article should be made as follows: Wu, Xiaogang. 2007. "Family Resources and Educational Stratification: The Case of Hong Kong, 1981–2001".

[1] The research project was supported by the Hong Kong Research Grants Council/Public Policy Research Fund (HKUST6003–PPR20051). I am grateful to Miss Alice Yeung, Mr. Stephen Wan, and Dr. Yuxiao Wu for research assistance, and an anonymous reviewer for comments and suggestions. Direct all correspondence to Xiaogang WU, Division of Social Science, Hong Kong University of Science and Technology, Clear Water Bay, Kowloon, Hong Kong SAR (Email: sowu@ust.hk).

stratification (Shavit and Blossfeld 1993): (1) the logit effects of social origins on educational transitions tend to be stronger at the beginning of an educational career and then decline in subsequent transitions, namely, social selection is most pronounced in the early stage of educational transitions (also see Mare 1980); (2) such patterns of association remain stable across cohorts, even in the context of a long-term educational expansion. Young pupils are dependent on the preferences of their parents and economic conditions of their families for school continuation decisions, but as they get older and advance to higher levels, they are increasingly able to decide on what they want and family (parental) resources become less important. In many countries, children from disadvantaged backgrounds encounter very severe selection barriers in early stages of transitions: only the brightest children from those backgrounds can make it to the higher levels, whereas children from advantaged families progress into secondary and tertiary schools with great ease. Consequently, school success is less and less affected by family socioeconomic background (Mare 1980; also see summary in Blossfeld and Shavit 1993).

The expansion of the educational system in many countries, reinforced by the educational reforms in the 20th century, seems to have had little impact on the role played by family background in its children's educational attainments, suggesting that an ever expanding pie of educational opportunities is always sliced in the same proportions among different social strata. The mechanism of distributing educational opportunities remains largely intact.

Family influence on education can be analytically separated into at least three components: economic capital, social capital, and cultural capital (Boudieu 1986; Coleman 1988). Economic capital, the physical resources that aid achievement, is commonly measured by the family's income or wealth. Social capital is less tangible because it exists only in social relationships among people. To understand the role of a family's social capital in its children's educational achievement, it is important to include the social relationships that are embedded in the larger community and through which parents can mobilize their organizational resources to facilitate children's socialization processes, such as social networks among parents and interactions with teachers, students, and other parents (Lin 1982; 1990). Cultural capital comes from the family's life style and consumption patterns, which provide valuable educational resources to foster children's motivation to learn and to improve academic performance. Empirical studies have found that all these aspects of family environments have independent effects on children's educational achievements in Western societies (Boudier 1986; Coleman 1988; DeGraaf 1986; DiMaggio 1982).

Educational inequalities partly result from the unequal distribution of these resources among different social classes. A constant relationship between family backgrounds and educational outcomes may indicate that mechanisms of redistributing those resources have remained more or less stable over time. Only radical institutional changes, such as the shift to state socialism, would yield visible impacts on educational stratification, not only directly through the implementation of educational policies that favour or discriminate against children of certain class backgrounds (e.g., Deng and Treiman 1997) but also indirectly through the redistribution of family resources that affect children's learning processes.

The latter process is more subtle than the former. While the temporal trend of educational stratification is often approximated by cohort variations corresponding to periods when a particular educational policy is implemented, historical information on the changing distribution of family resources is rarely available. Moreover, among the three forms of family resources mentioned above, only a family's economic capital, approximated by income or wealth, has a consistent measurement. The measurement of the distribution of social capital and cultural capital at the societal level is far from clear, but given the increasing income inequalities and rising employment rates, a changing distribution in non-economic resources among different families for their children's education can be expected.

Just as income growth does not necessarily lead to a more equal distribution of income, educational expansion has no intrinsic relation to changes in educational inequalities. This analogy suggests that the distribution of educational opportunities may resemble the distribution of other scarce resources that affect educational outcomes. Therefore, an examination of the change in educational stratification in the era of rapidly rising social inequalities not only helps us to identify the existence of such linkages but also to provide an in-depth understanding of how inequalities in family resources lead to social reproduction across generations.

In this paper, I investigate changes in educational stratification in Hong Kong from 1981 to 2001, a period when substantial socioeconomic and political transformations occurred. Using the one percent samples of the 1981 census and the 1986 by-census and the five percent samples of the 1991 census, the 1996 by-census and the 2001 census, I match school-age children (6–19) to their parents' background information within the same households and focus on changes in the effects of family resources on children's school enrolments and transitions over the past two decades.

In the following, I first present the historical background on economic development and educational expansion in Hong Kong in the past few decades and explain how the census/by-census data can be employed to analyze temporal trends in educational inequalities. I then demonstrate how family socioeconomic background affects children's educational outcomes, highlighting some unique features of Hong Kong's educational stratification that have not been found elsewhere. Finally, I discuss the implications of the case of Hong Kong for international comparative studies of educational attainment.

### *Increasing Inequality, Expanding Schools, and Educational Stratification in Hong Kong*

Hong Kong provides an interesting case for the study of social stratification and mobility. As one of the richest societies in Asia, Hong Kong is also among the most unequal economies in the world. From the 1960s to the 1980s, the at-that-time British colony successfully transformed itself from an entrepôt to a manufacturing center and then to a regional hub of business services. The GDP per capita increased from HK$49,075 in 1971 to HK$92,221 in 1981 to HK$151,969 in 1991 (adjusted by the fixed prices in 2000), with an annual growth rate of 5.8 percent. By 2001, despite the economic difficulties after the Asian financial crisis, the GDP per capita reached HK$192,465, putting Hong Kong among the advanced developed economies (Census and Statistics Department 1992, 2002; Lui 1997).

Hong Kong's economic miracle is often attributed to its world-renowned *laissez-faire* capitalism (Friedman 1982). Unsurprisingly, economic growth in Hong Kong has always been accompanied by increasing income inequalities (Chow and Papanek 1981). This defies the inverted U-shaped relationship between economic growth and income distribution observed in many countries, namely, the growth in income levels first leads to an increase and then, beyond a certain point, to a decrease in income inequalities (Kuznets 1955). As Figure 1 shows, the Gini coefficient, a common measure of income inequality, rose from

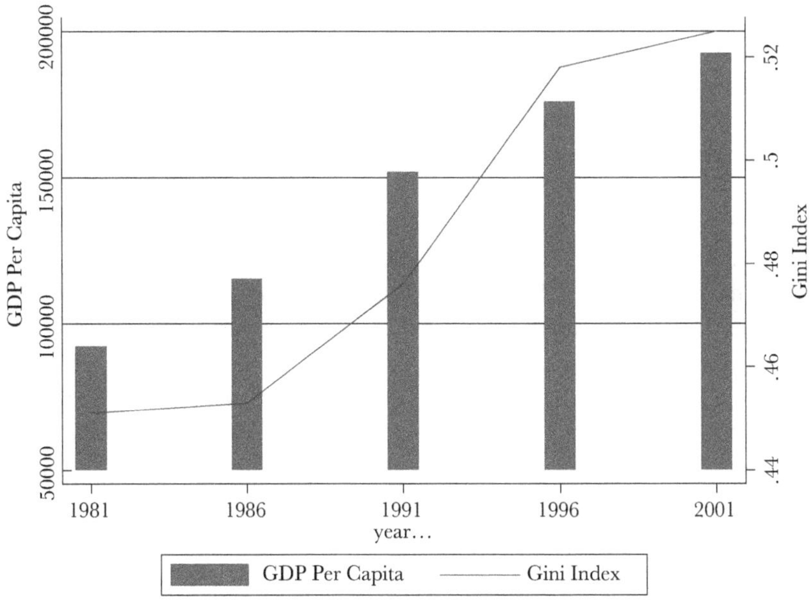


Figure 1: Growth of GDP Per Capita and Income Inequality in Hong Kong (1981–2001)

Note: GDP per capita is adjusted by the fixed price of 2000. Income inequality is measured by the Gini index.
*Data Source: Census and Statistics Department, Hong Kong SAR Government 1992, 2002*

0.43 in 1971 to 0.45 in 1981 and further to 0.48 in 1991 (Census and Statistics Department 1992). The income gap between the rich and poor was widened in the 1990s. The Gini increased further to 0.518 in 1996 and 0.525 in 2001 (Census and Statistics Department 2002), putting Hong Kong among the most unequal economies in the world.

Given this sharp disparity, Hong Kong provides a unique case for sociologists to investigate the issue beyond the relationship between economic growth and income distribution to understand the social implications of enlarging income and social inequalities on intergenerational social reproduction and mobility. As education is known as an important avenue for an individual to move away from poverty, how a family's economic resources affect its children's school performance and educational outcome has become a central issue of concerns for both academics and community members. Education could have a long-term impact on the evolution of social structures in Hong Kong. In the context of the increasing income inequalities, changes in the pattern of intergenerational mobility to a great extent are contingent upon how changes in these inequalities affect children's educational opportunities.

Over the past decades, education in Hong Kong has been expanded substantially in the course of economic development, being transformed from an elite-oriented system to a mass-oriented system. First, the structure of nine years of compulsory education, including six years of primary and three years of lower secondary education, was first implemented in the 1970s and expanded in the 1980s. Then, higher education has expanded since the late 1980s. In 1971, the government started providing free primary and also compulsory education to children aged 6 to 11 years old. Subsequently, the policy was extended to the lower secondary level in 1978. Legislation on compulsory education has been enacted to prohibit children aged 14 or younger from taking any form of employment in the labour market (Lui 1997; Post 1994). The expansion of secondary education put higher pressure on local higher education in the 1980s, since only children from rich families could afford overseas tertiary education. In 1989, the government decided to triple the enrolments in higher education; in the 1990s tertiary institutions expanded rapidly.[2]

The trend of educational expansion is clearly reflected in Figure 2, which plots the average years of schooling and the percentage of college graduates by gender for adults aged 25 or above. In general, Hong Kong people have become more educated over time. Men on average received 7.2 years of education in 1981 and 9.2 years of education in 2001, whereas women on average received 4.9 years of education in 1981 and 8.2 years in 2001. Figure 2 also plots the percentage of college graduates among men and women separately over the two decades (scale on the right Y-axis). While only 5.1 percent of men and 2.2 percent of women had college degrees in 1981, 13.4 percent of men and 9.4 percent of women received college degrees in 2001. Hence, it appears that the recent educational expansion probably has benefited women more than men—the gender gap in education has continued to shrink over time.

[2] Before the 1980s, there were only two universities in Hong Kong (HKU and CUHK) that offered Bachelor degrees. Each year fewer than 2000 places were available to students who completed upper secondary school, representing less than 3 percent of the age cohort (Post 2003:550).

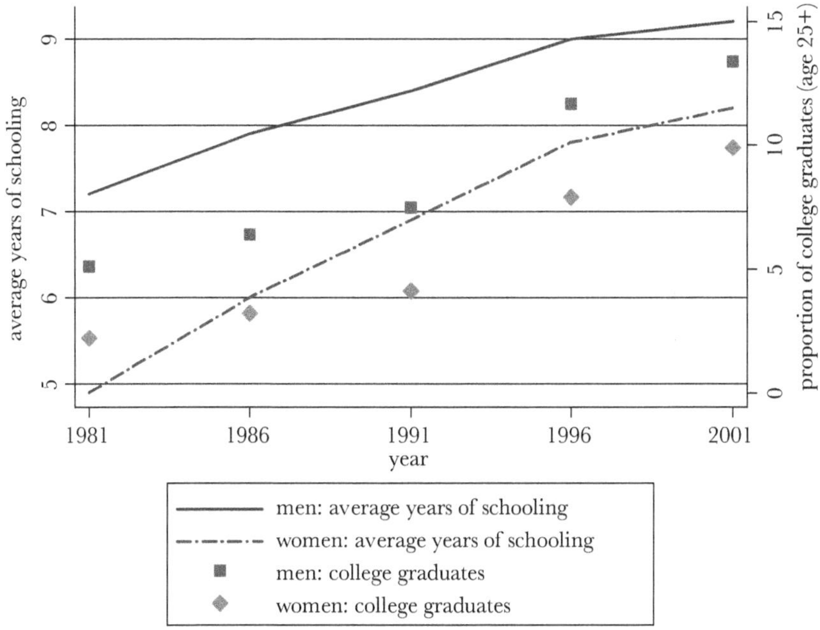


Figure 2: Educational Expansion in Hong Kong (by Gender), 1981–2001

The expansion of education in such a short period of time would naturally lead to another related but yet separate question—has educational inequality declined over the past two decades? In particular, how has the role of family resources in educational attainment changed in the expanding process along with social and economic changes? If primary and lower secondary education is provided for free, then family resources should not have much of an impact on educational achievement. At the school level beyond compulsory education (secondary 3), the government provided some subsidies to students to attend upper secondary school, but a nominal fee ranging from HK$5,000–8,000 per year continued to be charged. At the end of secondary 5, students take the Hong Kong Certificate of Education Examination (HKCEE), with a pass rate of around 30 percent in recent years; successful students then enter Forms 6 and 7 of secondary studies, which prepare them to take the Advanced Level (A Levels) examination for admission to university (Pong and Post 1991). A student's placement in a particular university and a particular academic program are contingent upon his/her examination scores. Students admitted to universities need to pay around HK$40,000–50,000 in tuition fees, with the remainder of the costs heavily subsidized by the government. In 1996, the Hong Kong University Grants Committee (UGC) stated that "no qualified students should be denied access to tertiary education through lack of means." Hence, it seems that the Chinese-style meritocratic examination system, together with a rapid expansion of educational opportunities, would reasonably wipe out to the effects of family resources on children's educational attainment, as has been found in other countries (e.g., the Netherlands, De Graaf 1986).

Up to now, little data has been collected to reveal the relationship between social mobility and educational inequalities in Hong Kong (except Chan, Lui and Wong 1995). Specifically, the parents' background information when the respondent grew up was seldom collected in most surveys. Using a one-percent sample of the micro data of the Hong Kong household censuses and by-censuses from various years, Pong and Post (1991) examined the educational attainment and transition for the four separate cohorts of youth aged 23–27 who had completed their educations but still lived with their parents. Their parents' information could therefore be identified. They found that, while linear regression results show that the effect of family background on educational attainment diminished over time, the effect of the same variables on the odds of educational transition *increased* at higher levels. These results indicate that the educational system in Hong Kong might have become more *socially* selective at the higher levels, a fact apparently at odds with the trends observed in most countries (Shavit and Blossfeld 1993).

Post (1994) analyzed the same data sets to address the impact of educational expansion (provision of free education) on school transitions at primary and secondary levels for youths aged 16–20. The effect of the father's monthly income, as a measure of family economic resources, declined in the transition from Primary 6 to Secondary 1 among both boys and girls, but remained unchanged in the transition from Secondary 5 to Secondary 6. In a recent article, Post (2004) specifically analyzed the role of family resources in access to tertiary education for individuals aged 19–20 from 1971 to 2001 and reported a diminishing role of family resources (including income) in access to all levels of education. However, the trend was reversed in the post-secondary level from 1991 to 2001; access to university education became more dependent upon family economic resources during this later period.

This method of utilizing the census data to address the issue of intergenerational transfer is innovative. However, as Pong and Post (1991) acknowledged, in the group between 23 and 27, only about half lived at home (Table 1, p. 256) and only the backgrounds of the parents of this half of the study population was available for analysis. Thus, the representativeness of their samples is questionable. Secondly, the family information included in the analysis was its status when the subjects were 23 to 27, rather than their status when they received or decided on the continuation of education. Furthermore, unlike in most educational stratification research, only three independent variables (gender, the mother's education, either the father's occupation or income, but not both) are included in the models. Finally, the data, measures used and age groups analyzed in a series of articles by Pong and Post (1991) and Post (1994, 2004) were not consistent among themselves. For instance, the measure of family income varied, ranging from the father's predicted earnings based on the simple human capital model for men (Pong and Post 1991), the father's monthly income (Post 1994), to the parents' income quartiles (Post 2004). Certain variables (such as the father's education, occupation, and the number of siblings) commonly used in the study of the effects of family background on educational stratification are missing. The age groups analyzed also vary from 23–27, 16–20, and 19–20. Hence these studies do not allow us to draw a comprehensive picture of the trends in the effects of family resources on educational attainment and transitions in Hong Kong.

This paper is an update and improvement based on the previous work by Pong and Post (1991) and Post (1994, 2004), with the focus on the effects of family economic, social and cultural resources on children's educational outcomes in Hong Kong since the 1980s. Rather than relying on cohort analysis of the snapshot census data, I analyze samples from the population census and by-census data for a specific age group from 1981 to 2001 to address temporal changes in educational stratification over the past two decades. I restrict the analysis to school age children between 6 and 19 years old in respective years so that I can obtain parents' information for most samples from the household records. Instead of analyzing those who have completed their educations, I investigate changes in family backgrounds (measured by the father's income, occupation, education, and the mother's education) in the children's enrolment status and educational transitions at various levels, an ongoing process of educational attainment in an era of rapid socioeconomic and political changes in Hong Kong.

## *Data Construction, Variables, And Statstical Methods*

### *Data*

The population census, conducted in every ten years in Hong Kong, and the by-census, conducted midway between two censuses, collects relatively detailed information on education, income, employment, and housing situations. Samples of the micro-data of population censuses are regularly made available to researchers by the Census and Statistics Department of the Hong Kong SAR Government. Prior to 1990, only the one percent sample was released to the public; since 1991, the sample has been increased to five percent to allow study of sub-populations.

I analyze the sample data of censuses and by-censuses from 1981 to 2001 for several reasons. First, substantial socioeconomic changes and educational expansion have occurred during the period, making it particularly interesting to link the changes in educational inequalities to the changes the distribution of family resources since 1981. Second, the five percent sample since 1991 greatly enhanced the utility of the census data in analyses targeting some specific age groups, for instance, school-age children. Finally, within the two decades, the school system has remained relatively stable, thus making education levels more comparable with one another.

The census and by-census prior to 2001 recorded individuals' education with two variables: school attendance and educational attainment. School attendance refers to whether a person is studying, has completed or has withdrawn from the highest level of educational attainment claimed. Educational attainment refers to the highest level of education ever attained by a person in a school or other educational institution, regardless of whether he or she had completed the course. Only formal courses are counted as educational attainment. The levels listed include "no schooling," "kindergarten," "lower primary (primary 1 to 4)", "upper primary (primary 5 and 6), "form 1" to "form 7," a variety of "sub-degrees" and "diplomas", "college," and "postgraduate" (22 categories in total). The education information collected in the 2001 census is basically comparable, but with more detailed information. For instance, "lower primary" is broken into "primary 1" to "primary 4.", and "upper primary" is broken into "primary 5 and 6). Educational level is measured separately by two indicators—highest level attended and highest level completed, in addition to school attendance status.

This paper employs educational level and school attendance status to construct variables related to school enrolment and transitions.

The household censuses have collected no information on the respondent's family background when the respondent was growing up (typically referring to the situation when he/she was at age 14), the information necessary for studying intergenerational inheritance and mobility. Certainly, one can match parents with adult children living within the same household (e.g., Deng and Treiman 1997), but the sample of multi-generational households is hardly representative of most modern societies with the dominance of nuclear families. In Hong Kong, over half of the cohort aged 23–27 who just completed their educations do not live with their parents (Pong and Post 1991, p. 256), making the study of educational attainment via analysis of census data rather problematic.

By slightly modifying the issue, this paper shifts the focus to a younger cohort—children ranging from 6 to 19 in age, who are more likely to be in school and live with their parents. Hence, on the one hand, we cannot conduct analysis on educational attainment because many respondents were still attending school. On the other hand, we can obtain a more representative sample of those who are currently receiving education, and the matched information of their parents is more suitable to addressing the effects of family resources (when children received their education) on educational outcomes, such as school enrolments and transitions.

In Hong Kong, children typically start schooling at age 6, and if proceeding smoothly, would enter university by age 19. This is confirmed in Figure 3, which presents the age-specific enrolment rates by gender from 1981 to 2001. In almost all years, children under age 14 almost reached full enrolment, clearly reflecting the effective implementation of 9 years of compulsory education in the territory since the 1980s. The enrolment rate for children/youth aged 15 or above (beyond Secondary 3 or Form 3) increased between 1981 and 2001. The age was capped at 19 because we are interested in those with entry into university but not completion of university education. Meanwhile, while extending the analysis to age 22 (typical age of completing college education) could include more college students in the sample, it also could include those who married and moved out of their parents' homes. The minimum age for legal marriage in Hong Kong is 18 years old.

Unlike Pong and Post (1991) and Post (1994, 2004), who matched children in their sample to their household heads to obtain a measure

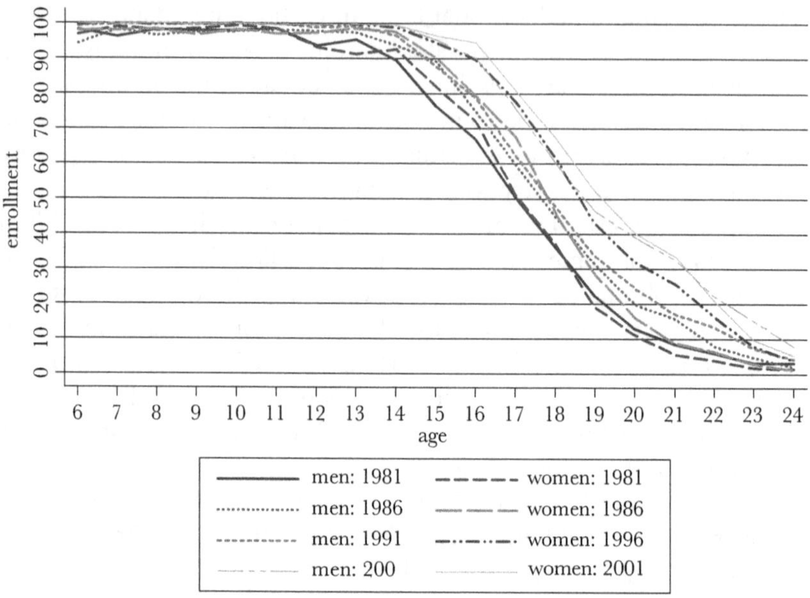


Figure 3: Age-specific School Enrolment Rates for Men and Women in Hong Kong, 1981–2001

of their family backgrounds, I adopt a more sophisticated method to construct the data for analysis. In the first step, records of married couples within the same household are constructed based on each individual's relationship with other household members. In the second step, the individuals who are in the 6–19 age group are linked to one of their parents through the variable that identifies the serial number of household members; and based on identified parents and their spouses (married couples), I further label them as "father" or "mother" on the basis of their gender. Through such data manipulations, I create a new data set containing individuals' educational information, matched with their parents' education, occupation and income.

Certainly, some children do not live with both parents; still others do not live with their parents at all. As Table 1 shows, except in 1981, at least 80 percent of children between 6 and 19 years old lived with both parents in all years. While the effect of the absence of at least one parent on children's educational achievement is an important topic, in this paper, I focus on the majority of children who live in "normal" (two-parent) family environments. I examine both fathers' and mothers' effects on children's education.

Table 1: Living Arrangements for Children/Youth Aged 6–19 in Hong Kong, 1981–2001

| Living arrangement | 1981 | 1986 | 1991 | 1996 | 2001 |
|---|---|---|---|---|---|
| Both parents present | 77.2 | 82.0 | 81.7 | 87.6 | 85.4 |
| Mother present | 13.6 | 8.4 | 8.3 | 6.3 | 8.0 |
| Father present | 7.3 | 4.2 | 2.3 | 2.7 | 2.5 |
| Parents missing | 1.9 | 5.5 | 7.7 | 3.4 | 4.1 |
| | 100% | 100% | 100% | 100% | 100% |
| N | 12,843 | 12,291 | 57,482 | 57,250 | 59,565 |

*Variables*

Most previous studies on educational attainment have used the father's occupation and education to approximate family resources (Shavit and Blossfeld 1991). In this paper, I consider four variables related to economic, social and cultural resources that a family possesses to assist in its children's educational attainment.

As pointed out in the earlier discussion, a family's economic resource is approximated by the father's monthly income. The father's occupation is typically employed to measure family socioeconomic status in the stratification literature (Blau and Duncan 1967; Hauser and Featherman 1978). As the economic dimension of family resources has been captured by father's income directly in the model,[3] it is believed that the father's occupation mainly represents the social resources that a family has, that is, the social networks embodied in the father's occupation (Lin 1982, 1990), which help children's learning. Parents' levels of education, especially the mother's education, are used to proxy for a family's cultural environment. The census data do not have other measures of cultural activities and consumption of families.

To be certain, the measures of the three dimensions of family resources overlap with each other, and separating one from another is only for analytical purposes, as I have previously pointed out. The goal of this paper is to demonstrate the multidimensionality of family

[3] A family's economic resources could be measured by household income. However, after completing their compulsory education (older than 14), children working to contribute to the household income and continuing schooling are two incompatible options. This is because in Hong Kong, men are the major bread earners for families, and females' labour market participation rate is lower than 60 per cent (Lui 1997).

influences on children's educational achievement and their changes over time.

Typically, family backgrounds when the respondent was at age 14 are employed to address the intergenerational transfer in educational attainment. Because this paper analyzes school-age children between 6 and 19, using their current family backgrounds would not lead to much bias.

In the following analysis, I employ only father's current monthly income from employment to directly measure a family's economic resources, father's current occupation to measure family social resources and parents' education to measure cultural resources available for children's education. Father's income is a continuous variable and I use its logarithm in the multivariate analysis. Father's occupation is coded into 5 categories: "manager/administrator," "professional," "self-employed" "non-manual worker," "manual worker." Both father's education and the mother's education are continuous variables measured by years of schooling they had completed.

The available resources are distributed among children in a family. Scholars have demonstrated that the number of siblings has a negative impact on educational attainment in western societies (e.g., Mare and Chen 1986), probably because economic resources and parents' attention are divided among all of the children (but see Post 1998). The number of siblings is treated as a continuous variable in the models.

As Figure 2 shows, educational inequalities in Hong Kong between men and women have been greatly reduced. Gender is included as a control variable and coded as a dummy variable (male=1) in the analysis.

Given the restricted age range of the sample, it is impossible to conduct linear regression analysis on years of schooling completed. Instead, I examine the determination of full-time school enrolment for school-age children. Based on the school attendance status, I create a dummy to indicate full-time enrolment (yes=1).

Table 2 present the descriptive statistics of the variables to be included in the analysis from 1981 to 2001. Noticeably, within the two decades, the overall enrolment rate increased from 77.5 percent in 1981 to 90.8 percent in 2001, mostly due to the rising enrolments in higher levels of school. The father's mean monthly income almost doubled, increasing from HK$7,669 in 1991 to HK$19,559 in 2001 (adjusted by prices in 2000). In 1981, 8.6 percent of fathers had no occupation, most of whom were presumably unemployed; in 2001, 13.9 percent had no occupation.

Table 2: Descriptive Statistics of School-Age Children (6–19) in Hong Kong

| | 1981 | 1986 | 1991 | 1996 | 2001 |
|---|---|---|---|---|---|
| Full-time school enrolment | 0.775 | 0.830 | 0.871 | 0.893 | 0.908 |
| Age | 13.03 | 12.76 | 12.53 | 12.63 | 12.73 |
| | (4.05) | (4.038) | (4.002) | (3.959) | (4.001) |
| Sex (male=1) | 0.517 | 0.523 | 0.520 | 0.516 | 0.520 |
| Father's total monthly income | 7669.0 | 9396.5 | 11008.2 | 13646.9 | 19558.9 |
| (2000 HK$) | (11564.2) | (13165.4) | (10562.5) | (17373.0) | (21994.7) |
| Father's monthly income | 8.666 | 8.906 | 9.135 | 9.325 | 9.579 |
| (logged) | (0.667) | (0.725) | (0.668) | (0.702) | (0.729) |
| Father occupation: | | | | | |
| Manager | 0.033 | 0.047 | 0.109 | 0.142 | 0.123 |
| Professional | 0.030 | 0.046 | 0.074 | 0.079 | 0.097 |
| Self-employed | 0.137 | 0.119 | 0.091 | 0.074 | 0.068 |
| Non-manual workers | 0.260 | 0.275 | 0.141 | 0.157 | 0.148 |
| Manual workers | 0.454 | 0.369 | 0.499 | 0.463 | 0.426 |
| No occupation (unemployed) | 0.086 | 0.145 | 0.087 | 0.087 | 0.139 |
| Father's schooling (years) | 6.257 | 7.343 | 7.894 | 8.379 | 8.587 |
| | (4.065) | (4.147) | (3.880) | (3.857) | (3.960) |
| Mother's schooling (years) | 4.366 | 5.777 | 6.767 | 7.524 | 8.114 |
| | (4.063) | (4.097) | (3.800) | (3.777) | (3.841) |
| Number of siblings | 2.509 | 2.019 | 1.610 | 1.383 | 1.206 |
| | (1.793) | (1.435) | (1.167) | (1.009) | (0.919) |
| Number of cases used analysis | 8801 | 8920 | 43780 | 45890 | 43881 |
| Total # of sample | 12843 | 12042 | 57482 | 57250 | 59565 |

Both father's and mother's mean years of schooling increased over the two decades. Father's schooling increased by 2.33 years, from 6.3 years in 1981 to 8.6 years in 2001. Mother's schooling increased even more, by 3.7 years, from 4.4 years in 1981 to 8.1 years in 2001. This change clearly reflects the expansion of education in Hong Kong since the 1970s, particularly for women. As a result of a decline in fertility, the average sibling number decreased from 2.5 in 1981 to 1.2 in 2001.

### *Methods*

The statistical analysis here is in three parts. First, I examine the effects of family backgrounds on school enrolments. Since children aged 14 or below reached almost full enrolment in school (see Figure 3), as stipulated by the compulsory education laws, I focus the analysis of children between 15 and 19 only.

Second, I model school attainment as a series of transitions to secondary 4 given the completion of secondary 3, to secondary 6 given the completion of secondary 5, and to university to given the completion of secondary 7 (Mare 1980). Given the full enrolment in compulsory education, I omit the analysis of the transition to secondary 1 given the completion of primary 6, as almost everyone makes this transition. Finally, I examine the probability of having some university education (attending university or completed university education) for people of the subsequent cohort (aged between 20 and 24). I compare the coefficients for a specific cohort from 1981 to 2001 rather than coefficients across cohorts in a specific year, to address the temporal changes.

Binary logit models are employed in the analyses. In the school enrolment model, the dependent variable is the probability of being enrolled as full-time students; in each of the school transition models, the dependent variable is the probability of success in the transition from a particular level of education, given the completion of the previous level (Mare 1980). The logits transformed from the probability are linearly determined by the family background variables, including the father's income, occupation, and education, and the mother's education, as well as the number of siblings and the respondent's gender.

Because the data analyzed are from household samples, two problems arise. First, individuals in households of different sizes have unequal probability of being included in the analysis: those from large households are more likely to be in the selected samples. I created a weight variable, which equals the inverse of the household size, to remedy the problem. Second, siblings from the same households in the samples could cause clustering problems; thus, an adjustment of standard errors is needed in the logistic regression analysis. All the models reported were estimated using Stata 9.0, with robust standard errors corrected for clustering effects (Stata Corporation. 2001).

## *Results*

### *The Effects of Family Resources on School Enrolment*

Table 3 presents the estimated coefficients for the logistic regression predicting full-time school enrolment for children aged between 15 and 19 on selected variables from 1981 to 2001. Results show that a family's economic resources, measured by the father's monthly earnings, are a significant predictor of school enrolments for children in all years. For every 10 percent increase in the father's monthly income, the children's net odds of being enrolled in school increase by 2.9 percent ($=10*[e^{0.302}-1]/100*[e-1]$) in 1981, 3.1 percent in 1986, 3.0 percent in

1991, 2.8 percent in 1996, and 2.6 percent in 2001, holding constant of other factors. Such an effect is highly significant ($p<.001$).

After controlling for the father's income, the father's occupation seems to have little effect on school enrolment. Except for manual workers in 1991 and 2001 and the self-employed in 1981, neither professionals nor non-manual workers differ from administrators/managers in the likelihood of their children's school enrolment. Statistical tests suggest that the joint effect of occupation dummies is significant only in 2001, dominated by the difference between manual workers and administrators/managers. The evidence suggests that the effect of the father's occupation on the likelihood of being enrolled in school for children aged between 15 and 19 is largely due to the economic resources that their families can afford to expend on for their continuation in school (without income in the equation, the effect of the father's occupation is statistically significant). On the other hand, the significant difference in the odds of being enrolled in school between an administrator's/manager's child and a manual worker's child in 2001 suggests that the determination of school enrolment goes beyond the economic resources of the family. Non-economic factors associated with father's occupation begin to play an independent and important role in 2001.

In the presence of the father's income and occupation, we identify parents' education levels as a proxy for a family's cultural capital. As the models show, both father's and mother's education (years of schooling) positively affect the children's likelihood of enrolment, and the effects are statistically significant (except for 1981). Other things being equal, an additional year of father's schooling increases the odds of enrolment in school by 1.8 percent ($e^{0.018}-1$) in 1981, 7.4 percent ($e^{0.071}-1$) in 1986, 4.0 percent ($e^{0.039}-1$) in 1991, and 4.2 percent ($e^{0.041}-1$) in 1996, and 5.7 percent ($e^{0.041}-1$) in 2001. Similarly, a year increase in mother's schooling leads to an increase of the odds of school enrolment by 5.0 percent ($e^{0.049}-1$) in 1981, 8.5 percent ($e^{0.082}-1$) in 1986, 7.5 percent ($e^{0.072}-1$) in 1991, 6.0 percent ($e^{0.058}-1$) in 1996, and 7.8 ($e^{0.075}-1$) in 2001. These results suggest that a family's cultural capital, particularly embodied in the mother's education level, is an important factor in addition to the family's economic background in determining their children's school enrolment.

In regard to the effects of family size and the gender of the children, the more siblings a child has, the less likely he or she is enrolled in school; and boys are less likely to be enrolled in school than girls after

Table 3: Logistic Models Predicting Full-time School Enrolment (aged 15–19), Hong Kong

| | 1981 | 1986 | 1991 | 1996 | 2001 |
|---|---|---|---|---|---|
| Father's income (logged) | 0.302*** | 0.370*** | 0.352*** | 0.266*** | 0.204*** |
| | (0.073) | (0.084) | (0.043) | (0.036) | (0.039) |
| Father's occupation [a] | | | | | |
| Professional | −0.340 | 0.033 | −0.011 | −0.047 | 0.211 |
| | (0.392) | (0.399) | (0.123) | (0.108) | (0.128) |
| Self-employed | −0.674* | −0.087 | −0.058 | −0.071 | −0.110 |
| | (0.330) | (0.307) | (0.101) | (0.092) | (0.111) |
| Non-manual | −0.135 | −0.276 | −0.088 | −0.109 | −0.183 |
| | (0.323) | (0.291) | (0.091) | (0.078) | (0.095) |
| Manual | −0.556 | −0.184 | −0.171* | −0.131 | −0.288*** |
| | (0.320) | (0.294) | (0.084) | (0.071) | (0.089) |
| Father's schooling | 0.018 | 0.071*** | 0.039*** | 0.041*** | 0.055*** |
| | (0.014) | (0.016) | (0.007) | (0.007) | (0.007) |
| Mother's schooling | 0.049*** | 0.082*** | 0.072*** | 0.058*** | 0.075*** |
| | (0.014) | (0.016) | (0.008) | (0.007) | (0.007) |
| male | −0.026 | −0.078 | −0.299*** | −0.307*** | −0.308*** |
| | (0.074) | (0.087) | (0.039) | (0.038) | (0.041) |
| No. of sibling | 0.009 | 0.009 | −0.022 | −0.087*** | −0.060* |
| | (0.024) | (0.031) | (0.018) | (0.019) | (0.023) |
| Constant | −1.880** | −2.907*** | −2.571*** | −1.613*** | −1.089** |
| | (0.680) | (0.764) | (0.405) | (0.358) | (0.395) |
| Pseudo R-square | 0.032 | 0.073 | 0.051 | 0.038 | 0.055 |
| Observations | 3227 | 2696 | 13598 | 15170 | 15389 |

Notes: a. Administrators/managers as reference group; Robust standard errors in parentheses; *** p<.001 ** p<.01 * p<.05 (two-tailed tests).

age 14. The gender difference has been statistically significant since 1991, whereas the effect of family size has been significant since 1996. For example, an additional brother or sister decreased the net odds of a child's school enrolment by 9.1 percent ($e^{-0.087}-1$) in 1996 and by 6.2 percent ($e^{-0.060}-1$) in 2001 ($p<.001$). This is because the more children a family has, the less resources (including economic, social and cultural) it can spend on each child. However, this does not mean that girls are always sacrificed, as one would typically expect in a Chinese society. Indeed, girls enjoy a clear advantage over boys in school enrolment: the net odds of boys' school enrolment were only 74.2 percent ($e^{-0.299}$) in 1991, 73.6 percent ($e^{-0.307}$) in 1996, and 73.5 percent ($e^{-0.307}$) in 2001, of those for girls. Figure 3 demonstrated a trend of narrowing the gender gap in educational attainment, and here girls seem to have surpassed boys in educational attainment among the young cohort. It seems that this reversed trend will continue, and women advantages over men in educational attainment are expected to increase in the future.

Table 4a: Logistic Model Predicting Transition to Secondary 4 Given Completion of Secondary 3

| | 1981 | 1986 | 1991 | 1996 | 2001 |
|---|---|---|---|---|---|
| Father's income (logged) | 0.592*** | 0.427*** | 0.411*** | 0.321*** | 0.402*** |
| | (0.168) | (0.140) | (0.075) | (0.076) | (0.079) |
| Father's occupation [a] | | | | | |
| Professional | — | −0.817 | 0.331 | 0.053 | 0.062 |
| | — | (1.223) | (0.306) | (0.265) | (0.268) |
| Self-employed | −16.32*** | −1.237 | −0.003 | 0.048 | 0.508* |
| | (1.219) | (1.056) | (0.207) | (0.202) | (0.249) |
| Non-manual | −15.93*** | −1.548 | −0.269 | −0.295 | 0.126 |
| | (1.263) | (1.037) | (0.191) | (0.168) | (0.209) |
| Manual | −16.29*** | −1.428 | −0.272 | −0.301* | 0.018 |
| | (1.266) | (1.039) | (0.179) | (0.152) | (0.195) |
| Father's schooling | 0.029 | 0.055* | 0.062*** | 0.063*** | 0.065*** |
| | (0.035) | (0.028) | (0.014) | (0.015) | (0.014) |
| Mother's schooling | 0.026 | 0.094** | 0.065*** | 0.085*** | 0.088*** |
| | (0.037) | (0.029) | (0.014) | (0.014) | (0.014) |
| male | −0.621*** | −0.454** | −0.842*** | −1.030*** | −0.813*** |
| | (0.219) | (0.163) | (0.077) | (0.082) | (0.089) |
| No. of sibling | −0.042 | 0.069 | −0.095** | −0.095* | −0.153** |
| | (0.068) | (0.057) | (0.035) | (0.040) | (0.049) |
| Constant | 14.77 | −0.541 | −1.021 | −0.184 | −1.088 |
| | (0.000) | (1.638) | (0.720) | (0.746) | (0.813) |
| Pseudo R-square | 0.050 | 0.071 | 0.074 | 0.0782 | 0.0710 |
| Observations | 1666 | 1948 | 10622 | 12701 | 13445 |

Notes: a. Administrators/managers as reference group; Robust standard errors in parentheses; *** p<.001 ** p<.01 * p<.05 (two-tailed tests).

### *The Effects of Family Resources on School Transitions*

The effects of family resources on school enrolment may differ by school levels. In this section, I turn to analyzing school transitions beyond the compulsory years of education, namely, the transition to secondary 4 given the completion of secondary 3; the transition to secondary 6 given the completion of secondary 5; and the transition to college given the completion of secondary 7, which are determined by a set of variables that measure family resource used in the previous analysis. Table 4a presents the estimated coefficients for a logistic regression on the school transition to secondary 4 given the completion of secondary 3, separated by years of censuses and by-censuses.

The patterns are largely similar to what has been observed for school enrolment. The father's income is a consistent predictor of the transition to secondary 4 after the completion of the compulsory lower secondary education. The father's occupation does not have a significant effect on the transition, except in 1981, in which the coefficients of self-employed, non-manual and manuals workers are inflated because only a few children of administrators/managers did not go to secondary 4, and essentially all children of professionals continued in school after secondary 4. Both the father's and mother's education levels have significant effect on the likelihood of continuing education beyond the lower secondary level. A 10 percent increase in the father's income increases the net odds of the transition by about 4.7 percent ($10*[e^{0.592}-1)/100*[e-1]$) in 1981, by 3.1 percent ($10*[e^{0.427}-1)/100*[e-1]$) in 1986, by 3.0 percent ($10*[e^{0.411}-1)/100*[e-1]$) in 1991, by 2.2 percent ($10*[e^{0.321}-1)/100*[e-1]$) in 1996, and by 2.9 percent ($10*[e^{0.411}-1)/100*[e-1]$) in 2001 ($p<.001$). Other things being equal, a year's increase in the father's schooling brings about an increase in the odds of the transition to secondary 4 after completing secondary 3 by 2.9 percent ($e^{0.029}-1$) in 1981, 5.7 percent ($e^{0.055}-1$) in 1986, 6.4 percent ($e^{0.062}-1$) in 1991, 6.5 percent ($e^{0.063}-1$) in 1996, and 6.7 percent ($e^{0.065}-1$) in 2001. Similarly, a year's increase in the mother's schooling brings about an increase in the odds of the transition to secondary 4 after completing secondary 3 by 2.6 percent ($e^{0.026}-1$) in 1981 (though statistically significant), 9.9 percent ($e^{0.094}-1$) in 1986, 6.7 percent ($e^{0.065}-1$) in 1991, 8.9 percent ($e^{0.085}-1$) in 1996, and 9.2 percent ($e^{0.088}-1$) in 2001. The effects of both parents' schooling are statistically significant in all years except for 1981.

Gender differences in the transition rate at this level persist, and boys are disadvantaged compared to girls. The effect of family size became statistically significant in 1991. Hence, while the expansion of the educational system does alleviate the effect of family background on education at the compulsory levels (saturated, see Figure 3), social selection starts playing an important role beyond the lower secondary level. This pattern becomes even clearer in the subsequent school transitions in recent years.

Table 4b presents the estimated coefficients for the logistic regression on the school transition to secondary 6 given the completion of secondary 5 from 1981 to 2001. In 1981, none of the factors had significant effects on the transition at this level except for gender. Boys regain an advantage over girls in the transition to secondary 6 on the academic track for university education in 1981—their odds are more than twice ($e^{0.709}-1$) those for girls ($p<.001$). This significant advantage lasted until 1991, after which the gender gap in the transition to secondary 6 was reversed: boys lost the advantage, and their net odds of transition were

Table 4b: Transition to Secondary 6 Given the Completion of Secondary 5

| | 1981 | 1986 | 1991 | 1996 | 2001 |
|---|---|---|---|---|---|
| Father's income (logged) | 0.233 | 0.235 | 0.323*** | 0.231*** | 0.134** |
| | (0.169) | (0.165) | (0.071) | (0.061) | (0.052) |
| Father's occupation[a] | | | | | |
| Professional | –0.804 | 1.141 | –0.155 | –0.026 | 0.245* |
| | (0.759) | (0.785) | (0.193) | (0.159) | (0.147) |
| Self-employed | –0.743 | –0.332 | –0.280 | –0.031 | –0.013 |
| | (0.669) | (0.566) | (0.170) | (0.147) | (0.139) |
| Non-manual | –1.162 | –0.542 | –0.072 | –0.046 | –0.235* |
| | (0.651) | (0.536) | (0.157) | (0.116) | (0.118) |
| Manual | –1.083 | –0.350 | –0.303* | –0.149 | –0.297** |
| | (0.653) | (0.539) | (0.144) | (0.108) | (0.110) |
| Father's schooling | 0.008 | 0.089** | 0.028* | 0.042*** | 0.045*** |
| | (0.033) | (0.032) | (0.013) | (0.011) | (0.010) |
| Mother's schooling | 0.053 | 0.024 | 0.046*** | 0.051*** | 0.055*** |
| | (0.032) | (0.033) | (0.013) | (0.011) | (0.010) |
| Male | 0.709*** | 0.333* | 0.430*** | –0.205*** | –0.292*** |
| | (0.178) | (0.170) | (0.073) | (0.062) | (0.057) |
| No. of sibling | –0.038 | –0.111* | –0.053 | –0.129*** | –0.093** |
| | (0.060) | (0.065) | (0.032) | (0.033) | (0.034) |
| Constant | –1.153 | –1.474 | –2.649*** | –1.721** | –0.801 |
| | (1.562) | (1.482) | (0.670) | (0.604) | (0.535) |
| Pseudo R-square | 0.054 | 0.079 | 0.046 | 0.038 | 0.045 |
| Observations | 561 | 645 | 3559 | 4962 | 6216 |

Notes: a. Administrators/managers as reference group; Robust standard errors in parentheses; *** p<.001 ** p<.01 * p<.05 (two-tailed tests).

only 81.4 percent ($e^{-0.205}$) of girls' odds in 1996 and 74.7 percent ($e^{-0.205}$) in 2001 (p<.001).

Family economic resources started to play a significant role since 1991. The father's income is still a strong predictor of success in the transition to secondary 6: every 10 percent increase in the father's income will bring an increase in the odds of making the transition by 2.2 percent ((10*[$e^{0.323}$–1)/100*[e–1]) in 1991, 1.5 percent ((10*[$e^{0.231}$–1)/100*[e–1]) in 1996, and 0.8 percent 2.2 percent ((10*[$e^{0.134}$–1)/100*[e–1]) in 2001. The effect is highly significant (p<.001) for all three years.

Although the magnitude of the coefficient for the father's income declined from 1991 to 2001, the father's occupation became a significant factor in determining success in the transition in 2001. Children of both non-manual and manual workers faced significant disadvantages in the transition to secondary 6, compared to children of administrators/managers. Their respective odds of making the transition were only 79.1 percent ($e^{-0.2235}$) and 74.3 percent ($e^{-0.297}$) of the odds for administrators'/managers' children. On the other hand, the children of professionals indeed were more likely than the children of administrators/managers to make such a transition ($p<.05$). As proceeding to secondary 6 clearly leads to the academic track, it is understandable that professionals' children are more likely to succeed. A family's cultural resources indicated by father's and mother years of schooling are significant predictors of the transition, especially in 2001.

The divergent patterns become even more evident in the transition to university given the completion of secondary 7. Table 4c presents the estimated coefficients for the logistic regression on the transition to university from 1981 to 2001. Results show that family economic resources have no significant effect on the entry into university from 1981 to 1996, but the effect becomes significant in 2001. Every 10 percent increase in the father's income leads to 3.3 percent ($10*[e^{0.446}-1)/100*[e-1]$) increase in the net odds of entry into university for those who have completed secondary 7 ($p<.001$). Meanwhile, the father's occupation also makes a great difference in determining the children's entry into university in 2001 (as well as in 1991). For example, other things being equal, manual workers' children's odds of entry into university are only 43.3 percent ($e^{-0.838}$) of those of administrators'/manager's children ($p<.01$). In addition, the mother's education and gender are significant determinants of entry into college.

Comparing the coefficients across transition models reveals an even more interesting shift in the patterns of school transitions from 1981 to 2001. Beyond compulsory education, while the effects of family background—the father's income and occupation—decline in the progression to higher levels of schooling in the 1980s, they indeed increased in the 1990s, especially in 2001.

In 1981, the coefficient of the father's income declined from 0.592 for the transition to secondary 4, to 0.233 for the transition to secondary 6, and then to −0.821 for the transition to university; and the last two are insignificant. Similar patterns hold for 1986, 1991, and 1996. In 2001, however, the coefficient of the father's income declined from 0.402 for the transition to secondary 4, to 0.134 for the transition to secondary 6, but it bounced back to an even higher level of 0.446 for the transition to university. The effect on all the three levels of transition is statistically significant ($p<.001$).

Most previous studies of school transitions have demonstrated that severe social selection tends to occur at lower levels, and social back-

Table 4c: Transition to College Given Completion of Secondary 6/7

| | 1981 | 1986 | 1991 | 1996 | 2001 |
|---|---|---|---|---|---|
| Father's income (logged) | −0.821 | 1.039 | 0.237 | 0.128 | 0.446*** |
| | (0.650) | (0.613) | (0.180) | (0.135) | (0.133) |
| Father's occupation [a] | | | | | |
| Professional | −0.877 | — | −0.566 | −0.378 | −0.174 |
| | (1.944) | — | (0.370) | (0.294) | (0.301) |
| Self-employed | — | −1.128 | −0.543 | 0.063 | −0.422 |
| | — | (1.447) | (0.395) | (0.311) | (0.362) |
| Non-manual | −1.427 | −0.434 | −0.950** | −0.395 | −0.493 |
| | (2.053) | (0.752) | (0.360) | (0.246) | (0.292) |
| Manual | −1.648 | −1.577 | −0.701* | −0.339 | −0.838** |
| | (1.975) | (0.935) | (0.297) | (0.236) | (0.275) |
| Father's schooling | 0.068 | −0.106 | 0.026 | 0.063* | 0.036 |
| | (0.208) | (0.120) | (0.036) | (0.025) | (0.029) |
| Mother's schooling | 0.075 | 0.125 | −0.001 | 0.024 | 0.084** |
| | (0.261) | (0.112) | (0.037) | (0.024) | (0.029) |
| male | 0.041 | 0.811 | −0.037 | −0.189 | −0.430** |
| | (0.883) | (0.698) | (0.187) | (0.140) | (0.161) |
| No. of sibling | −0.143 | −0.084 | −0.181 | −0.132 | 0.159 |
| | (0.342) | (0.496) | (0.101) | (0.076) | (0.092) |
| Constant | 4.651 | −10.46* | −3.210 | −2.384 | −5.000*** |
| | (6.745) | (4.782) | (1.752) | (1.384) | (1.334) |
| Pseudo R-square | 0.071 | 0.163 | 0.038 | 0.035 | 0.130 |
| Observations | 100 | 152 | 1135 | 1187 | 769 |

Notes: a. Administrators/managers as reference group; Robust standard errors in parentheses; *** p<.001 ** p<.01 * p<.05 (two-tailed tests).

grounds matter less in the progression to higher levels of school (e.g., Mare 1980; Shavit and Blossfeld 1994). Scholars have proposed two explanations for this. The life course thesis argues that, as children get older and advance to higher levels, they become more independent in deciding on what they want and parental resources become less important. The differential selection thesis posits that severe selection barriers tend to occur in early stages of the transition, and only those brightest children from disadvantaged backgrounds can make to the higher levels. Consequently, it is scholastic aptitude and other unobserved characteristics of students (e.g., motivation) that determine educational success in higher levels (Shavit and Blossfeld 1994). Hong Kong's situation most of the time fits this pattern quite well. However, the pattern in 2001 shifts to a new one, which is certainly at odds with the common pattern of how family backgrounds affect educational transitions at different levels. Family resources, particularly economic resources, become even more important in the progression to higher levels of education, particularly to university, in the era of rapid expansion of higher education but also worsening income inequalities.

*The Effects of Family Resources on Receiving University Education*

The above analysis is restricted to those aged between 15 and 19 across 20 years. In the final analysis, I analyze the attainment of university education for the successive cohort, most of whom still live with their parents so that the information on the family backgrounds can be obtained. I define the dependent variable as whether one is either studying in university (in Hong Kong the university completion rate is high, which means that he or she is expected to have a university education), or has completed university education. It is coded as a dummy (yes=1). Table 5 presents the estimated coefficients for the logistic regression on the same set of variables examined previously, which shed light on how family resources affect attainment of university education over time from another perspective.

Table 5: Logistic Models Predicting Entering College (Aged 20–24)

| | 1981 | 1986 | 1991 | 1996 | 2001 |
|---|---|---|---|---|---|
| Father's income (logged) | 0.905*** | 0.762*** | 0.398*** | 0.458*** | 0.373*** |
| | (0.204) | (0.163) | (0.070) | (0.074) | (0.045) |
| Father's occupation [a] | | | | | |
| Professional | 0.139 | −0.870 | 0.171 | −0.257 | −0.041 |
| | (0.857) | (0.535) | (0.146) | (0.141) | (0.099) |
| Self-employed | −0.847 | −1.118* | −0.049 | −0.577** | −0.324** |
| | (0.942) | (0.567) | (0.162) | (0.216) | (0.111) |
| Non-manual | 0.345 | −0.919* | −0.327* | −0.476** | −0.332*** |
| | (0.721) | (0.418) | (0.155) | (0.154) | (0.092) |
| Manual | −0.133 | −1.409** | −0.296* | −0.886** | −0.515*** |
| | (0.800) | (0.420) | (0.136) | (0.146) | (0.086) |
| Father's schooling | 0.088 | 0.024 | 0.039** | 0.033 | 0.075*** |
| | (0.063) | (0.043) | (0.014) | (0.018) | (0.009) |
| Mother's schooling | 0.046 | 0.029 | 0.051*** | 0.091*** | 0.079*** |
| | (0.047) | (0.046) | (0.013) | (0.017) | (0.008) |
| male | 0.235 | 0.289 | 0.067 | 0.031 | −0.166*** |
| | (0.286) | (0.240) | (0.078) | (0.092) | (0.046) |
| No. of sibling | −0.050 | −0.054 | −0.088** | −0.251*** | −0.142*** |
| | (0.081) | (0.075) | (0.034) | (0.056) | (0.028) |
| Constant | −11.45*** | −8.860*** | −6.096*** | −7.296*** | −4.964*** |
| | (1.999) | (1.634) | (0.673) | (0.747) | (0.451) |
| Pseudo R-square | 0.119 | 0.124 | 0.070 | 0.137 | 0.106 |
| Observations | 2134 | 2135 | 9097 | 11399 | 11038 |

Notes: a. Administrators/managers as reference group; Robust standard errors in parentheses; *** p<.001 ** p<.01 * p<.05 (two-tailed tests).

As the model shows, a family's economic resources are consistently important and significant in predicting attainment of university education, although the magnitude seems to decline from 1981 to 2002. For example, every 10 percent increase in the father's income will improve the net odds of having a university education by 8.5 percent ($10*[e^{0.905}-1)/100*[e-1]$) in 1981, 6.7 percent ($10*[e^{0.762}-1)/100*[e-1]$) in 1986, 2.8 percent ($10*[e^{0.398}-1)/100*[e-1]$) in 1991, 3.4 percent ($10*[e^{0.458}-1)/100*[e-1]$) in 1996, and 2.6 percent ($10*[e^{0.373}-1)/100*[e-1]$) in 2001.

Despite the decline in the effect of a family's economic resources, a family's social and cultural resources seem to become more important. For example, the father's occupation and the parents' education levels have significant effects, independent of family economic resources, on university education attainment. In particular, the great divide is between the administrative or professional elite and the rest. Both father's and the mother's level of schooling also play a significant role in the 1990s. Looking at the equations from 1981 to 2001, it seems that the family resources that determine a university education become more diverse for this specific age group.

### *Summary and Conclusion*

Based on analyses of sample data from censuses in 1981, 1991 and 2001 and by-censuses in 1986 and 1996, this paper examines the trends in the effects of family resources on educational outcomes in Hong Kong, focusing on the effects of economic, social and cultural resources on school enrolments and transitions for children aged 6–19. As summarized in Table 6, results show that, over the two decades, the effect of the father's income on full-time enrolment has declined but the effect of the father's occupation has increased to some extent. As to school transitions, the effects of the father's income and occupation both decline in the transitions to higher levels of education beyond the compulsory level from 1981 to 1996, but become even more important in the progression to higher levels of education, particularly to university, in 2001.

The case of Hong Kong defies the general pattern of educational stratification previously found in many industrialized economies in three ways. First, while results of the linear regression show a decline in the effect of all family backgrounds on educational attainment in those countries, the effect of family resources on student enrolment has

Table 6: Summary of Findings from Regression Models

| | Age 15–19 | | | | Age 20–24 |
|---|---|---|---|---|---|
| | School Enrolment | Transition to Secondary 4 | Transition to Secondary 6 | Transition to University | University Education Attainment |
| Economic resource (father's income) | + + + + + | + + + + + | o o + + + | o o o o + | + + + + + |
| Social resource (father's occupation) | o o o o + | + o o o o | o o o o + | o o o o + | o o + + + |
| Cultural resource (father's education) | o + + + + | o + + + + | o + + + + | o o o + o | o o + + + |
| Cultural resource (mother's education) | + + + + + | o + + + + | o o + + + | o o o o + | o o + + + |

o statistically insignificant
+ statistically significant
Each symbol stands for one year, from left to right, 1981, 1986, 1991, 1996, and 2001

indeed increased in Hong Kong in the past two decades. Second, while the logit effects of family backgrounds on educational attainment are found constant elsewhere, the effects of the father's occupation on the likelihoods of transition to secondary 6 and to university are greater in 2001 than in previous years, and so is the effect of the father's monthly income on the likelihood of a transition to university. Third, while the effect of family backgrounds decline across the level of school transition in many countries as well as in Hong Kong before the mid-1990s, such an effect is strengthened rather than weakened in the transition to school beyond the compulsory level in 2001.

The pattern of educational stratification in Hong Kong also echoes some findings from other countries. For instance, Smith and Cheung (1986) reported that, in the Philippines, although the effects of the father's education on the educational transition declined over the stages of transitions, the effect of the fathers' occupation is among the highest for the transition to tertiary education and lowest for the transition to primary school. Gerber and Hout (1995) demonstrated that the effect of social origin on entering university in Soviet-era Russia increased after 1965, since higher education failed to keep pace with the rapid expansion of secondary education. The case of Hong Kong offers another case supporting the thesis of "maximally maintained inequality" (Raftery and Hout 1993), which argues that inequality in educational opportunity is maximally maintained, namely, in modern societies, the effect of social origin at all levels of education does not change, except when the enrolment of the advantaged groups is already so high at a given level, that further expansion is only feasible by increasing the opportunity of disadvantaged groups to make the transitions.

The implications of the findings in this paper may go beyond the thesis of maximally maintained inequality. While the thesis predicts that educational expansion does not lead to better chances for disadvantaged groups to make the transition and will not change the association between family backgrounds and the given level of school transitions, my analysis has demonstrated that the effects of family backgrounds have increased (rather than remained constant and decreased conditionally), and educational opportunities for the disadvantaged groups were reduced in 2001.

As the late Dudley Duncan (1968) once argued, to study social change, one has to distinguish between change that occurs owing to change in the distribution of variables and structural change—change in the fundamental social process underlying the associations among variables. To seek a better understanding of this pattern of educational stratification found in Hong Kong, I point to the change in broader socioeconomic contexts, particularly the increasing income inequalities in the 1990s. While there is no direct evidence showing that the observed change in educational stratification was caused by increasing income inequalities, given the existing strong impact of the father's income in children's educational opportunities, the enlarged gap between rich and poor in the 1990s would certainly bring about more educational inequalities. One can reasonably foresee that the rising educational inequality among students of different socioeconomic backgrounds in the 1990s could lead to increasing earnings inequality after they complete their education and enter the labour market. In the long run, intergenerational transmission is enhanced; the role of education as an important channel for socioeconomic mobility is weakened. The society may become increasingly polarized as a result.

## *References*

Blau, Peter and Otis Dudley Duncan. (1967). *American Occupational Structure.* New York: Academic Press

Boudier, Pierre. (1986). "The Form of Capital." Pp. 241–58 in *Handbook of Theory and Research for the Sociology of Education*, edited by John G. Richardson. New York: Greenwood.

Boudon, Raymond. (1974). *Education, Opportunities and Social Inequality*. New York: Wiley.

Chan, Tak Wing, Tai Lok Lui and Thomas W. P. Wong. (1995). "A Comparative Analysis of Social Mobility in Hong Kong." *European Sociological Review* 11:135–55.
Census and Statistics Department of the Hong Kong Government. (1992). *1991 Population Census Main Report.* Hong Kong, Government Printer.
—— (2002). *Population Census 2001 Main Report: Volume 1.* Hong Kong, Printing Department.
Chow, C. Steven and Gustav F. Papanek. (1981) "Laissez-Faire, Growth and Equity—Hong Kong." *The Economic Journal* 91:466–85.
Coleman, James S. (1988). "Social Capital in the Creation Human Capital." *American Journal of Sociology* 94 (suppl.): S 95–S120.
De Graaf, Paul M. (1986). "The Impact of Financial and Cultural Resources on Educational Attainment in the Netherlands." *Sociology of Education* 59:237–46
DiMaggio, Paul. (1982). "Cultural Capital and School Success: The Impact of Status Cultural Participation on the Grades of U.S. High School Students." *American Sociological Review* 47:189–201
Duncan, Otis Dudley. (1968). "Social Stratification and Mobility: Problems in the Measurement of Trend." Pp 675–719 in *Indicators of Social Change: Concept and Measurements*, edited by Eleanor Bernert Sheldon and Wilbert E. Moore. New York: NY, Russell Sage Foundation.
Ishida, Hiroshi, Walter Muller, and John M. Ridge. (1995). "Class Origin, Class Destination, and Education: a Cross-National Study of Ten Industrial Nations." *American Journal of Sociology* 101:145–93.
Featherman, David L., and Robert M. Hauser. (1978). *Opportunity and Change.* New York: Academic Press.
Friedman, Milton. (1982). *Capitalism and Freedom.* Chicago: University of Chicago Press.
Hong Kong University Grants Committee. (1996). *Higher Education in Hong Kong.* Hong Kong, Government Printer.
Kuznets, Simon. (1955). "Economic Growth and Income Inequality." *American Economic Review* 45:1–28.
Lam, David A, and Deborah Levison. (1992). "Declining Inequality in Schooling in Brazil and Its Effects on Inequality in Earnings." *Journal of Developmental Economics*, 37: 199–225.
Lin, Nan. (1982). "Social Resources and Instrumental Action." Pp. 131–45 in *Social Structure and Network Analysis*, edited by Peter Marsden and Nan Lin. Beverly Hills, CA: Sage.
Lin, Nan. (1990). "Social Resources and Social Mobility: a Structural Theory of Status Attainment." Pp. 247–71 in *Social Mobility and Social Structure*, edited by Ronald L. Breiger. Cambridge, England: Cambridge University Press.
Lui Hon-Kwong. (1997). *Income Inequality and Economic Development.* City University of Hong Kong Press.
Mare, D. Robert. (1980). "Social Backgrounds and Educational Continuation Decisions." *Journal of the American Statistical Association.* 75:295–305.
Mare, Robert D., and M. D. Chen. (1986). "Further Evidence on Number of Siblings and Educational Stratification." *American Sociological Review* 51: 403–412.
Post, David. (1994). "Educational Stratification, School Expansion, and Public Policy in Hong Kong." *Sociology of Education* 67:121–138.
——, (2003). "Hong Kong Higher Education, 1981–2001: Public Policy and Re-emergent Social Stratification." *Oxford Review of Education* 29:545–570.
——, (2004). "Family Resources, Gender, and Immigration: Changing Sources of Hong Educational Inequality: 1971–2001." *Social Science Quarterly* 85: 1238–58.
Pong, Suet-ling and David Post. (1991). "Trends in Gender and Family Background Effects on School Attainment: The Case of Hong Kong" *The British Journal of Sociology* 42: 249–271.

——, (1998). "The Waning Effect of Sibship Composition on School Attainment in Hong Kong." *Comparative Education Review* 99–117.
Raftery, Andrian E. and Michael Hout. (1993). "Maximally Maintained Inequality: Expansion, Reform, and Opportunity in Irish Education: 1921–1975." *Sociology of Education* 66:41–62.
Ramirez, Francisco and Marc Ventresca. (1992). "Building the Institution of Mass Schooling: Isomorphism in the Modern World." Pp. 47–61 in *The Political Construction of Education*, edited by Bruce Fuller and Richard Robinson. New York: Praeger.
Shavit, Yossi and Hans-Peter Blossfeld. (1993). *Persistent Inequality.* Boulder, CO.: Westview Press.
Smith, Herbert L., and Paul P. L. Cheung. (1986). "Trends in the Effects of Family Backgrounds on Educational Attainment in the Philippines." *American Journal of Sociology* 91:1387–1408.
Stata Corp. (2001). *Stata Reference Manual: Volume 3*, Stata Corporation. College Station, Texas.
Treiman, Donald. (1970). "Industrialization and Social Stratification." Pp. 207–34 in *Social Stratification: Research and Theory for the 1970s*, edited by Edward Laumann. Indianapolis: Bobbs-Merrill.
Zhao, Xiaobin, Zhang Li and Sit Tak O. Kelvin. (2004)."Income Inequalities under Economic Restructuring in Hong Kong." *Asian Survey* XLIV (3) 442–73.

# THE TRANSNATIONAL LINKAGES OF CHINESE IN TORONTO*

Eric Fong, Cao Xingshan and Chen Wenhong[1]

## *Introduction*

In recent decades, there has been considerable interest among researchers in immigrant adaptation patterns (Alba and Nee 2003; Portes, Guarnizo, and Landolt 1999; Waldinger and Fitzgerald 2004; Zhou 1997). In particular, there has been heated discussion about the applicability of the assimilation perspective to explain recent immigrant adaptation experiences. Many commentators argue that the assimilation perspective was developed at the beginning of the last century to explain the integration patterns of European immigrants in an industrialized society, and that it is now outdated (Levitt, DeWind, and Vertovec 2003; Portes, Guarnizo, and Landolt 1999). Today, a majority of recent immigrants have come from non-European countries to a postindustrial economy. In addition, the increasingly low cost and easy access to information and communication technologies has transformed the ability of immigrants to maintain contacts in their home countries, which may complicate the integration patterns.

In light of these social developments, a growing number of researchers have adopted the transnational perspective to understand the immigrant adaptation process. The transnational perspective recognizes the transnational activities of immigrants (Glick Schiller, Basch, and Szaton-Blanc 1992). It postulates that immigrants maintain frequent and strong connections with the home country as they adapt to the new country (Glick Schiller 1995; Portes 2001; Waldinger and Fitzgerald 2004). While this perspective opens a new avenue for understanding the immigrant adaptation process, it has also generated a wide debate. Critics raise doubts about the applicability and validity of the perspective. Many

---

* Reference to this article should be made as follows: Fong, Eric; Cao, Xingshan and Chen, Wenhong. 2007. "The Transnational Linkages of Chinese in Toronto".

[1] This research was supported by the Social Sciences and Humanities Research Council of Canada. Direct Correspondence to Eric Fong, Department of Sociology, 725 Spadina Avenue, University of Toronto, Ontario, Canada. M5S 2J4.

have questioned the extensity and intensity of immigrants participating in transnational contact (Foner 2001; Kivisto 2001; Portes 2001). They argued that most studies on the transnational contacts of immigrants are based on in-depth case studies (Alba and Nee 2003). Results from these studies may exaggerate the significance of transnational contact among immigrants, and their findings are difficult to generalize.

Some critics also argue that there is nothing new about immigrant transnational contacts (Levitt, DeWind, and Vertovec 2003). There have always been immigrants involved in such activities when they first arrive in the new country. Transnational contact slowly and steadily submerges as immigrants stay and establish themselves in the new country (Alba and Nee 2003). Given that most case studies about transnational activities are based on the experiences of recent immigrants, their findings simply describe the beginning period of the immigrant adaptation process and cannot make further implications regarding integration patterns in the long run.

Facing considerable criticism, researchers using a transnational perspective to study immigrant integration patterns further refined their conceptual and methodological issues. Although there have been more empirical studies, most of them still employ the ethnographic approach of studying a few cases. Therefore the concerns remain unanswered. There have been efforts to collect large scale survey data, but they focus on specific transnational activities, such as entrepreneurial participation (Portes, Haller, and Guarnizo 2002), political activities (Guarnizo 1997), or the second generation (Raijman and Tienda 2000). Surprisingly, there is a lack of basic information about transnational contact among immigrants, due to an absence of large scale survey data. Therefore, there is no systematic evaluation of the transnational contact occurring among immigrants when they first arrive.

Our study fills this important gap in the literature. Drawing from data collected in a recent systematic survey of immigrant adaptation in Toronto, we explore the transnational contact of Chinese, a major recent immigrant group in Canada. Transnational contact here refers to the communication with individuals and information obtained from the home country. It is not about social networks but it can be viewed as the basic activity from where social networks may be emerged. We show that only a small proportion of Chinese immigrants and Canadian born Chinese are involved in intensive and extensive transnational contact. We further demonstrate that immigrants participating in transnational contact are those who have arrived recently and lack local social support. Our findings suggest that transnational contact has not been a widespread practice among immigrants, and that these activities may be just the initial stage of the larger assimilation process.

## *Literature Review*

The emergence of the transnational perspective as an alternative explanation for immigrant integration patterns has generated considerable discussion. As Levitt and Waters (2002b) pointed out, the transnational perspective is a generic term covering a range of topics related to the connection between communities of origin and destination. In our discussion, we focus on the transnational adaptation process, which is confined to "occupations and activities that require regular and sustained social contact over time across national borders for their implementation." (Portes, Guarnizo, and Landolt 1999) Rather than perceiving immigrants as gradually losing their ties to home as they settle in the new country, as suggested by the assimilation perspective, the transnational perspective sees immigrants as simultaneously maintaining contact with the sending community while integrating with the receiving community (Levitt and Schiller 2004). The emphasis on transnational activities redraws and expands the "social field" of the immigrant (Menjivar 2002). Subsequently, this perspective highlights a distinctive mode of transnational adaptation among immigrants.

The maintenance of social connections with the home country is the cornerstone of all transnational activities. Transnational activities, including political and economic, cannot really take place without transnational contact. Given the advancement of information and communication technologies, transnational contact can be made in various ways with easy accessibility and reasonably low cost. Thus, transnational contact, as suggested by the transnational perspective, should be frequent and widespread (Foner 2000).

Since the introduction of the transnational perspective to sociologists, there have been considerable challenges to the notion of frequent widespread transnational contact among immigrants (Alba and Nee 2003; Waldinger and Fitzgerald 2004; Chan 2000; Chan and Ng 2000). The issue is important because if the transnational contacts of most immigrants are rare and infrequent, or only a small proportion of immigrants are actively and regularly involved in transnational contacts, the significance of the perspective to explain immigrant integration is considerably diminished. However, the study of the intensity and extensity of transnational contact can be complicated, because modern technologies allow immigrants to maintain contact through various means. To obtain an accurate picture, comprehensive information on transnational contact through various means is needed.

Most research exploring the issue is based on ethnographic studies. They have shown that connections with the sending communities are well spread among immigrants. Levitt (2001) showed that Dominican immigrants in Boston had active transnational linkages with their sending communities. Studies on Haitian (Horst 2006) and Pilipino (Igancio 2005) immigrants also suggest that immigrants are actively involved in transnational communication with people back home through internet facilities. Earlier studies also documented the transnational networks of Chinese in Australia (Lever-Tracy et al. 1991) and Montreal, Canada (Chan 1991). However, a comprehensive picture of transnational contact among immigrants cannot be obtained from these ethnographic case studies. Studies based on large scale survey data on transnational contact are limited. Published studies based on survey data show that only a small proportion of immigrants participate in transnational activities. Portes, Haller, and Guarnizo (2002) studied transnational entrepreneurs and found only a relative small percentage participated in transnational activities. Similarly, a study of transnational political participation by immigrants showed only a small percentage of immigrants participating (Guarnizo 2001). However, these studies explored specific transnational activities that require a certain level of financial or political commitment. How much these survey findings can apply to casual transnational contact remains unclear.

With limited systematic data available on transnational contact, we have also drawn from large scale survey and census data collected in recent decades which explore immigrant integration patterns over time to discuss the patterns of transnational contacts among immigrants. However, it is important to be aware that these studies do not have information of transnational contacts among immigrants.

Drawing from these two sets of literature, we suggest that various social forces pull immigrants away from maintaining regular and intensive transnational contact. In particular, findings obtained from surveys suggest that immigrants integrate into society and establish themselves in the labour market through different pathways over time. One reason suggested by Alba and Nee (2003) is the increasing racial tolerance in society. Policies such as affirmative action in the US and multiculturalism in Canada are an attempt to prevent unequal racial treatment. Some observers also argue that the increase in educational opportunities and the importance of education credentials in the labour market allow more immigrants to gradually and steadily achieve economic integration (Farley 1996). Subsequently, as they integrate into society, they spend less time and fewer resources maintaining transnational contacts.

We further expect that immigrants who maintain transnational contact are those who do not have strong social support in their local community. Since social support is usually channeled through social contacts, immigrants turn to transnational contacts if they are not able to develop local social support. Horst's (Horst 2006) study of Jamaican mobile phone transnational use showed that most calls back home were to family members for various kinds of social support. Similarly, Smart and Smart (1998) reported that Chinese immigrants perceive their transnational social networks as "competitive advantages" for survival in a new country. Transnational support thus takes many forms.

Drawing from the results of large scale surveys, we expect that transnational contact will diminish as immigrants stay in the new country longer. Over time, immigrants will gradually develop their own local support. Their ability to develop social support will be further enhanced as they become more familiar with the local institutions and culture and are able to network beyond their own ethnic community.

Thus, our expectation is in line with the assimilation perspective, which suggests that, albeit with variations, immigrants gradually achieve more integration with their receiving communities and lose their transnational connections as they stay in the new country longer. As Piore (1979) described Mexican migrants in the *Birds of Passage*, immigrants may think about and consciously do things for their families and friends back home when they first arrive. As they gradually meet more people and develop social ties in the local receiving community, they spend more time with friends in the local community and send less money back home.

We further argue that the second-generation experiences decline more in transnational contact than do their parents, though some still maintain their transnational contacts. A growing body of literature seems to support the pattern implied by the transnational perspective and suggests that these ties extend over generations (Levitt and Waters 2002; Rumbaut 2002; Lever-Tracy et al. 1991). These writers argue that the identities constructed though transnational networks perpetuate the transnational connection. It is well documented that transnational ties among Chinese families in the first generation of immigrants usually extend over future generations. Recent studies exploring the transnational activities of the children of some new immigrant groups from Mexico, Vietnam, Philippines, mainland China, Taiwan, Cambodia and Laos also showed that a large percentage of them maintains active contact with their parents' countries (Rumbaut 2002).

Although there is no dispute that transnational contact extends beyond the first generation of immigrants, ongoing transnational contact among immigrant children is affected by various contextual factors (Waldinger and Fitzgerald 2004). Once these factors are removed, the transnational contacts of immigrant children will gradually be reduced. The transnational ties among Chinese families discussed earlier are noted by some researchers as being a response to discriminatory immigration laws in various countries (Chan 2000; Alba and Nee 2003). Once these laws are lifted, transnational activities are reduced, and there is instead the familiar pattern of assimilation and establishment in the labour market of succeeding generations. Study of Koreans in Japan also showed that the continuation of their Korean contact is largely related to their marginal position in a society where they do not find satisfaction (Kim 2003).

In short, we argue that only a small proportion of immigrants are intensively and extensively involved in transnational contacts. Those who are involved in transnational contacts are more likely to be those who have recently arrived and do not have strong social support in the local receiving community. Immigrant children will have fewer transnational contacts than their parents.

In the following sections, we explore transnational contact patterns based on recently collected data on Chinese in Toronto. Before discussing the findings, we first describe Chinese in Toronto to provide a context for understanding the results.

## *Chinese in Toronto, Canada*

Chinese have a long history in Canada. Local records of Chinese arrivals date back to 1858 (Lai 1988). During the early 1900s, anti-Chinese sentiments were very strong (Lai 1988). In 1923, the Chinese Immigration Act was passed, which eventually almost completely stopped Chinese immigration (Fong 1996). As the political environment and racial attitudes gradually changed after the Second World War, various discriminatory laws were repealed, including the repeal of the Chinese Immigration Act in 1947. Despite these changes, the number of Chinese immigrants still remained low throughout the 1950s (Li 1998).

Chinese immigration began to increase when Canada adopted immigration policies that admitted applicants based on their labour market adaptability and human capital. According to Li (Li 2005), about 170,000 Chinese immigrated to Canada between 1968 and 1984. Consequently, the Chinese population in Canada rapidly increased, from118,630 in 1971 to 288,825 in 1981 (Fong 1993). Most of these immigrants, about 43%, settled in Toronto.

The volume of Chinese immigrants continued to expand in the 1980s and 1990s. The Chinese population in Canada rose to 633,933 in 1991 (Li 1998) and 1,029,395 in 2001 (Statistics Canada 2005), while the Chinese population in Toronto reached 409,535 in 2001. The increase between the 1980s and the mid-1990s was largely a result of the exodus of many people from Hong Kong, triggered by the uncertainty surrounding the anticipated return of that colony back to China in 1997 (Fong and Ooka 2006). Concern about the future of Hong Kong was further heightened when the Chinese government used force to suppress the student demonstration in Tiananmen Square in 1989. This concern led to greater emigration. In 1990 alone, the number of immigrants to Canada from Hong Kong was about 30,000 (Li 2005). The upward trend of immigration from Hong Kong continued, and the number reached 44,000 in 1994 (Li 2005). Immigration from Hong Kong dropped dramatically after 1997, and the flow of Chinese immigrants was gradually replaced by immigrants from mainland China. In 1998, immigration from Hong Kong was only about 8,000. By 2001, the number was about 2,000 (Li 2005).

A large number of these immigrants from Hong Kong in the late 1980s and 1990s arrived in Canada with financial and human capital. About 88,674 immigrants arrived in Canada between 1983 and 1990 under the investment category (Li 1993). It is natural that they were the group who worried about possible loss due to the return of Hong Kong to communist China in 1997. However, there were no major changes in the economic and political arrangements in Hong Kong after the return. This situation provided incentives for many emigrants to maintain contact with Hong Kong.

During the same period, immigration from mainland China was about 13,000 in 1995; steadily increased to about 29,000 in 1999 and jumped to 40,000 in 2001 (Li 2005). However, it is noteworthy that immigration from Taiwan at the end of the 1990s rose for a short period to about 13,000 and quickly dropped back to 2,000 in 2001. The increased immigration flow from China actually began in the late 1980s when the Canadian government granted landed immigrant status to all students from mainland China after the Tiananmen Square Incident (Fong, Ooka, and Luk 2005). Most of these students took advantage of the opportunity and applied for immigration. In the next few years, they completed their studies in Canada and started their careers. As they established themselves, they began to sponsor their relatives to immigrate to Canada. This growth was further enhanced by a considerable number of students from mainland China who had studied in other countries and professionals from China who moved to Canada in response to the emphasis on human capital requirements in Canadian immigration policies (Wang and Lo 2005). The business opportunities and the vibrant economy in China in recent years became a strong magnet to attract immigrants from mainland China to maintain various contacts back home.

As the Chinese population grows, so do Chinese businesses. The increase in the Chinese population and businesses in Toronto fosters the development of a strong and vibrant Chinese ethnic economy. The critical mass also allows the development of ethnic newspapers, radio, and TV. The Chinese community is increasingly institutionally complete.

With the low costs of transportation, advances in technology, and the tradition of maintaining close family ties and friendship networks, there should be considerable potential for Chinese immigrants to become involved in transnational contact. At the same time, the well-established Chinese community in Toronto, with ethnic newspapers, radio and TV stations, and the growing business ties between Canada and China should promote transnational contact.

## *Data and Methods*

The data for this study were drawn from the New Economy and Immigrant Adaptation Survey, conducted in 2005 in Toronto, Canada. The data was collected through telephone interviews based on random digital dialing. Individuals were selected to be interviewed if the person is between age 18 and 65. The response rate is about 91%. The full sample includes 1539 cases. Among them, we only included Chinese respondents (i.e. 494 cases). Our sample closely reflects the Chinese population by immigration status as reported in the census. For example, while the sample has about 12% of Canadian born Chinese between age 18 and 65, the 2001 census recorded 13% between age 15 and 64. We selected only Chinese because they are the ideal group for studying transnational contacts. The economic and political environments encourage transnational contacts, and Chinese have been documented as maintaining close networks.

In this study, we are particularly interested in the transnational contacts of immigrants. We include a wide range of activities to capture these contacts, from visiting the home country, which requires considerable expenditure, to email messages, which require a degree of computer literacy, to telephone calls. We also include reading online newspapers and listening to online radio from the home country, as well as reading local ethnic newspapers. The frequency of using these various means of transnational contact will be reported separately. In addition, we also compute the summary information to report the overall intensity and extensity of using these various forms of information and communication. The overall intensity level is a scale based on five different means of transnational contacts (using telephone, writing email, listening online radio, reading online newspaper, and local ethnic newspaper), and the overall extensity variable level is the counts of how many of these technological means are used.

The list deliberately excludes the contacts with family members because it is quite natural that family members maintain contacts despite being in different locations. The study attempts to focus on maintaining transnational contacts of the wider social circle and obtaining information of the home country. Although the list covers a wide range of forms of information and communication, it has no means to be comprehensive. For instance, we include reading the local ethnic newspaper but not watching local ethnic television. In addition, some forms of communications are more likely to be used by certain age groups, such as the younger generation is more likely to access the internet. Thus, our interpretation has to be with caution. Nevertheless, the list represents considerable forms of maintaining contacts with the home country and is able to portray a general picture of transnational contacts.

We performed an analysis to explore factors related to the frequency of involvement in transnational contact. Drawing from our previous discussion, we expect that the immigrants who are more likely to be involved in transnational contact are those who have been in the country for a short time and lack local social support. Duration in the country is assessed from the question asking for their year of arrival. We used three proxies to approximate social support: presence of family members in the local community, extensity of local social networks, and language ability. Having family members in the local community suggests that immigrants are more likely to obtain support from family members. Larger local social networks imply greater likelihood of obtaining social support from a variety of sources. The social networks of individuals are measured by a variable derived from the position generator, a survey instrument commonly used to capture the extent of a respondent's social network (Lin 2001; Lin and Dumin 1986). It is the range between the highest and the lowest occupation to which the respondent has access, thus showing the extent of the individual's social network. The occupational prestige score is based on the SES scores from Ganzeboom and Trieman's findings (1966). Finally, immigrants with better language ability are more likely to extend their networks beyond their own ethnic community and to obtain more resources.

When we present our descriptive information, we provide separate information on immigrants from Hong Kong, mainland China, and other locations. As Waldinger and Fitzgerald (Waldinger and Fitzgerald 2004) has pointed out, transnational activities can be affected by the nature of the nation-state. Hong Kong has been a capitalistic society, while mainland China is experiencing a transitional economy with considerable governmental control of various aspects of society.

In our multivariate analysis, we also control for age, gender, being a business owner, and place of origin, i.e., Hong Kong, mainland China, other places. We did not run separate analyses for the immigrants from "other places" because the samples were not large enough to permit sensible analysis. Ordered logit regression model is used in most of these analyses. However, two dependent variables, including home visit and extensity of transnational contacts, are Count Data and Poisson Regression Model are used. In addition, the intensity of transnational contacts is based on the OLS regression model.

## *Results*

Table 1 presents the frequencies with which Chinese from different places use a variety of information and communication technologies to

Table 1: Frequencies with which Chinese from different places use Different Technologies to Maintain Home Country Contact

| | Immigrants | | | Canadian Born | |
|---|---|---|---|---|---|
| | From Mainland | From Hong Kong | From Other Places | | Total |
| Visit Home Country in the Last Two Years | | | | | |
| 0 time | 55.14 | 50.69 | 70.42 | 81.54 | 59.51 |
| 1 time | 33.18 | 30.56 | 21.13 | 15.38 | 28.34 |
| 2 times | 8.41 | 15.97 | 7.04 | 1.54 | 9.51 |
| 3 times or above | 3.27 | 2.78 | 1.41 | 0.00 | 2.43 |
| Contact Friends by telephone in the Last Two Years | | | | | |
| Daily | 1.91 | 1.49 | 1.64 | 2.44 | 1.80 |
| About 2 or 3 times a week | 5.74 | 2.24 | 3.28 | 2.44 | 4.04 |
| About once a week | 7.66 | 2.24 | 1.64 | 0.00 | 4.49 |
| About once every two weeks | 6.22 | 6.72 | 1.64 | 2.44 | 5.39 |
| About once a month | 31.58 | 21.64 | 8.20 | 4.88 | 22.92 |
| Rarely | 23.92 | 29.10 | 19.67 | 19.51 | 24.49 |
| Never | 22.97 | 36.57 | 63.93 | 68.29 | 36.85 |
| Contact Friends by email in the Last Two Years | | | | | |
| Daily | 3.83 | 0.00 | 4.92 | 2.44 | 2.70 |
| About 2 or 3 times a week | 5.74 | 2.24 | 3.28 | 4.88 | 4.27 |
| About once a week | 7.18 | 5.22 | 6.56 | 7.32 | 6.52 |
| About once every two weeks | 7.18 | 7.46 | 1.64 | 4.88 | 6.29 |
| About once a month | 15.79 | 20.15 | 11.48 | 4.88 | 15.51 |
| Rarely | 18.66 | 19.40 | 8.20 | 17.07 | 17.30 |
| Never | 41.63 | 45.52 | 63.93 | 58.54 | 47.42 |
| Listent Online Radio from Home Country in the Last Two Years | | | | | |
| Daily | 1.86 | 6.29 | 1.41 | 0.00 | 2.83 |
| About 2 or 3 times a week | 2.33 | 2.80 | 1.41 | 0.00 | 2.02 |
| About once a week | 4.65 | 1.40 | 2.82 | 0.00 | 2.83 |
| About once every two weeks | 2.33 | 0.70 | 0.00 | 0.00 | 1.21 |
| About once a month | 2.33 | 3.50 | 1.41 | 1.54 | 2.43 |
| Rarely | 3.26 | 11.19 | 1.41 | 3.08 | 5.26 |
| Never | 83.26 | 74.13 | 91.55 | 95.38 | 83.40 |
| Read Online Newspaper from Home Country in the Last Two Years | | | | | |
| Daily | 17.21 | 7.69 | 12.68 | 4.62 | 12.15 |
| About 2 or 3 times a week | 8.37 | 6.29 | 2.82 | 1.54 | 6.07 |
| About once a week | 7.91 | 4.20 | 4.23 | 1.54 | 5.47 |
| About once every two weeks | 2.33 | 2.10 | 2.82 | 0.00 | 2.02 |
| About once a month | 6.05 | 4.90 | 1.41 | 1.54 | 4.45 |
| Rarely | 6.51 | 9.79 | 7.04 | 0.00 | 6.68 |
| Never | 51.63 | 65.03 | 69.01 | 90.77 | 63.16 |
| Read Local Ethnic Newspaper from Home Country in the Last Two Years | | | | | |
| Daily | 24.19 | 46.15 | 9.86 | 0.00 | 25.30 |
| About 2 or 3 times a week | 16.28 | 7.69 | 7.04 | 1.54 | 10.53 |
| About once a week | 20.93 | 17.48 | 15.49 | 3.08 | 16.80 |
| About once every two weeks | 6.05 | 0.70 | 4.23 | 1.54 | 3.64 |
| About once a month | 8.37 | 4.20 | 7.04 | 4.62 | 6.48 |
| Rarely | 7.44 | 6.99 | 7.04 | 3.08 | 6.68 |
| Never | 16.74 | 16.78 | 49.30 | 86.15 | 30.57 |
| N | 215 | 143 | 71 | 65 | 497 |

maintain contact with the home country. The first three communication technologies facilitate transnational contact in person. Transnational contact through these three different technologies and communication media involve different levels of financial commitment, ranging from email communication to visiting the home country. The results show that although Chinese who have immigrated from various places and those born in Canada maintain certain transnational contacts back home, most of them have only infrequent contact even considering various technologies. About half of respondents have never visited their home country in the last two years. Among those who visited their home countries, most of them have visited their home country only once. The low frequency of visiting the home country may be affected by the high cost of traveling to Asia. However, even considering the two other communication technologies, telephone and email, which are less costly, the frequency of contact remains low. About 61% and 65% respectively have rarely or never called or sent email messages to friends back home. Only about 10% and 13% respectively contact their friends back home at least once a week using telephone or email.

Another dimension of maintaining contact with the home country is to keep up to date with news and developments back home through news media. The survey again reveals that Chinese in Toronto do not listen often to on-line radio or read online newspapers. About 89% and 70% respectively reported they rarely or never get updates on news and developments back home through on-line radio or on-line newspapers. Listening to radio and reading newspapers on-line require familiarity and access to the internet. Reading an ethnic local newspaper is convenient for most people. A substantial proportion of respondents read a local ethnic newspaper daily or at least a few times a week. However, reading local ethnic newspapers does not necessarily indicate an interest in news from back home. Local ethnic newspapers also have major sections on local news.

The tables also provide information about Chinese in Toronto using various information and communication technologies to maintain contact back home by place of origin and nativity. We have reported the transnational contacts of Chinese immigrants from different places separately to explore the possibility of different patterns due to the different economic and social contexts of the sending places. In general, there are only minor differences between Chinese immigrants from mainland China and those from Hong Kong, except in frequency of reading local ethnic newspapers. However, the results show a consid-

Table 2: Overall Intensity and Extensity of Chinese from different places use Different Technologies to Maintain Home Country Contact

| | N | Mean | Std. Error | F-test |
|---|---|---|---|---|
| Intensity of Transnational Contact | | | | |
| Immigrants | | | | |
| From Mainland China | 215 | 6.80 | 0.29 | |
| From Hong Kong | 143 | 6.04 | 0.34 | 34.08*** |
| From Other Places | 71 | 3.70 | 0.54 | |
| Canadian Born | 65 | 1.38 | 0.41 | |
| Total | 494 | 5.42 | 0.20 | |
| Extensity of Transnational Contact | | | | |
| | N | Mean | Std. Error | F-test |
| Immigrants | | | | |
| From Mainland China | 215 | 2.95 | 0.10 | |
| From Hong Kong | 144 | 2.66 | 0.11 | 51.682*** |
| From Other Places | 71 | 1.62 | 0.18 | |
| Canadian Born | 65 | 0.78 | 0.14 | |
| Total | 495 | 2.39 | 0.07 | |

erable difference between immigrant and Canadian-born Chinese. Canadian-born Chinese are much less likely to contact their ancestral country. An overwhelming proportion never or rarely uses any information or communication technology to contact their ancestral country. These results point to the general assimilation pattern of the second generation.

Table 2 shows the overall intensity and extensity of transnational contact. We created an overall intensity index of transnational contact, which is based on the frequencies of different transnational contacts. The overall extensity variable indicates in the last two years how many technological means have used to maintain transnational contact. Possible means are ranging from zero to six.

The results show that Chinese immigrants, whatever their place of origin, have more intense contact with the home country than Canadian-born Chinese. The intensity of contact by Chinese immigrants from both mainland China and Hong Kong is about six times greater than that of Canadian-born Chinese. The results also show that Chinese immigrants from mainland China, in comparison to Chinese immigrants from Hong Kong, consistently have slightly more intensive transnational contacts and use more extensive information and communication technologies to maintain contact back home.

Table 3: Coefficients of Ordinal/Poisson Regression on Different Transnational Contacts among Chinese Immigrants in Toronto

| | Home Country Visit | Telephone | Email | Online Radio | Online Newspaper | Local Newspaper |
|---|---|---|---|---|---|---|
| **Immigrants** | | | | | | |
| Intercept[threshold = .00] | | –1.194** | –0.350 | 0.098 | 0.439 | –2.839*** |
| Intercept[threshold = 1.00] | | 1.378** | 1.360** | 0.872 | 1.023* | –2.008*** |
| Intercept[threshold = 2.00] | | 1.975*** | 1.920*** | 1.076* | 1.136* | –1.822*** |
| Intercept[threshold = 3.00] | | 2.670*** | 2.660*** | 1.467** | 1.526** | –0.762 |
| Intercept[threshold = 4.00] | | 3.887*** | 3.614*** | 2.135*** | 2.142*** | –0.069 |
| Intercept | –0.562 | | | | | |
| Age | 0.001 | 0.015 | –0.013 | –0.031** | 0.011 | 0.037*** |
| Sex (Female =1) | 0.379* | 0.304 | 0.149 | 0.245 | –0.458 ** | –0.269 |
| Good English Ability | –0.204 | –0.791*** | 0.654** | –0.130 | –0.173 | –1.243*** |
| Years in Canada | –0.004 | –0.052*** | –0.072*** | –0.009 | –0.091*** | –0.052*** |
| Business Owner | –0.003 | –0.191 | 0.281 | 0.421 | 0.026 | 0.127 |
| Occupational Range | 0.006 | 0.005 | 0.026*** | 0.022** | 0.035*** | –0.005 |
| Proportion of family member in same city | –0.560** | –0.807* | –0.549 | –1.238* | –0.959** | –0.163 |
| Borin in Mainland China | –0.139 | 0.153 | –0.261 | –1.148*** | –0.097 | –1.032*** |
| Born in Hong Kong (r.c.) | | | | | | |
| Born in Other Places | –0.380 | –1.068*** | –0.609* | –1.753*** | –0.039 | –1.961*** |
| Chi square | 0.027** | 0.092*** | 0.077*** | 0.066*** | 0.079*** | 0.1*** |
| Pseudo $R^2$ | 20.86 | 75.54 | 67.24 | 35.69 | 71 | 115.39 |
| N | 348 | 328 | 328 | 347 | 347 | 347 |
| **Canadian Born** | | | | | | |
| Intercept[threshold = .00] | | 2.205 | 2.604 | | 4.867* | 3.134 |
| Intercept[threshold = 1.00] | | 4.191** | 4.074* | | 5.088* | 4.138 |
| Intercept[threshold = 2.00] | | 4.669** | 4.533* | | | 4.466 |
| Intercept[threshold = 3.00] | | | 5.479* | | 5.351* | 5.649 |
| Intercept[threshold = 4.00] | | 5.456*** | 6.712*** | | 5.675** | |
| Intercept | 0.053** | | | | | |
| Age | –0.921* | 0.045 | 0.003 | | 0.101 | 0.037 |
| Sex (Female =1) | 2.094*** | –1.056 | –2.030** | | –1.360 | –1.110 |
| Business Owner | 0.019 | 0.367 | 0.792 | | –0.907 | 0.663 |
| Occupational Range | 1.058 | 0.035 | 0.087* | | 0.026 | 0.024 |
| Proportion of family member in same city | –3.927*** | –2.422* | –0.968 | | –5.042* | –1.094 |
| Chi square | 0.426 | 0.108 | 0.151** | | 0.142 | 0.086 |
| Pseudo $R^2$ | 71.91 | 7.56 | 14.81 | | 7.73 | 6.22 |
| N | 62 | 39 | 39 | | 62 | 62 |

Note: * P<0.1, ** P<0.05, *** P<0.01

With Table 3, we explore how the level of integration and the social support at the immigrant destination are related to transnational contact. We controlled for the demographic background of respondents, age and gender, and place of origin. Our analysis did not include listening to on-line radio among Canadian-born Chinese because an overwhelming large percentage do not listen on-line radio. As mentioned earlier, ordered logit regression is used for most analyses. Since the dependent variables report the usage frequency levels of different technologies to maintain transnational contacts, an intercept for each level of the dependent variable will be reported. The estimated coefficients can be interpreted when the level of the dependent variable is changed by the coefficient in the ordered log-odds scale as a unit increases in the independent variable.

The results show that duration in the country, with two exceptions, is usually negatively related to the frequency of contact with the home country using information and communication technologies. Specifically, more time in the new country is related to less frequent contact with the home country through various information and communication technologies, except listening to online radio from home and visiting the home country. Listening to on-line radio may not relate to the number of years in the country because listening to radio programs requires a considerable amount of time. Immigrants who have jobs, no matter what their level of integration, may not be able to afford the time to listen to radio programs. This interpretation is supported by the negative effect of age on frequency of listening to online radio. Immigrants who are younger may not have entered the labour market and may therefore be more likely to listen to online radio.

The results suggest that having local social support reduces transnational contact. The results show that Chinese immigrants with family members living in the same city have considerably less frequent contact with the home country. The presence of family members in the same city implies that local social support is easily accessible, so those immigrants no longer need to maintain frequent contact with friends back home. In addition, though language ability is not always related to transnational contact, it is usually negatively related to transnational contact when it is statistically significant. However, the results also show that immigrants with a more extensive local social network are more likely to maintain contacts back home, except for home country visiting, calling friends in the home country, and reading local ethnic newspaper. Nevertheless, these effects are minimal.

Finally, the results show that having local social supports are more to be associated with less transnational contact among Canadian-born Chinese. In other words, having more family members in the same city is negatively related to transnational contact of the group.

Table 4 reports the intensity and extensity of transnational contacts using various information and communication technologies among

Table 4: Coefficient of OLS/Poisson Regression on Extensity of Transnational Contacts in Two Years among Chinese

| | Immigrant | Canadian born |
|---|---|---|
| **Extensity** | | |
| AGE | 0.012*** | 0.013*** |
| Sex (Female = 1) | −0.044*** | −0.186*** |
| Good English Ability | −0.164*** | — |
| Years in Canada | −0.007*** | — |
| Business Owner | −0.300*** | −0.549*** |
| Occupational Range | 0.008*** | 0.018*** |
| Proportion of family member in same city | −0.116*** | −0.497*** |
| Borin in Mainland China | −0.229*** | — |
| Born in Hong Kong (r.c.) | *** | — |
| Born in Other Places | −0.352*** | — |
| Intercept | 3.948*** | 3.113*** |
| Chi Square | 1443.51 | 291.34 |
| Pseudo $R^2$ | 0.048*** | 0.083*** |
| N | 348 | 62 |
| **Intensity** | | |
| AGE | 0.018 | 0.071 |
| Sex (Female = 1) | −0.257 | −2.805* |
| Good English Ability | −1.349** | — |
| Years in Canada | −0.132*** | — |
| Business Owner | 0.199 | 2.723 |
| Occupational Range | 0.049*** | 0.078 |
| Proportion of family member in same city | −2.021** | −2.351 |
| Borin in Mainland China | −0.708 | — |
| Born in Hong Kong (r.c.) | | — |
| Born in Other Places | −2.249** | — |
| Intercept | 7.908*** | −0.703 |
| $R^2$ | 0.212*** | 0.291** |
| N | 328 | 39 |

Note: * P<0.1, ** P<0.05, *** P<0.01

Chinese immigrants from various places and among Canadian-born Chinese. For Chinese immigrants, controlling for place of origin, duration in the country is positively related to both intensity and extensity of transnational contacts. In other words, staying in the country reduces the intensity and extensity of transnational contacts. In addition, lacking local social support also reduces the intensity of transnational contacts. Poorer language ability and fewer family members residing in the local community are associated with lower intensity and extensity of transnational contact. Although a wider local social network, in an unexpected direction, is positively related to both the intensity and extensity of transnational contact, the effect is minimal. As for the

Canadian-born Chinese, local social support affects only the extensity but not the intensity of transnational contact.

## *Conclusion*

At one time, research showed that immigrants gradually achieve full social and economic integration the longer they stay in the country. Research on previous immigrant generations suggests that although they may maintain transnational contact when they first arrive, this contact steadily fades away as they take root in the new country and have increased access to local social support. In recent years, however, the transnational perspective, which emerged as an alternative explanation of the immigrant adaptation process, has argued that transnational contacts are widespread among recent immigrants. Thus, these contacts should be considered in any analysis of immigrant integration patterns, because to a large extent they shape the integration patterns.

Our findings based on the Chinese in Toronto clearly do not show strong support for the transnational perspective to explain immigrant experiences. Our results show that only a small proportion of immigrants are intensively and extensively involved in transnational contact. In addition, our analyses demonstrated that recently arrived immigrants or those who lack local social support are more likely to be involved in transnational contacts. This study echoes the suggestion that maintaining transnational contacts may be just the initial stage of the assimilation process.

However, our results have shown positive relationships between social networks and transnational contacts, though the effects are consistently small. One possible reason is that the variable only measures the accessibility of various occupations. It may not well capture the availability of social support, rather how the respondents or professional networks developed through jobs.

Although Chinese *guanxi* (networks) are important elements of their social fabric, and the existing elaborated structures of the Chinese community in Toronto should foster the development of transnational contacts, the level of transnational contact among Chinese immigrants and their children remains low. Thus, the findings indicate that the transnational perspective has limited applicability to the immigrant experience. However, it is important to point out that our study is based on one ethnic group in one city characterized as having high level of institutional completeness of the Chinese community. The findings should be generalized only with caution. Besides maintaining transnational contact can also be related to the lucrative economic benefits among entrepreneurs as suggested by the literature (Lever-Tracy at el 1996; Chan 2000), it is important in future analyses to differentiate how the integration process is related to transnational contact due to economic consequences among these entrepreneurs. In addition, some recent studies have pointed out previous experiences, such as occupations in the home country, and the life stage at immigration, such as age at immigration, can affect the likelihood of transnational contacts. Further analyses should include this information in the analysis.

## *References*


Alba, Richard and Victor Nee. (2003). *Remaking the American Mainstream: Assimilation and Contemporary Immigration.* Cambridge: Harvard University Press.

Chan, Kwok Bun. (1991). *Smoke and Fire: The Chinese in Montreal.* Hong Kong: Chinese University Press.

——. (2000). "State, economy and culture: Reflections on the Chinese business networks." Pp. 1–13 in *Chinese Business Networks: State, Economy and Culture*, edited by K.B. Chan. Singapore: Prentice Hall and Copenhagen: Nordic Institute of Asian Studies.

Chan, K. B. and B. K. Ng. (2000). "Myths and misperceptions of ethnic Chinese capitalism." Pp. 285–302 in *Chinese Business Networks: State, Economy and Culture*, edited by K. B. Chan. Singapore: Prentice Hall and Copenhagen: Nordic Institute of Asian Studies.

Farley, Reynolds. (1996). *The New American Reality: Who We Are, How We Got There, Where We Are Going.* New York: Russell Sage Foundation.

Foner, Nancy. (2000). *From Ellis Island to JFK: New York's Two Great Waves of Immigration.* New Haven: Yale University Press.

——. (2001). "Transnationalism, Then and Now: New York Immigrants Today and at the Turn of the Twentieth Century." Pp. 35–57 in *Migration, Transnationalization, and Race in a Changing New York*, edited by H. Cordero-Guzman, R. Smith, and R. Grosfoguel. Philadelphia: Temple University Press.

Fong, Eric. (1993). "Racial Residential Segregation in American and Canadian Cities." Ph.D. Dissertation. University of Chicago.

——. (1996). "A Comparative Perspective of Racial Residential Segregation: American and Canadian Experiences." *Sociological Quarterly* 37:501–528.

Fong, Eric and Emi Ooka. (2006). "Assessing Patterns of Social Integration Among Immigrants." *International Migration Review* 40:348–374.

Fong, Eric, Emi Ooka, and Chiu Luk. (2005). "Suburban Spatial Distribution of Ethnic Businesses." *Social Science Research* 34:215–235.

Glick Schiller, Nina. (1995). "From Immigrant to Transmigrant: Theorizing Transnational Migration." *Anthropological Quarterly* 68:48–63.

Glick Schiller, Nina, Linda Basch, and Cristina Szaton-Blanc. (1992). *Towards a Transnational Perspective on Migration: Race, Class, Ethnicity, and Nationalism Reconsidered.* New York: New York Academy of Science.

Guarnizo, Luis E. (1997). "The Emergence of a Transnational Social Formation and the Mirage of Return Migration among Dominican Transmigrants." *Identities: Global Studies in Cultural and Power* 4:281–322.
——. (2001). "On the Political Participation of Transnational Migrants: Old Practices and New Trends." in *E Pluribus Unum? Contemporary and Historical Perspectives on Immigrant Political Incorporation*, edited by G. Gerstle and J. Mollenkopf. New York: Russell Sage Foundation.
Horst, Heather A. (2006). "The Blessings and Burdens of Communication: Cell Phones in Jamacian Transnational Social Fields." *Global Networks* 6:143–159.
Igancio, Emily Noelle. (2005). *Building Diaspora*. New Brunswick: Rutgers University Press.
Kim, Myungsoo. (2003). "Ethnic Stratification and Inter-Generational Differences in Japan: A Comparative Study of Korean and Japanese Status Attainment." *International Journal of Japanese Sociology* 12:6–16.
Kivisto, Peter. (2001). "Theorizing Transnational Immigration: A Critical Review of Current Efforts." *Ethnic and Racial Studies* 24:549–577.
Lai, David Chuenyan. (1988). *Chinatowns: Towns within Cities in Canada*. Vancouver: University of British Columbia Press.
Lever-Tracy, Constance, David Ip, Jim Kitay. Irene Phillips, and Noel Tracy. (1991). *Asian Entrepreneurs in Australia*. Canaberra: OMA/AGPS.
Levitt, Peggy, Josh DeWind, and Steven Vertovec. (2003). "International Perspectives on Transnational Migration: An Introduction." *International Migration Review* 37:565–575.
Levitt, Peggy and Nina Glick Schiller. (2004). "Conceptualizing Simultaneity: A Transnational Social Field Perspective on Society." *International Migration Review* 38:1002–1039
Levitt, Peggy and Mary C. Waters. (2002). "The Changing Face of Home: The Transnational Lives of the Second Generation." New York: Russell Sage Foundation.
Li, Peter. (1993). "Chinese Investment and Business in Canada: Ethnic Entrepreneurship Reconsidered." *Pacific Affairs* 66:219–243.
——. (1998). *Chinese in Canada*. Toronto: Oxford University Press.
——. (2005). "The Rise and Fall of Chinese Immigration to Canada: Newcomers from Hong Kong Special Administrative Region of China and Mainland China, 1980–2000." *International Migration* 43:9–32.
Lin, Nan. (2001). *Social Capital: A Theory of Social Structure and Action*. New York: Cambridge University Press.
Lin, Nan and Mary Dumin. (1986). "Access to Occupations Through Social Ties." *Social Networks* 8:365–385.
Menjivar, Cecilia. (2002). "Living in Two Worlds? Guatemalan-Origin Children in the United States and Emerging Transnationalism." *Journal of Ethnic and Migration Studies* 28:531–552.
Piore, Michael J. (1979). *Birds of Passage: Migrant Labor and Industrial Societies*. New York: Cambridge University Press.
Portes, Alejandro. (2001). "The Debates and Significance of Immigrant Transnationalism." *Global Networks* 1:195–217.
Portes, Alejandro, Luis E. Guarnizo, and Patricia Landolt. (1999). "The Study of Transnationalism: Pitfalls and Promises of an Emergent Social Field." *Ethnic and Racial Studies* 22:217–237.
Portes, Alejandro, William J. Haller, and Luis Eduardo Guarnizo. (2002). "Transnational Entrepreneurs: An Alternative Form of Immigrant Economic Adaptation." *American Sociological Review* 67:278–298.
Raijman, Rebeca and Marta Tienda. (2000). "Training Functions of Ethnic Economies: Mexican Entrepreneurs in Chicago." *Sociological Perspectives* 43:439–456.

Rumbaut, Ruben G. (2002). "Severed or Sustained Attachments? Language, Identity, and Imagined Communities in the Post-Immigrant Generation." in *The Changing Face of Home: The Transnational Lives of the Second Generation*, edited by P. Levitt and M. C. Waters. New York: Russell Sage Foundation.

Waldinger, Roger and David Fitzgerald. (2004). "Transnationalism in Question." *American Journal of Sociology* 109:1177–1195.

Wang, Shuguang and Lucia Lo. (2005). "Chinese Immigrants in Canada: Their Changing Composition and Economic Performance." *International Migration* 43:35–71.

Zhou, Min. (1997). "Segmented Assimilation: Issues, Controversies, and Recent Research on the New Second Generation." *International Migration Review* 31:825–858.

# REDISCOVERING CHINESE SOCIETY IN THE SOCIALIST ERA: USING THE PAST TO SERVE THE PRESENT*

JONATHAN UNGER**

## *Introduction*

Sociologists who specialize in China focus almost all of their research attention on the here and now. When we go to China to conduct research, we organize surveys and carry out interviews regarding contemporary concerns. As a consequence, during the past quarter of a century very little sociological research has been conducted about the extraordinary social changes that occurred during the period of Mao's rule.

This lamentably leaves us with too little knowledge of the first three decades of PRC history, with large areas of important research still left undone. Under Mao, China did not contain a single Sociology Department, and no sociological research of any kind was carried out during most of that period. The only sociological studies of China necessarily were conducted from abroad, by fewer than a dozen sociologists, who largely interviewed émigrés in Hong Kong. The two books co-authored by William Parish and Martin K. Whyte on rural and urban society are examples of the excellent work that could be done using this methodology.[1] Nonetheless, it is obvious that conducting research inside China can provide more accurate information than was available to this earlier generation of scholars. Since the 1980s we have held the opportunity, but we have not taken much advantage of it to interview people about their social circumstances during the Maoist period.

* Reference to this article should be made as follows: Unger, Jonathan. 2007. "Rediscovering Chinese Society in the Socialist Era: Using the Past to Serve the Present".

** This paper was presented as the keynote address at the annual conference of the Hong Kong Sociological Association, held at Shue Yan College, Hong Kong, on 2 December 2006. I am indebted to the organizers of the conference, Professor Harold Traver and Dr Selina Chan, and also to Dr Anita Chan and the referees of *Social Transformations of Chinese Societies* for their advice.

[1] William L. Parish and Martin K. Whyte, *Village and Family in Contemporary China* (Chicago: University of Chicago Press, 1978); Martin K. Whyte and William L. Parish, *Urban Life in Contemporary China* (Chicago: University of Chicago Press, 1984).

The 1950s, 1960s and 1970s witnessed major government experiments to reshape society that are almost unparalleled anywhere in history. The chances to examine this are now dwindling. The memories of people about their lives and the social situations and mores under Mao are fading, and the older generation has begun to pass away. If such research is ever to take place, it needs to be conducted soon. And if we do not sufficiently understand those decades, we will never adequately understand current-day Chinese society, which has evolved out of that recent past and still bears its imprint in current institutional settings, social mores, and deep-seated attitudes.

It can almost be guaranteed that practically every sociological issue has been under-studied for the Maoist period, be it on any aspect of family life, or any gender studies topic, or any topic concerning social stratification, social mobility, criminology, you name it. Some topics are unique to China. One that I think warrants renewed research involves the grassroots social upheaval of the Cultural Revolution in 1966–68. The factional conflicts that erupted between contending groups within society provided a window into the hidden social tensions and antagonisms that had built up during the years leading up to the Cultural Revolution.[2] After the mass upheavals were suppressed in 1968 and a political system of tight hierarchical controls was reinstituted, many of the same tensions and frustrations re-emerged and persisted throughout the 1970s. Thus examining what was exposed in each sector of Chinese society during those two years of social upheaval during the Cultural Revolution can provide us with a means to better understand the hidden tensions and grievances of almost the whole sweep of the Maoist period.

Rural China provides a second example. Fortunately, there is a worldwide social-science tradition that village studies should trace social change in a modern community over time. As a consequence, a considerable number of village studies have probed back in time into the Maoist period and even earlier.[3] These can present us with

---

[2] I discuss this in some detail in "The Cultural Revolution at the Grass Roots", *The China Journal* 57 (January 2007): 109–137.

[3] Village studies that contain substantial material on social and political change in the Maoist period include Zhang Letian, *Gaobie lixiang: Renmin gongshe zhidu yanjiu* (Departing from Ideals: Research into the System of the People's Commune) (Shanghai: Dongfang Chubanshe, 1998); Zhu Xiaoyang, *Zuiguo yu chengfa: Xiaocun gushi 1931–1997* (Crime and Punishment: The Tale of a Small Village 1931–1997) (Tianjin Guji Chubanshe, 2003); two books by Edward Friedman, Paul G. Pickowicz and Mark Selden, *Chinese*

information and insights directly relevant to the present day. One particular illustration involves the secret land allocations that currently go on among villagers across China.[4] In most of China's villages—despite the government's opposition—extra plots of land periodically are being given free-of-charge to households that have gained new members, and land is periodically taken away from families in which one or more members have died or moved away. Such land redistribution is not a traditional Chinese practice. A new conception of land ownership, a new means of coping as household economies, and a new community strategy have developed in rural China since the return to household farming in the early 1980s. Since the government forbids these land transfers, China's news media have never publicized the practice. Yet it has taken hold in tens of thousands of villages across China without the permission of the authorities.

Where, then, did this unusual idea of periodically redistributing land come from? Our knowledge of practices in the period of collective agriculture can provide an answer. In the Maoist period, under the collectives, farmers had been assigned small plots (*ziliudi*) on which to grow vegetables for their own consumption, and the size of these plots expanded and contracted as families added and lost members. In addition, families had obtained grain "on loan" from their agricultural production team when their children were young, and then, years later,

*Village, Socialist State* and *Revolution, Resistance and Reform in Village China* (New Haven: Yale University Press, 1991 and 2005); Mobo Gao, *Gao Village: Rural Life in China Since the Revolution* (London: Hurst & Co.; Honolulu: University of Hawaii Press, 1999); Anita Chan, Richard Madsen and Jonathan Unger, *Chen Village Under Mao and Deng* (Berkeley: University of California Press, 1992); Richard Madsen, *Morality and Power in a Chinese Village* (Berkeley: University of California Press, 1984); Philip Huang, *The Peasant Family and Rural Development in the Yangzi Delta* (Stanford: Stanford University Press, 1990); Huang Shu-min, *The Spiral Road: Change in a Chinese Village Through the Eyes of a Communist Party Leader* (Boulder: Westview Press, 1989); Jun Jing, *The Temple of Memories: History, Power, and Morality in a Chinese Village* (Stanford: Stanford University Press, 1996); Ellen R. Judd, *Gender and Power in Rural North China* (Stanford: Stanford University Press, 1994); Sulamith Heins Potter and Jack M. Potter, *China's Peasants: The Anthropology of a Revolution* (Cambridge: Cambridge University Press, 1990); Gregory A. Ruf, *Cadres and Kin: Power, Authority, and Corporatism in a West China Village, 1937–1991* (Stanford: Stanford University Press, 1998); Helen F. Siu, *Agents and Victims in South China* (New Haven: Yale University Press, 1989); and Yunxiang Yan, *The Flow of Gifts: Reciprocity and Social Networks in a Chinese Village* (Berkeley: University of California Press, 1996); Hok Bun Ku, *Moral Politics in a South Chinese Village* (Lanham: Rowman and Littlefield, 2003).

[4] Jonathan Unger, "Family Customs and Farmland Reallocations in Contemporary Chinese Villages", *Social Transformations in Chinese Societies* Vol. 1, No. 1 (March 2006), pp. 113–130.

the cost of the grain was repaid when the children became teenagers who worked in the fields and augmented the family's earnings. Although some elements of collective agriculture were disliked, interviews about the past reveal that these two aspects were popular among farmers. After the return to household farming in the 1980s, many farmers have faced problems in raising families on limited amounts of land, and so they have, as communities, turned to what they had grown accustomed to under the collectives. If we are not aware of the practices of the Maoist past and do not know farmers' attitudes in that period, the Chinese farmers' current resort to reallocating fields would seem inexplicable to us.

### *The Maoist Past of Urban Work Communities*

Whereas rural communities and their experiences in the Maoist period are being studied, no similar studies of urban communities are available. Yet we have just as much need to understand the past of urban communities as we do of rural ones. As is well known, urban people during the Maoist period were enveloped by their work units (*danwei*). These provided lifelong employment, accommodation, and for better or worse, political study, because they were also political communities. But in contrast to the wealth of information that is available from village studies, there is not a single published monograph on the social history of a factory, the quintessential urban work unit. In this journal article I wish to focus on this topic, and I will attempt to show the relevance of such research for understanding the attitudes and worldviews of employees today.

Anita Chan and I have been conducting research at a distillery in China that produces a type of strong liquor, *qujiu*. The distillery's history goes back in time to before the Communist ascension to power, and it became a state enterprise owned by the city government early in the Communist era. The distillery is not a "model" enterprise, and there was no effort by Chinese authorities to steer us to it.[5] During 2002–2004 Anita Chan and I undertook full-time research there at three different

[5] We were granted access to the enterprise through a Chinese academic who sits on its board of directors. We visited the distillery and interviewed there about twenty times. Even more frequently, we conducted interviews in the residential compounds and homes of workers and retirees.

times for a total of four months, and were able to conduct unsupervised interviews with dozens of its employees and retirees. Through recording their oral histories, we sought to examine life and attitudes at the enterprise starting in the mid-1930s, through its nationalization in the 1950s, the Great Leap Forward and its aftermath, the Cultural Revolution, and onward into the period of post-Mao industrial reforms up to the present day.

Briefly stated, the message that the older employees and the retirees derive today from their conception of the past is that for decades they had served loyally, had endured the hardships of poverty, and had engaged in bone-jarring labour to build up the enterprise. They believe that the enterprise today, having become profitable, owes them solicitous concern and a good livelihood in recompense for all that they had sacrificed in the past. It will be observed later in this paper that they hold to a type of "moral economy" perspective of their past and present.

*Earliest Memories*

The views of these workers in the Maoist period had been influenced by what they had experienced before the revolution, and their sense of whether they had benefited or not from the Communists' rise to power. The two oldest interviewees had become apprentices at two different distilleries in 1936, and they recall a world of constant work prior to the Communist victory. They had laboured every single day of the week for almost as long as they were awake, starting at the break of dawn. One of them recalls that it was not until the city watchman's second gong sounded at around 10 PM that he and his exhausted fellow workers finally could climb up into the distillery's loft to sleep. It was a Spartan existence. Twice a month at one distillery and three times a month at the other, they had a dish containing meat, the only times they ever ate meat. In addition to a small wage, every year they each received one simple set of clothing and one pair of cloth shoes. But in recollecting to us their work lives of those years, there was no noticeable rancor. They had accepted their lot at the time as normal, and only measured it in comparison to the conditions of their families in the countryside, whose lives were just as impoverished.

At the time of the Communist Party's ascension to power after 1949, our dozen elderly interviewees who were adults at the time made a shift in the way they interpreted their past. A striking example was provided by one of the two former apprentices. In the early 1950s he began participating actively in the nascent labor union that the new Communist government was organizing. He recalls that one evening in early 1950 the distillery owner cursed at him when he left work to attend a union meeting, and the owner's wife did not save his dinner for him that night. He complained to the union, which sent someone to speak with the owner, and thereafter dinners always awaited his return. It had been a trivial incident, but he insisted on recounting this small victory to us several times. It held great significance to him as a defining moment, signaling a change in power and in his own circumstances. In recounting to us his life as an apprentice he had expressed respect for the owner as a knowledgeable distiller who had passed on valuable skills to him. He had referred to the man as *Shifu*, a respectful term for a skilled mentor. But from his new perspective of the early 1950s he could begin to perceive of the man as an exploiter. He fluctuates in his recollections between an appreciation of the *Shifu*'s abilities and, at other times, from the vantage point of the new regime, in simple rigid pejorative terms as a "capitalist". More than half a century of Party teachings long ago habituated him to speak in such terms. He proudly played for us a videotape of a TV documentary that was filmed a few years ago, in which he appears on screen as an honoured working-class elder recounting how cruel it was to labour under a capitalist before the revolution. He feels no sense of hypocrisy in speaking this way. From his life experience, he is of two minds today about his relationship with his former employer. And in his conversations, he keeps his two minds separate and intact.

Both of the former apprentices first learned to read and write at free night classes that the new regime established. So, too, in fact did all of our elderly blue-collar interviewees. We interviewed eight women who began working at the distillery during the 1950s, and all of them have similar recollections about the early years of that decade: of free literacy classes, the establishment of neighbourhood health clinics, and enthusiastic volunteer work cleaning up their neighbourhoods. Whatever complaints they variously expressed to us about later times of Mao's rule, they all look back with very positive feelings to the changes in their lives for the better in the early 1950s.

As just one example, a now-elderly woman recalls her feelings about entering the distillery. Born into a very poor family, at the age of 12 in 1948, a year before the Communist victory, she had been sold into bonded labour to a better-off family to work as an unpaid maid. She remained in that situation until 1954, five years after the Communist victory, when at the age of 18 her employer arranged for her to marry a worker at a shoe factory. Within a year she gave birth to her first son. She, too, became a volunteer in her neighbourhood and began learning to read and write. When recruited by the local neighbourhood committee in 1957 to go work at the distillery, she responded with enthusiasm:

> We had been told by the street committee that men and women are equal, that our status should be the same, and that I could live on my own income, with no need to rely on others. I lived quite far from the factory. There was no bus. I had to walk for an hour to go to work, while my mother-in-law took care of my small children. A whole group of us women walked there together for our first day of work. I felt very moved and excited. After I received my first pay, I took it home to my husband. I had made 12 yuan. He said, 'you worked hard for it, you should do whatever you wish with it'.

Memories of initial feelings of commitment were held by almost all of our elderly interviewees, women and men alike. One consequence is that even when times turned bad in the following years, they did not become cynical. Throughout, they largely accepted the new Party-led system.

### *Doing It Tough*

Even though they largely supported the new political order, the distillery workers quickly became discomfited by never-ending rounds of "political study" and by a succession of campaigns that often puzzled them, sometimes worried them, very frequently bored them, and only occasionally aroused any enthusiasm. This was true even of the first of the campaigns that affected the distillery, the Three-Anti (*San Fan*) Campaign of 1952. The Three Antis referred to anti-corruption, anti-waste, and anti-bureaucratism, and the campaign was used by the new government to enforce its control early on in its rule.[6] No one at the then-tiny distillery was targeted, but daytime production stopped for several weeks, during which all of the staff had to attend massive public rallies with thousands of other spectators. They shouted out slogans

[6] A good description of the campaign and its effects is contained in Kenneth Lieberthal, *Revolution and Tradition in Tientsin, 1949–1952* (Stanford: Stanford University Press), 153–178.

criticizing corrupt capitalists and officials, day after numbing day. "Sitting there was awful," one of them recalls, "It was better to be working." To make up for the lost time, they had to labour at night. Even when the campaign ebbed and they returned to daytime production, political meetings after work hours relating to the campaign droned on for some months. Over the next quarter century, one campaign was to follow another, "sometimes one every year, sometimes two a year". The tedium of the meetings sapped their enthusiasm and patience.

There was also another way in which the workers could feel disadvantaged. Throughout the decades under Mao, work at the distillery involved dirty, hard, low-status physical labour. In the Marxist worldview, this type of work does not have the prestige of modern heavy industry, and thus during the period of Mao's rule the salaries and perquisites were noticeably poorer at the distillery than in high-status industries such as steel production.

Looking back from their present circumstances, the oldest generation recalls that throughout the decades of Mao's rule they had endured a subsistence living standard, very crowded run-down housing, and exhausting labor. In many cases, three generations of a family were packed into one or two small, dank rooms, without any kitchen space or nearby tap water.

### *The Great Leap and its Aftermath*

The Great Leap Forward of 1958–59 involved extended labour and extended political study to an extreme degree and aroused conflicted feelings among almost all of the interviewees. They believed in the government, wanted to remain committed, yet the campaign demanded far too much of them. They recollect exhaustion, concerns among the women about not having the time to care for their children, and a period so tense that no one dared complain. One woman, for instance, related to us a series of incidents in which one or another employee got into trouble for complaining or for telling politically incorrect jokes, and she indicated that people were held in line by this tension, concluding "It was severe in the time of Grandpa Mao." Yet later in the same interview, when asked about why she worked so hard in the 1950s and 1960s, she replied, "It was the teachings. If the Party called on you to work at something you worked at that, as though you were a Party member. Because we were of impoverished birth, it didn't matter whether you were or weren't a Party member, we still should work like this, and do so independently."

Most of our other interviewees similarly expressed confused, contrary feelings about the Great Leap Forward, and about later periods. My sense from the interviews is that they had held such complex self-contradictory feelings *at the time*. Surprisingly, the recollections by employees who were favoured by the political system and became Party members and those who were disfavoured politically were somewhat similar. A woman whose husband had been sent in 1957 to labour in the countryside for two decades as punishment for being a Rightist recalls bouts of crying and misery over her family's personal fate, but she also remembers a mood of commitment at the distillery.

### *From Cultural Revolution to Mao's Death*

During the Cultural Revolution of 1966–68, the manager and two of the foremen who were known for strictness had aroused enough disgruntlement that they were locked up briefly in one of the storerooms, on a concocted accusation that before the revolution they had belonged to a working-class secret society, the Elder Brothers Society. But there was no violence or turmoil at the distillery. Practically all of the factory's employees supported the Rebel faction, *en masse*, but no interviewee could explain what each of the Cultural Revolution factions stood for, or why they wore Rebel-faction armbands to work. However, the fact that the distillery was solidly Rebel was not a random choice. Throughout much of China, workers at the core high-status enterprises largely supported the so-called Conservative faction, while workers at the enterprises that received unfavourable treatment and relatively low wages largely supported the Rebel faction.[7] The impoverished over-worked distillery workers presumably understood this at some semi-conscious level—that people like themselves fit into this Cultural Revolution Rebel faction. But the great majority of them, and all of the women interviewees, recall simply a time of chaotic violence in the streets, worries about their children, and personal bafflement. These

[7] As examples, in Changsha, the capital of Hunan province, handicraft workers, construction workers (who were also poorly paid) and the transport coolies who pulled the handcarts that manhandled freight through city streets all heavily supported the Rebel faction. (Jonathan Unger, "Whither China? Yang Xiguang, Red Capitalists, and the Social Turmoil of the Cultural Revolution," *Modern China* 17, 1 (January 1991): 20.

distillery workers' views presumably were shared by many tens of millions of ordinary middle-aged people across China.

After the turmoil was suppressed by the national leadership in the latter part of 1968, recriminations and factionalism continued for some years at many of China's factories, especially the larger ones.[8] But not at the small and politically peripheral distillery. For the most part, the level of anxiety was subdued. Employees no longer competed to seem politically active when discussion sessions were held to determine each others' wages, and they no longer criticized each other when asked to do so. They preferred to get along with others while at work, and they were exhausted by anything that smacked of "politics". Even so, they did not become noticeably cynical or disaffected. The unanimous opinion among interviewees is that most of the employees had remained conscientious in their work.

Nevertheless, outside of the workplace all of the distillery employees confronted the daily grind of poverty. To a large extent, it was a poverty shared by most urban Chinese, which at least made it more palatable. Few goods were available in stores, and even basic necessities were rationed, including cloth. As a consequence, most urban people needed to keep mending their old clothes until these were full of patches. As one elderly woman recalls, "People would look down at you if you were dirty and didn't regularly wash your clothes, but not if your clothes were full of patches. If the patches were sewn on nicely, people even complimented you on your sewing skill." But in many other respects, including their abysmal housing, the distillery workers were worse off than most other state-enterprise workers, as was their status, and it sometimes grated. As one of our interviewees observes, "In our industry, there was a saying: 'a distillery guy has to guard an empty bedroom.' It was hard for distillery workers like us to find a wife. We were looked down upon by others." Looking back in time, the distillery employees today consider that their prior poverty, back-wrenching work, and even difficulties in getting married were sacrifices that they had patiently endured, at a time when workers were told, decade after decade, that they needed to make sacrifices for the

[8] Liu Guokai, "A Brief Analysis of the Cultural Revolution", *Chinese Sociology and Anthropology*, 19, 2 (Winter 1986–87), esp. 130–145; also Keith Forster, *Rebellion and Factionalism in a Chinese Province: Zhejiang, 1966–1976* (Armonk, N.Y.: M. E. Sharpe, 1990); Elizabeth J. Perry and Li Xun, *Proletarian Power: Shanghai in the Cultural Revolution* (Boulder: Westview Press, 1997).

good of the revolution. In short, the memories of the Maoist period of most of our interviewees are not nostalgic.

### *The Post-Mao Era: Enterprise Profits and New Expectations*

Under the command economy of Mao's time, the enterprise leadership did not have the leeway to decide on the salaries and living conditions of the employees, which were largely determined by the state plan. The concerns of the management had to focus more on meeting the targets of the Party-state and of the food-processing-industry bureau that stood directly above the enterprise rather than the needs and pressures of the work community. They had little scope to be the benefactors of their workforce. But after Mao's death, under the economic reforms of Deng Xiaoping, this began to change.

To be sure, the distillery and other state-owned enterprises retained many of the attributes of a Mao-era work-unit (*danwei*). But starting in the 1980s, there was no longer any regular Maoist-style political study or strong political controls over the workforce, and the distillery managers were no longer under strong command-economy pressures to serve the interests of the state. Reforms to industry in the 1980s allowed enterprises to retain much of their profits and gave far greater discretion to management on how to spend the funds. The distillery benefited greatly from this. Up through the 1980s, good liquor was in short supply, especially since officials throughout China were increasingly lavish when banqueting at public expense. The distillery was permitted to sell its production at high market prices, and in such circumstances there was a feeling among the blue-collar employees, including the workshop heads and foremen, that a debt was owed to them—that since the workers had put in many years of loyal service, in poverty, the distillery leadership was in turn duty-bound to be paternalistic and to share out the enterprise's new-found profits with them.

The distillery responded by boosting their standard of living. It was not unique in doing this. A great many state-owned enterprises in the mid-1980s began to bestow on their workers cash bonuses, extra in-kind compensation, and new housing.[9]

---

[9] On this phenomenon of the mid-1980s, see, e.g., Andrew Walder, "Factory and Manager in an Era of Reform", *The China Quarterly* 118 (June 1989): 249, 251. Notably, at the start of the reforms to industry in 1982, 54 percent of all of China's urban

Some China specialists today are under the impression that almost all of China's state enterprises turned sharply away from such paternalistic and benevolent managerial behaviour during the following decades. Certainly, many enterprises did, but a distillery director who understood the employees' values had recently been appointed from within the bureau. The distillery was making good money, and he felt under no financial pressure to clamp down on the employees' conditions of employment. Instead, he was able to implement a series of enterprise policies that were in keeping with the employees' moral economy perspective.

## *The Moral Economy*

This term "moral economy", as employed in the writings of E. P. Thompson, James C. Scott and many others, refers to a community demand that those who control resources should abide by a shared notion of economic justice, often grounded in a vision by subordinates of what they insist are honoured traditions of what is right and wrong. The concept encapsulates several important features of the work-community ethos that prevails in a Chinese enterprise such as the distillery.

Thompson first used the term in a famous paper analysing food riots in 18th century urban England. He noted that the riots cannot be explained simply as an effort by hungry people to grab food; rather, their actions were in protest against the violation of a "moral economy" in which they held a right to subsistence:

> ...the men and women in the crowd were informed by the belief that they were defending traditional rights or customs; and in general, that they were supported by the consensus of the community...as to what were legitimate and what were illegitimate practices.... An outrage to these moral assumptions, quite as much as actual deprivation, was the usual occasion for direct action.... [These 'moral-economy' notions] found some support in the paternalist tradition of the authorities; notions

housing stock was work-unit owned. Work units built so much new accommodation for employees during the 1982–85 period, in the first flush of enterprise autonomy, that by 1985 75 percent of all urban housing was work-unit owned. Fulong Wu, "Changes in the Structure of Public Housing Provision in Urban China", *Urban Studies* 33, 9 (1966): 1603.

> which the people re-echoed so loudly in their turn that the authorities were, in some measure, the prisoners of the people.[10]

James Scott extended the moral economy concept to pre-capitalist Southeast Asian villages, which were tightly bound social communities unlike the urban environments in which Thompson's food riots occurred. In Scott's portrait, the moral-economy perceptions held by poor farmers in such villages (what Scott calls "their notion of economic justice...—their view of which claims on their product were tolerable and which intolerable")[11] often proved effective without any need for explicit, organized protests. Through the pressure of opinion in the community, the richer farmers and landlords felt constrained to meet that notion of economic justice by acting in a redistributive fashion through charitable acts, or through lowering land rents at times of drought, or through sponsorship of community celebrations.

Both Thompson and Scott presumed that the rise of capitalism and of the commercialization of relationships spelled an end to the environment in which a 'moral economy' could prevail, and a main focus of their writings was on the desperate protests that arose during that particular historical period of change. But several scholars have fruitfully employed the 'moral economy' framework to analyse late 20th century situations.[12] (Thompson himself has used the concept to describe the British miners' strike of 1984.)[13] Most of these contemporary studies focus, like their predecessors, on incidents of mass protest, but there is no necessary reason why studies that use a 'moral economy' framework need to be restricted to conflicts. In some cases, a leadership may share the community's premises about a 'moral economy' and may give in

---

[10] E. P. Thompson, "The Moral Economy of the English Crowd in the Eighteenth Century," *Past and Present*, 50 (February 1971): 78–9. Although Thompson was focusing on riots as a means to make these people's voices heard about violations to a moral economy, he also noted that such rioting is not "the only or the most obvious form of collective action—there may be alternatives such as mass petitioning of the authorities". See E. P. Thompson, *Customs in Common* (London: Merlin Press, 1991), 263.

[11] James C. Scott, *The Moral Economy of the Peasant* (New Haven: Yale University Press, 1976), 3.

[12] See, for example, Paul Bagguley, "The Moral Economy of Anti-Poll Tax Protest" [on Thatcher's England], in Colin Barker and Paul Kennedy, eds, *To Make Another World: Studies in Protest and Collective Action* (Aldershot: Avebury, 1996), 7–24; Marsha Pripstein Posusney, "Irrational Workers: The Moral Economy of Labor Protest in Egypt," *World Politics* 46 (October 1993): 83–120; John Walton, *Western Times and Water Wars: State, Culture and Rebellion in California* (Berkeley: University of California Press, 1992); and Stefan Svallfors, *The Moral Economy of Class* (Stanford: Stanford University Press, 2006).

[13] E. P. Thompson, *Customs in Common*, 340, fn. 1.

to community pressures willingly. The core of the 'moral economy' premise rests, after all, not on antagonistic confrontation *per se*, but on a community's insistence that those in power abide by the preservation, in James Scott's words, of "the structure of a shared moral universe, a common notion of what is just".[14]

The crux of the 'moral economy' premise applies to the Chinese enterprise we have discussed. As will be observed, it possesses an enterprise ethos in which a "shared moral universe" and, in Scott's phrasing, a "notion of economic justice" advocated by subordinates has obliged the top management to bend redistributive policies more in their favour.

### *The Shared Moral Universe at the Distillery*

The distillery workers justify (and have used pressures to help shape) their fortunate present circumstances by drawing upon a specific moral interpretation of the past. There have been reports from China's rustbelt regions, where many state-enterprise workers have been laid off or do not receive their full pay on time, that workers there have carried Mao portraits in protest demonstrations and proclaim nostalgia for the period of Mao's rule. Because the distillery workers' current situation differs dramatically from that of rustbelt workers, their *evaluation* of the past is far less favourable than that of the currently disgruntled rustbelt workers.

In at least some respects, though, the "moral economy" discourse of the distillery workers bears a similarity to the perspective of workers in the rustbelt. One similarity is in borrowing from the official rhetoric of the Maoist era, which preached that workers were the masters of the country and that a debt of gratitude was implicitly owed to them. This notion was remembered and taken to heart by workers at the distillery during the post-Mao reform era, and they have made strategic use of it. Their memories of having remained faithfully committed to the good of the enterprise and the country, of having worked themselves to the bone decade after decade, and having been continuously materially deprived contributes to their moral discourse of having earned favoured treatment in the present day.

[14] James C. Scott, *The Moral Economy of the Peasant*, 167.

While this discourse contains some of the elements of the Maoist ethos about the superiority of the proletariat and of the industrial working class, it also contains elements that go against the Maoist vision. Unlike workers in the rustbelt, the distillery employees do *not* project the Maoist period as fairer to the working class than the present day. Indeed, their collective view is that they are entitled today to generous treatment by the enterprise precisely because they had materially sacrificed and been deprived during the decades under Mao. Notably, in visits to several dozen homes I did not see a single Mao portrait or other memento of Mao, nor did I see any at the distillery.

The argument that the distillery paternalistically owes the workers benefits has been implicitly generalized to cover all of the distillery employees, including those who started working after the Maoist period had already ended. These younger workers today comprise the great bulk of the workforce, especially since the distillery has expanded from some 400–500 employees at the time of Mao's death in 1976 to close to 2,000 today. A generalized aura surrounds the notion that paternalistic treatment is owed to all of the employees, young as well as old, as recompense for the workforce's sacrifices of past times, highlighted by the special debt owed to the older workers in their ranks.

The enterprise director accepts the employees' feelings and expectations of paternalism. So do most of the middle-level managerial staff, who largely have risen from the ranks of the blue-collar employees. Their own sense of economic justice is in line with the manual workers'. Reinforcing this is the fact that, similar to the rich farmers and landlords in James Scott's traditional village communities, all of the distillery's managers have lived intermixed with the employees in distillery-built housing, that is, in the same tight-knit community. Through this, the employees have been able to reach managers' ears and can bring the community's sentiments to bear.

In many other state enterprises, especially those that have been losing money, as in the rustbelt, top managers have sealed themselves off from work-community feelings and pressures and have narrowly looked only to their own interests. But with substantial profits flowing in from high-priced liquor starting in the late 1980s, the distillery directors have had considerable scope to respond with sympathetic generosity.

The work community's capacity to influence enterprise policies in a "moral economy" direction is well illustrated by the debates that arose in 1994 when the distillery built a new housing estate containing more than three hundred nice apartments in a landscaped setting.[15] It was central government policy to sell off enterprise apartments, and a rumour spread that several of the distillery managers proposed to favour themselves by reserving the best of the new apartments for top management. A group of middle-ranking cadres who had entered the distillery in the early 1970s drew up a petition protesting against the rumoured proposal. The petition asked that the main criterion when selling the apartments should be longevity at the enterprise. Large numbers of ordinary workers and most of the production workshop heads and foremen and older white-collar staff signed the petition.

When the enterprise director—who was simultaneously the Party secretary—received the petition, he convened a meeting and emotionally conceded the justice of the employees' position. In the following days, he let it be known that the issue was of such importance that, rather than have the enterprise leaders simply decide from above how the apartments would be allocated, the decision would be given over to the enterprise's Staff and Workers Representative Council (*Zhi Gong Daibiao Dahui*).

Over a period of several months, influenced by repeated discussions on the workshop floors, the Council's deliberations bent the sale of the new apartments in a 'moral economy' direction. It was decided that the best 3-bedroom apartments should all be sold at a subsidized rate to those who had worked at the enterprise the longest, out of respect for their decades of toil. Based on this criterion, they would go first in selecting the apartments they wanted, and then others would be able to choose their own smaller and less well-located apartments, going in the order of their work-year seniority. It was also decided that employees who had worked for over 30 years (and they alone) should get a substantial price reduction for the portion of their apartment over 60 square meters. For each year that they had worked, they would receive a 2 percent reduction, and thus those in their late 50s, with some 40 years of work under their belts, would obtain an 80 percent discount. This reduction violated government regulations. But as one interviewee—the director of the enterprise's Administrative Office—expressed it, "The older you are the more you had contributed to the enterprise. Before,

[15] This discussion of the distribution of these flats draws upon Jonathan Unger and Anita Chan, "The Internal Politics of an Urban Chinese Work Community: A Case Study of Employee Influence on Decision-Making at a State Owned Factory," *The China Journal* 52 (July 2004): 1–24.

they just worked and worked, with no bonuses, and their wages were low, so all they did was to contribute. And that's why the special discount was passed."

This subsidized sale of enterprise-built apartments clearly illuminates a shared moral-economy ethos in which enterprise leaders acceded to work-community desires that housing distributions should be made in what employees deemed an equitable fashion. But there was a special twist to the meaning here of "equitable". This was not strictly a needs-based equity. Acting in accordance with genuine needs would not have granted the largest 3-bedroom apartments to older workers whose children had already left home. Instead, a needs-based equity would have prioritized the new young workers with young children who need the extra space. The sense of "equity" that prevailed at the distillery was derived instead from the particular moral-economy perspective that had evolved during China's recent history: that a debt of gratitude was owed, as "just" and "fair" reciprocity, to those who had faithfully, in poverty, served the enterprise longest—especially those who had engaged in hard physical labour, the kind of labour that was hailed as "proletarian" and superior in the Maoist ethos. The older employees' interpretation of the past has served them well.

The enterprise management's sense of its responsibility extends to a special show of paternalistic benevolence toward retirees. At Chinese New Year in 2003, 210 out of the 240 retirees turned up at a restaurant to be honoured at an annual celebration on their behalf, at which the distillery's leaders thanked them in emotional speeches for the decades of hard work they had given to the enterprise. Each was handed a red envelope containing 300 yuan, along with apologies that the amount was 100 yuan less than the previous year, which had been more profitable for the company. In another show of appreciation, up until recently all of the retirees and their spouses were given free overnight sightseeing tours every year to famous scenic landmarks.

The enterprise is not an anomaly among state enterprises in providing such benefits. With the Chinese economy expanding healthily year after year, we should not assume that all state enterprises are in financial difficulties. Interviewees relate that many of the state-owned enterprises in their city's food-processing industry have continued to show profits and have sought to look after the interests of their workforce in a similarly paternalistic fashion.

*Going Private*

Such expenditures, as expressions of paternalistic concern, may be drawing to a close. The central government has been promoting the privatization of many of the state enterprises—and the distillery was no exception. Its privatization occurred in 2003, and the top enterprise directors have been able to buy the lion's share of the new stocks under the guise that this is a combined employee/management buyout. In reality, the ordinary employees have been restricted to a maximum of only 13 percent of the enterprise's shares.

Notably, the concerns of the employees—including the workshop heads and middle-level officials who were interviewed—did not focus on their enterprise's change of ownership, even though the great bulk of the shares went to a small number of executives at a discounted price. This is a matter well beyond their normal concerns or understanding. They accepted without questioning when told that they themselves would only be able to purchase a few stocks in the complicated buyout, even though a larger block of shares might conceivably have made them well off. What instead concerns them most is whether the benevolent, paternalistic moral-economy ethos will continue as before. The horizons of their wishes and demands are quite limited. Their mentality is akin to the "subsistence ethic" of James Scott's moral economy—"The test for the peasant is more likely to be 'What is left?' than 'How much is taken?'"[16] The privatization had to be approved by the Staff and Workers Representative Council, and it sailed through without objections in a single afternoon. Having adopted a "moral economy" paradigm as their framework, the employees had trapped themselves within that paradigm, and as a result had forfeited opportunities for self-advancement when an entirely different set of opportunities arose.

Even after its privatization, the enterprise has continued to provide employees and retirees with gifts, subsidies and other benefits. And the employees, despite their quiet fears, declare their continued "trust" in the good heart of the enterprise director. But if he does not live up to their trust, or after he retires, they may well find that less is "left" for them than they believe is their due. Already, most of the enterprise

[16] *The Moral Economy of the Peasant*, 7. A very good discussion of this "subsistence ethic" among laid-off Chinese workers is Feng Chen, "Subsistence Crises, Managerial Corruption and Labour Protests in China", *The China Journal* 44 (July 2000): 41–63.

managers have sold their flats in the distillery's housing complexes and have moved into fancy high-rise housing estates scattered across the city. They no longer live in the same community as the employees, and no longer so readily come under the community's influence. However much the older employees justify their present-day treatment in terms of their commitment and sacrifices in the past, they now have far less capacity to influence the managers' policies than they have previously enjoyed. In short, it seems unlikely that the moral-economy consensus that has guided corporate behaviour in this and kindred enterprises can be sustained much longer in the face of corporate sell-offs and a shift in management's lifestyle. Nevertheless, whatever occurs, the collective memories, beliefs, and attitudes of the older employees are not likely to quickly disappear. They are part of the worldview of that generation of workers.

## *Summing Up*

This discussion of the distillery helps illuminate ways in which the past and the present are interrelated. It would not be possible to comprehend management-worker relations in the current era without any reference to the attitude-set held by both the employees and the enterprise director. And it would not be possible to comprehend these attitudes outside of the context of the experiences of the employees during the period of Mao's rule and the 'moral economy' perspective that they developed as a consequence. We should not, as sociologists, cut ourselves off from the recent Maoist past through a lack of research.

One of Chairman Mao's famous quotes was 'Use the Past to Serve the Present'. As we have been discussing the Maoist period, let me borrow this quotation from the Great Helmsman. We as sociologists ought to study the past for its own sake, before it is lost to history. But doing so also places us in a position, as the Chairman urges, to use the past to serve the present: to better understand present-day Chinese society by understanding the impact of the past on the present.

## *References*

Bagguley, Paul. (1996). "The Moral Economy of Anti-Poll Tax Protest." Pp. 7–24 in *To Make Another World: Studies in Protest and Collective Action*, edited by Colin Barker and Paul Kennedy. Aldershot: Avebury.

Chan, Anita; Richard Madsen and Jonathan Unger. (1992). *Chen Village Under Mao and Deng*. Berkeley: University of California Press.
Feng Chen. (2000). "Subsistence Crises, Managerial Corruption and Labour Protests in China." *The China Journal* 44: 41–63.
Forster, Keith. (1990). *Rebellion and Factionalism in a Chinese Province: Zhejiang, 1966–1976*. Armonk, N.Y.: M. E. Sharpe.
Friedman, Edward; Paul G. Pickowicz and Mark Selden. (1991/2005). *Chinese Village, Socialist State* and *Revolution, Resistance and Reform in Village China*. New Haven: Yale University Press.
Gao Mobo. (1999). *Gao Village: Rural Life in China Since the Revolution*. Honolulu: University of Hawaii Press.
Huang, Philip. (1990). *The Peasant Family and Rural Development in the Yangzi Delta*. Stanford: Stanford University Press.
Huang Shu-min. (1989). *The Spiral Road: Change in a Chinese Village Through the Eyes of a Communist Party Leader*. Boulder: Westview Press.
Judd, Ellen R. (1994). *Gender and Power in Rural North China*. Stanford: Stanford University Press.
Jun Jing. (1996). *The Temple of Memories: History, Power, and Morality in a Chinese Village*. Stanford: Stanford University Press.
Ku, Hok Bun. (2003). *Moral Politics in a South Chinese Village*. Lanham: Rowman and Littlefield.
Lieberthal, Kenneth. (1980). *Revolution and Tradition in Tientsin, 1949–1952*. Stanford: Stanford University Press.
Liu Guokai. (1986/7). "A Brief Analysis of the Cultural Revolution." *Chinese Sociology and Anthropology* 19(2):130–145.
Madsen, Richard. (1984). *Morality and Power in a Chinese Village*. Berkeley: University of California Press.
Parish, William L., and Martin K. Whyte. (1978). *Village and Family in Contemporary China*. Chicago: University of Chicago Press.
Perry, Elizabeth J., and Li Xun. (1997). *Proletarian Power: Shanghai in the Cultural Revolution*. Boulder: Westview Press.
Posusney, Marsha Pripstein. (1993). "Irrational Workers: The Moral Economy of Labor Protest in Egypt." *World Politics* 46: 83–120.
Potter, Sulamith Heins and Jack M. Potter. (1990). *China's Peasants: The Anthropology of a Revolution*. Cambridge: Cambridge University Press.
Ruf, Gregory A. (1998). *Cadres and Kin: Power, Authority, and Corporatism in a West China Village, 1937–1991*. Stanford: Stanford University Press.
Scott, James C. (1976). *The Moral Economy of the Peasant*. New Haven: Yale University Press.
Siu, Helen F. (1989). *Agents and Victims in South China*. New Haven: Yale University Press.
Svallfors, Stefan. (2006). *The Moral Economy of Class*. Stanford: Stanford University Press.
Thompson, E. P. (1971). "The Moral Economy of the English Crowd in the Eighteenth Century." *Past and Present* 50: 78–9.
——. (1991). *Customs in Common*. London: Merlin Press.
Unger, Jonathan. (1991). "Whither China? Yang Xiguang, Red Capitalists, and the Social Turmoil of the Cultural Revolution." *Modern China* 17(1): 3–37.
——. (2006). "Family Customs and Farmland Reallocations in Contemporary Chinese Villages", *Social Transformations in Chinese Societies* 1(1): 113–130.
——. (2007). "The Cultural Revolution at the Grass Roots." *The China Journal*. 57: 09–137.
Unger, Jonathan, and Anita Chan. (2004). "The Internal Politics of an Urban Chinese Work Community: A Case Study of Employee Influence on Decision-Making at a State Owned Factory." *The China Journal* 52: 1–24.

Walder, Andrew. (1989). "Factory and Manager in an Era of Reform." *The China Quarterly* 118: 242–264.

Walton, John. (1992). *Western Times and Water Wars: State, Culture and Rebellion in California.* Berkeley: University of California Press.

Wu, Fulong. (1996). "Changes in the Structure of Public Housing Provision in Urban China." *Urban Studies* 33(9): 1601–1627.

Whyte, Martin K., and William L. Parish. (1984). *Urban Life in Contemporary China.* Chicago: University of Chicago Press.

Yan, Yunxiang. (1996). *The Flow of Gifts: Reciprocity and Social Networks in a Chinese Village.* Berkeley: University of California Press.

Zhang Letian. (1998). *Gaobie lixiang: Renmin gongshe zhidu yanjiu* (Departing from Ideals: Research into the System of the People's Commune). Shanghai: Dongfang Chubanshe.

Zhu Xiaoyang. (2003). *Zuiguo yu chengfa: Xiaocun gushi 1931–1997* (Crime and Punishment: The Tale of a Small Village 1931–1997). Tianjin: Guji Chubanshe.

# BOOK REVIEWS

*Commerce and Capitalism in Chinese Societies*, by Hamilton, Gary G., London, New York: Routledge, 2006. 309pp. ISBN: 9–7804–1515–705–6.

This book is a collection of Gary Hamilton's previously published articles, with a new introduction. Cast in historical and comparative perspectives and rearranged thematically, these articles offer a highly illuminating account of the evolution of capitalism in Chinese societies. The book begins with a discussion of the theoretical and methodological challenges posed by the economic transformations of Chinese societies in the wake and shadow of Western industrialization. It then traces the roots of Chinese capitalism by examining production, commerce, and consumption in the late-imperial period. Expanding on the ideas and arguments laid out in the preceding chapters, the remaining chapters of the book analyses the trajectories of capitalist development in Hong Kong, Taiwan, and Chinese communities in Thailand; the internal and external organisation of Chinese business firms; and the relationship between Asian business networks and the remaking of the global capitalist economy. Three related themes recur throughout the book.

First, the author identifies a major flaw in many comparative studies of capitalism. The problem, he argues, is that these studies use ideal types based on the experiences of Western capitalist development as the benchmark to gauge the level and vitality of capitalist development in non-Western societies. According to Hamilton, capitalism involves predominantly private, for-profit activities to address growing consumer demands from domestic and, increasingly, international markets. In the West, the organisation of such activities initially took the form of the factory system, which culminated in the Fordist mode of production. Such organisation was anchored in a co-evolving legal-rational political system. These organisational and institutional features are products of Western history. But they are not the only internal and external arrangements whereby capitalism can be developed.

The book illustrates this by discussing two widely noted debates. The first concerns the "sprouts of capitalism" in China. Using the Western model as the benchmark, many scholars have concluded that capitalism did not develop indigenously in China because before the mid-19th century, neither the factory system nor anything close to the modern Western political system could be found there. They then attribute this absence to various "culprits", such as constraints and disincentives from the political system, market rigidities, pressure of population growth, the inheritance system and other social and cultural institutions. The second debate is about the causes of the Asian financial crisis in the late 1990s. A popular explanation claims that the lack of well-established legal-rational institutions and free markets in East and Southeast Asian economies, where informality permeated business practices and transactions, fostered a "cronyism" that led to the debacle of their financial and currency systems.

What these lines of reasoning have in common is that they seek to establish causality by looking for "what is not there" in light of a Western model of capitalism. This tends to blur rather than clarify the picture. A more useful approach, Hamilton argues, is to explore how capitalism might have developed through alternative avenues in civilisations that are quite different from those in the West, and to examine how "what was there" actually shaped the process and outcome of such development. This leads to the second theme of the book: the development of capitalism in Chinese societies.

The title of the book, *Commerce and Capitalism in Chinese Societies*, captures the gist of the story. Hamilton shows that an essential feature of capitalism in Chinese societies is that it has been in large part a merchant-driven process instead of a producer-driven process. In contrast to the factory system where the division of labor is highly internalised and formalised, market-oriented industrial production in China was initially organised through extensive external division of labor among very small social units, such as families working as sub-contractors, and coordinated through a network of merchants that interlinked producers with markets. Also, despite the lack of legal-rational state authority, communal organisations such as native-place associations and merchant associations evolved into an influential force in fostering trust, enforcing shared norms and business codes, and regulating transactions, thereby creating an institutional environment in which a certain level of calculability, reciprocity and relational stability could be sustained for the recurrence and expansion of commercial pursuits.

It was with these organisational and institutional features that capitalism had its beginnings in China, which Hamilton dates back to the mid-Ming period (between the 15th and 16th centuries). This form of capitalism gradually grew during the Qing dynasty (1644–1911) and spread to Chinese societies outside the mainland. While adapting to changes in the political and socio-economic environments of these societies and co-evolving with other types of economic organisation into the modern era, it has never been absorbed by the Western mode of capitalist production. Interestingly, since the mid-1960s, the "retail revolution" led by increasingly powerful retailers and brand-name merchandisers in the West has shifted the organisation of the global economy from producer-driven manufacturing to merchant-driven, demand-responsive chains of commodity production. Such development converges with the historical trajectory of Chinese capitalism, thereby stimulating the growth of the economies where it has a significant presence and integrating these economies more closely with the global economic system. This new dynamism continues to draw extensively on socially embedded, informal business networks and reciprocities. Hamilton argues that such interactions do not amount to collusion that prevents competition and, therefore, it is wrong to equate them to "cronyism" and treat them as the cause of the Asian financial crisis. On the contrary, they have in fact enabled Chinese-dominant capitalist economies to weather the storm of the crisis better than some other regional economies. The main cause of the crisis, instead, lie elsewhere. It resulted (and then spilled over) from interplays among organisational rigidities in Japan and South Korea, weak financial institutional infrastructure in Southeast Asia, and speculation in capital and property markets.

The third theme of the book concerns the notion "Chinese capitalism". This is an ideal type defined in the Weberian tradition. In Hamilton's view, it is misleading to use the Western model as the common reference point for comparative study of capitalism in societies shaped by vastly different "civilisational forces". He identifies two defining features that set the ideal-typical Chinese capitalism apart from its Western counterpart. Its internal organisation is held together by an authoritarian structure based on family ownership and control, and what reinforces the hierarchical role differentiation among family members at the decision core is the value of *xiao* (filial piety). The external organisation of this type of capitalism is lodged in socially embedded business networks, where the norm of *renqing* (interpersonal indebtedness and obligations) plays a central role in sustaining reciprocity and facilitating cooperation. The ideas of *xiao* and *renqing* are both deeply rooted in Chinese civilisation, yet they have also been cannibalised as essential elements in the evolving organisation and governance of capitalism since the late-imperial period. Despite the diverse paths of development subsequently taken by different Chinese societies, the ideal type still epitomises their shared historical and cultural heritage that continues to be influential in social and economic life, thus serving as a far more useful benchmark for making comparisons among these societies and with other societies.

The substantive chapters of the book contain ample and wide-ranging evidence and examples that persuasively substantiate the themes summarised above. Although crafted separately over the span of nearly three decades, these articles form a remarkably coherent set of scholarship. The book is masterfully written, cogently argued, and full of insights. It is a must-read for anyone interested in the study of global capitalism, as well as economic development and social change in East and Southeast Asia. It is also an excellent source of materials for courses on economic sociology, comparative economic systems, economic history, international management, and the Chinese diaspora.

Lin Yi-min Hong Kong University of Science and Technology

*As Borders Bend: Transnational Spaces on the Pacific Rim*, by Chen Xiangming, Lanham, M. D.: Rowman & Littlefield Publishers, 2005. 360pp. ISBN: 0–7425–0094–2.

One of the most important implications of the globalisation thesis is that the status and role of the nation-state have been significantly re-shaped in the context of macro socio-economic, political, cultural, technological, and environmental changes. Some, like Kenichi Ohmae (1990, 1995), suggest that globalisation has brought about a borderless world and thus the end of the nation-state. Chen, being prudent and having his observations firmly grounded in rigorous historical and comparative analysis, is cautious when making generalisations about what has been going on in local and regional development in the past twenty years. He argues that the nation-states in different parts of the world have been de-bordered and re-bordered simultaneously. It is not that national borders have disappeared. Rather, they have been reconfigured—from the previous function of a barrier to a new bridging role in connecting sub-regions whose activities are no longer confined to the boundary of the nation states.

Chen's analysis is based upon empirical studies of seven cases of trans-border sub-regions in the Asia Pacific. These trans-border subregions are: a) the Greater Southeast China Sub-region (covering China's Guangdong and Fujian provinces, Hong Kong, Macau, and Taiwan); b) the Bohai/Yellow Sea Sub-region (including China's Liaoning and Shandong provinces, South Korea, the southwestern region of Japan, and possibly North Korea); c) the Greater Tumen Sub-region (involving China's Jilin province, North Korea's Free Trade Zone, and Russia's Far East Khasan region); d) the Greater Mekong Sub-region (covering China's Yunnan province, Myanmar, Lao People's Democratic Republic, Thailand, Vambodia and Vietnam); e) the Indonesia-Malaysia-Thailand Growth Triangle; f) the Indonesia-Malaysia-Singapore Growth Triangle; and g) the Brunei-Indonesia-Malaysia-Philippines East ASEAN Growth Area. These seven cases are individually analysed in detail and are also examined comparatively. On one hand, Chen emphasises the commonalities of the spread of economic activity and cultural linkage across borders; emerging economic and political interdependence among nation states in the context of globalisation; and the rise of trans-border sub-regions in different parts of the Asia Pacific. On the other, he is quick to point out the diversity among the trans-border sub-regions in the Asia Pacific and elsewhere. The rise of these trans-border sub-regions is uneven, shaped by varying institutional thickness at the local and regional levels, and is moving towards both integration and fragmentation. The theoretical framework put forward by Chen promises to unravel the complexity and diversity among these emerging sub-regions of rapid economic growth, the flows of economic activity and the people in the context of globalisation.

Chen develops a framework for his comparative analysis with an emphasis on what he calls the four analytical lens, namely a geo-economic lens (the global-local nexus), a political-institutional lens (the decentering of the state), a socio-cultural lens (cross-border social capital), and a spatio-infrastructure lens (proximity and transportation). The framework is designed for analysing diversity in the configuration of the pattern of development among the selected cases of trans-border sub-regions. Furthermore, this is a tool for analysing the regional and local outcomes of the development of these trans-border sub-regions. Chen suggests that "underlying this synthetic framework is a harmonious hypothesis: if the main factors suggested by each analytical lens not only are favorable but also complement one another across the four dimensions, they will induce generally beneficial outcomes for a trans-border sub-region, such as rapid growth and close integration.... This harmonious hypothesis suggests not that these factors must and always will work well together, but that the extent to which they do helps explain the differences and similarities across the cases. The ultimate objective of this synthetic explanation is to shed light on the central argument about the changing role of borders in bridging previously isolated border areas into the linked transborder subregions verses the remaining or recurring barrier effect of borders on these transborder subregions" (pp. 54–5).

On the whole, Chen has provided a forceful analysis on the emergence of trans-border sub-regions in the Pacific Rim. Particularly, drawing upon the work of macro-historical studies (e.g. Hamashita), he has demonstrated the longer term historical roots of economic, cultural as well as political connections among the sub-regions. Indeed, one of the strengths of his analysis lies in his inclusion of population movement (especially the Chinese diaspora) into his analytical framework and the analysis of how the flows of people in a longer historical perspective explain the building of connections and cooperation across nation-states. Chen is also aware of the need for a comparison between, and this he does briefly, trans-border sub-regions in the Pacific and the Atlantic.

If there are questions that Chen has not dealt with adequately, it would be the evaluation of social and economic outcomes found in these sub-regions. His harmonious hypothesis and its testing also require further elaboration. For instance, Chen is very positive in his evaluation of the Greater Southeast China Subregion, praising it as "the most mature and successful in growth and integration" (p. 99). Such evaluation alerts us to the question concerning the sociological basis of his judgment. The impact of economic restructuring (such as relocation of manufacturing activity and the resultant changing employment opportunities for the less educated) on the local economies, say Hong Kong and Taiwan, are by no means unproblematic. More critical analysis of the unevenness of development and underlying inequalities in the structuring of cross-border socio-economic integration is in order.

*As Border Bends* is an informed analysis of an emerging pattern of local and regional development in the world. Both students (seniors at the undergraduate level and the postgraduates) and researchers in sociology, geography, urban studies, economics, politics, development studies and Asia-Pacific area studies would find it informative, stimulating and useful. Xiangming Chen has successfully shown how the global and the local have shaped the de-bordering and re-bordering processes in the contemporary world.

*References*

Ohmae, Kenichi. (1990). *The Borderless World: Power and Strategy in the Interlinked Economy*. New York: Collins.
——. (1995). *End of the Nation State: The Rise of Regional Economies*. New York: The Free Press.

Lui Tai-lok The Chinese University of Hong Kong

*Alternate Identities: The Chinese of Contemporary Thailand*, edited by Tong Chee Kiong and Chan Kwok-bun, edited by. Singapore: Times Academic Press; Leiden, The Netherlands: Brill Academic Publishers, 2001. 329pp. ISBN: 9–8121–0142–X.

As a graduate student, I read with rapt attention G. William Skinner's *Chinese Society in Thailand: An Analytical History*. Although published in 1957, this story of the love-hate relationship between the Thai rulers and their Chinese immigrants is still intriguing. The crackdowns under the Plaek Phibunsongkhram government and the alternating repressions and alliances with the Chinese made this long academic book a real page turner. One of my professors, an expert on China, said this book was a prime example of solid research and analysis—the best of anthropology. I think he contrasted Skinner's study to the post-modern theories, which were then sweeping universities and tended toward deconstruction and questioning of truths. I was delighted, therefore, to find this volume on Chinese in Thailand tackling this topic almost a half century later.

Through my research on spirit mediums in southern Thailand, I encountered strong beliefs in Chinese folk Taoism and Mahayana Buddhism. Thus the construction of Thai-Chinese identity is of great interest. *Alternate Identities: The Chinese of Contemporary Thailand* by Tong and Chan contains 12 academic articles which range from the meaning of the Chinese pigtail in Thai history to the symbolism in Sino-Thai weddings in Bangkok. The editors, Tong Chee Kiong and Chan Kwok-bun, from sociology departments at the National University of Singapore and the Hong Kong Baptist University, respectively, begin the book with two key themes that hold it together.

First, they argue that "...ethnicity and ethnic identity straddle, boundary-cross, alternate and perhaps mutate in the face of a multitude of influences" (p. 1). They stress that overseas Chinese in Thailand, as well as Thais, are not a homogeneous ethnic group. Different Chinese dialect groups immigrated at different times and settled into cities and provinces. In theorising identity, the editors take a middle path between scholarly schools of thought. Identity is not just based on primordial factors, ingrained at birth. It is not just based on a particular situation, when people put on different identities like donning clothes. Identity encompasses both those factors and also is constructed by groups for unification at celebrations and rituals.

Second, the editors maintain that Chinese culture has certainly blended with Thai culture but not following Skinner's one-way assimilation model. Skinner's theory was that the Chinese in Thailand would be totally assimilated into the dominate culture by the fourth generation. All the contributors to the volume had problems with this idea. While integration is clearly evident, especially seen in the ability of many Chinese to speak Thai fluently, some writers also observe a resurgence of Chinese identity. There is also a respect in the country for what are considered Chinese skills in business and now politics.

Much of the earlier Western research on this issue was based on the American melting pot model in which a minority group would blend with the dominant group and lose its separate ethnic identity. Skinner theorised that the Chinese would assimilate because they were attracted to the independent Thai culture, which had avoided colonisation, and were free to live among the Thai and travel the country. The Chinese also believed in Buddhism, although they followed the Mahayana sect rather than Thai Theravada Buddhism. Except for some brief periods of repression, the Thai government treated Chinese immigrants fairly well and promoted integration, according to the editors. So there were many reasons for the Chinese to get along with the Thai. Indeed, over the years the Chinese came to speak Thai, profess Thai values and pledge allegiance to Thailand, rather than China. Yet, they still kept a separate Chinese identity.

There have been three waves of theories on Chinese adjustment to living in Southeast Asia. Promoted by Victor Purcell in 1965, the Chinese were thought to be focused on going home to China and on holding tightly to their ethnicity. In opposition to this idea, Skinner proposed that the Chinese would integrate rather quickly, over a few generations, and would in essence disappear as a distinct group. As these were rather extreme opposite arguments, a third theory emerged stressing plurality or hybridity. The Chinese of Thailand are believed to have many identities, which are influenced by globalisation, capitalism, nationalism, localism and other factors. The editors suggest that perhaps it is time for academics to stop talking about the Chinese as an outside group but rather consider them as "deeply embedded" in Thai society. In this two-way exchange, both Chinese and Thai borrow from each other.

One of the first articles in the book is now a well-known classic. Kasian Tejapira wrote that problems with the overseas Chinese were created by both China and Thailand at the beginning of the 20th century. He stated that the concept of "Chineseness" did not exist before the reign of King Rama VI (r. 1910–1925). Kasian tackled this subject from an unique perspective by looking at the Chinese pigtail (*queue*). Countering Skinner's assessment that the pigtail was equivalent to being Chinese in Thailand, Kasian showed how this hair style had many meanings in different contexts. He argued that earlier kings accepted the Chinese as Thai, as one of many ethnic groups in the kingdom, although they wore pigtails. But King Rama VI, in his drive to promote nationalism, identified the Chinese as a threatening racial group, even though the pigtails had been shorn. He argued that the Chinese had not changed, but the way they were viewed by royalty had.

Bringing us into the modern world, the article by Richard Basham, "*Ethnicity and World View in Bangkok*," explores how Thai and Sino-Thai Bangkokians view each other. Although the research was done in 1987, and the "world view" idea has now gone out of fashion, the findings seem to hold true today, according to my Sino-Thai friends in the south. Those interviewed described differences between Thai and Sino-Thai especially in marriage ceremonies and funeral customs, but they thought merit-making ceremonies were fairly similar. Many informants thought the Sino-Thai were more strict in raising children, while the Thais seemed to divorce more. As to be expected, most female informants in both groups criticised mistresses or "minor wives" while the males were more sympathetic. Most of the informants spoke positively of Sino-Thai men as hard workers and heads of families while Thai males were heavily criticised for being irresponsible and too fun loving. Basham was surprised to find this admiration and lack of resentment toward the Sino-Thai, who were widely thought to dominate the business world. He thought the antipathy toward the Chinese was higher in Malaysia and Indonesia. Thai culture has a heavy emphasis on polite speech and movement, and criticised Sino-Thais for poor manners and physical awkwardness.

Although stereotypes about outsiders are common, I found this study valuable in identifying views which were shared between Thai and Sino-Thai. The strong negative view of Thai men was particularly informative. Early in the article, Basham defined Sino-Thai as people who looked Chinese, said they had Chinese heritage and spoke Thai without an accent. Throughout this volume, I had difficulty understanding the differing definitions for Chinese, Thai-Chinese and Sino-Thai. I think the terms reflect changing academic views on identity.

Michael Montesano explored Chinese provincial merchants and suggested they are missing the benefits of the economic growth of the past few decades. He questioned the assumption that Chinese are part of a "merchant culture" and that there is a continuity from the small businesses of the 1940s to major companies of the 1990s. He found that many of those who immigrated during the period of heavy influx from China, from 1918–31, remained small merchants in Bangkok and around the country. Many have not adjusted to the industrial international economy and are not today's business leaders.

Jieman Bao did an admirable job exploring and critiquing the definition of Sino-Thai by Western academics over a 30-year period. The author also described the self-definitions of Sino-Thai people, who identified important factors of blood lineage, dialect, place of birth, and symbolic kinship. These complex definitions show that the term "Chinese" has many meanings and cannot be reduced to describe a uniform group. For instance, earlier generations of Chinese in Thailand were more influenced by Confucian values while later generations identified more with Thai Buddhism. Bao then "unpacks" a Bangkok Sino-Thai wedding to show the influences of Western consumerism, Chinese Confucianism and Thai Buddhism, thereby giving insight into the complex construction of Sino-Thai identity. I was fascinated to read how all these rituals were combined—ancestor worship, tea service, a Buddhist monks' blessing, spirit house homage and a Catholic wedding. Bao showed how each tradition contains symbols that illustrate a belief in hierarchy with females in the lower position. While anyone who reads the *Bangkok Post* social page can see the importance of class and political connections at high society weddings, this article provides fascinating details about the role of the media, gift giving and elite ties.

For my own research interests, I enjoyed reading about the building of a traditional Chinese temple in Chiang Mai within the grounds of a respected Theravada Buddhist monastery, supported by the royal family. Ann Maxwell Hill used this case to illustrate the syncretism of Chinese popular religion. A Chinese funeral is described as another example of Chinese borrowing from Thai traditions. At the funeral, some of the deceased's sons and grandsons were temporarily ordained as novices into the monkhood to dedicate merit to the departed. While the rituals needed to be performed correctly, issues of ideology and whether the traditions were Thai or Chinese were not very important. What was significant was that blended ceremonies helped identify the Chinese as a community. Hill said these examples illustrate the strengthening of Chinese identity within Thailand and the larger globalised economy since the 1980s.

An article titled "Wang Thong: Civic Identity and Ethnicity in a Thai Market Town" by P. Tarkulwaranont, Chan Kwok-bun and Tong Chee Kiong is particularly insightful on the matter of identity. While many second- and third-generation Chinese identify themselves as Thai, others call themselves Chinese. So which is true? The authors found that both ethnic groups influenced each other. Significantly, both were also affected by Western culture and thus came to share many of the same beliefs in modernity and capitalist practices. This article makes a major contribution to questions of ethnicity by breaking down the homogeneous categories of Thai and Chinese, and also Lao. In a case study, the authors found 10 distinct groups of Thai, Chinese and Lao who had settled into one area at different times.

As part of dealing with the "past," the paper also explores how a local myth on the founding of the area has been adapted or manipulated by the Thai, Lao and Chinese groups to highlight their contribution, thereby causing history to influence the present. The Chinese community has been the most successful at claiming the past by holding a major annual ceremony to a Hainanese goddess, who is now honored as a local deity. Meanwhile local Thai rituals have declined partly because the central government has supported new traditions like boat racing. The authors conclude that the Chinese have not been assimilated but rather have merged with a local identity.

This is an important book. I appreciate the listing of authors and their universities at the beginning. I also value the long footnotes on research methods, which provide insight into the findings. Although it was necessary, the references to Skinner's theories in most articles became repetitive. Hopefully, future volumes will build on the new theories in this one.

Marlane Guelden — Anthropologist
(Currently an independent researcher)

*Chinese Business in the Making of a Malay State, 1882–1941: Kedah and Penang (Chinese Worlds)*, by Wu Xiaoan, London, New York: Routledge-Curzon, 2003. 239pp. ISBN: 0–4153–0176–9.

This book examines the dynamic historical processes of the formation of a Kedah-Penang Chinese business network at the turn of the 20th century through detailed case studies of a group of prominent Chinese families. The period under study was an epoch of rapid transformation in the history of Malaya, which, economically, was transformed from a Chinese-dominated revenue farming system to a colonial capitalist economy; and politically, from a Siamese suzerainty to British rule. While taking Chinese business networking as a focus, the author has consistently related Chinese business activities to larger socio-economic structure and historical processes. In other words, the author does not study Chinese business network per se, but rather takes it as a pair of "zoom lens" via which the intricate interplay between ethnicity, state, the region and the Southeast Asian's modernisation is examined.

Guided by the framework above and based on cogent historical analysis, Wu makes two major arguments that add new insights into the study of Chinese Diaspora. First, through delineating the multi-ethnic interactions and shifting power relations in the formation of Chinese business network, this study convincingly indicates that Chinese business cannot be purely defined by "Chineseness" but is deeply embedded in processes of social construction in specific place and time. Chinese business network is situational and opportunistic. It is meaningless to talk about Chinese network in general terms because it can only be addressed in terms of specific historical and social contexts. Such a view contrasts sharply with many primordial conceptions of Chinese networks prevalent in the literature, such as "global tribe", "bamboo networks" and "invisible empire of Overseas Chinese".

Second, and more importantly, this study demonstrates the crucial role played by Chinese immigrants in the transformation and modernisation of Southeast Asia, and presents another type of Chinese immigrant economy. In contrast to the works based on North American experiences that depict Chinese immigrants as an underclass and a marginalised category under the dominant structure of host countries, this study suggests that Chinese immigrants actively participated and played a major role in shaping the expanding economy and emerging new society in Malaya. The involvement was made possible by the sheer size and heavy impact of Chinese immigrants in Malaya, and was also due to the timing of the Chinese's arrival that was at a historical juncture of Malay's socio-economic transformation. As most Southeast Asian countries followed a similar path of social advancement as Malaya and had Chinese immigrants involved in the process, the findings of the study can be relevant to the whole region. As the author argues, "the important historical roles of Southeast Asian Chinese should be reassessed as an indispensable and inseparable element in shaping Southeast Asian history and society, like that of the other communities comprised of Europeans or the indigenous people" (p. 10).

Methodologically, this book showcases a good example of how a regional perspective and a family approach can be incorporated into the study of Chinese Diaspora. Firstly, region is found to be a constructive analytical unit especially when considering the nature of Chinese networks, which is characterised by trans-border mobility and wide linkages that transcend political and administrative boundaries, and the social reality of maritime in Southeast Asia, where many economic activities centered at geo-economic and geo-political regions rather than operate within fixed national boundaries. As Wu rightly indicates, many supra-national zones that played important roles in the past "are re-emerging as ASEAN's growth triangles and becoming main bases for ASEAN regional economic co-operation" (p. 3). Therefore, a regional perspective is not merely a suitable tool for a historical research like this; it is equally valuable in the study of contemporary transnational migrations in Southeast Asia and elsewhere.

Secondly, this work shows the effectiveness of a family approach in the study of Chinese business. The merit of this approach lies in its manageability as a research method and its richness as data source. For example, the reconstruction of the histories of Lim Leng Cheak's family and Kedah Choong Cheng Kean's family in Penang is weaved nicely into the investigation of broader socio-economic transformation. In the analysis, a variety of critical issues like ethnicity, state and region are also identified and discussed. Undoubtedly, more parallel research on Chinese families in other social settings should be done in the same manner.

An ambitious project like this has inevitable shortcomings. First, in most part of the study, the term ethnicity is treated as a fixed entity defined by sharing common primary characteristics, be it Chinese or Malay. Less attention is given to how different ethnic groups have been continuously defined by changing boundaries. By the mid-1880s, many Chinese immigrants had lived there for generations and assimilation had taken place at different levels. From a Southeast Asian perspective, there was perhaps a more fluid and complicated picture of ethnicity, which might generate further insights into the study of Southeast Asian history. Second, the author has firmly proved the existence of an interlocking relationship between migration, ethnicity, state and the region with detailed historical evidence. However, a framework that states theoretically how these various elements interplay with each other still has to be seen.

All in all, this book is a major contribution to the study of Chinese in Southeast Asia. It has greatly enhanced our knowledge and understanding of the formation of Chinese business networks in Southeast Asia in general and Malaya in particular. Students in the study of Southeast Asia and Chinese Diaspora will find this book a valuable reference.

Wang Cangbai University of Hong Kong

*Foreign Communities in Hong Kong, 1840's–1950's*, edited by Chu Yik-yi, Cindy. New York: Palgrave Macmillan, 2005. 209pp. ISBN: 2–0050–4343–3.

This edited volume sets itself the ambitious task of trying to understand some of the history of Hong Kong through the experiences of a few of the foreign resident communities. The approach focuses on communities, assessing both internal dynamics of these communities and their interactions with other communities, especially the local Chinese and British colonial authorities. Not all the chapters hold completely together in following this approach, but for an edited work, it comes extremely close to accomplishing this task, and certainly makes a major contribution to our understanding of foreign communities in Hong Kong. The authors have all put in valuable research time working with primary sources, and the results of their efforts provide much inspiration for further research on the history of the foreign communities in Hong Kong.

The introduction chapter is extremely well done, providing the reader with a clear explanation of the approach of the volume as well as short examples demonstrating how the various chapters fit into the overall scheme of the book. This is extremely handy in assessing how well each of the chapter fits into the scheme.

The introduction stresses the chronological order of the chapters, but does not clearly explain why this is important. Most of the goals of the volume do not rely on this type of organisation, and several of the chapters seem to fit in pretty much at any point. The first and last chapters do have the feel of bookends. The book begins with two chapters on the early British settlement, administration of and attitudes toward Hong Kong, both written by Gillian Bickley. What Bickley makes clear in these two chapters is that British control in the 19th century had as its aim to "integrate or convert others to their worldview." Bickley shows us that by the end of the century, British authorities had created a modern city that did partly reflect success of this aim, and also the adaptation of the British community to local circumstances.

The chapters on the German, Japanese, and Indian communities are all wonderful discussions of how these communities grew, adapted, and contributed to Hong Kong's history. Very effectively for a short essay, Ricardo K.S. Mak traces the development of the German community. In the early decades of the community, the Germans tended to not only affiliate with the British, but also often came to see themselves as almost part of the British community. Still, as Mak demonstrates, the Germans at the same time maintained certain aspects of a self-aware and proud community. The chapter would have been enhanced by more discussion of the examples of the increased tension between the German and British communities in the decades after German unification.

The early Japanese resident experience in Hong Kong as presented by Benjamin Wai-ming Ng stands out for a presentation of the great shift in the class of Japanese who settled in the colony. The majority of the resident Japanese in the early decades were prostitutes, and the most influential Japanese in the colony were gang bosses. As Japan underwent industrialisation, and engaged in greatly increased trade relations with the rest of the world, the makeup of the resident Japanese population of Hong Kong also transformed. In some ways the Japanese community of the early 20th century resembled the German community of the 19th century, being closely allied with the colonial British while also maintaining their own cultural institutions. The growing tensions between the Japanese and British in the years leading up to World War II resemble the growing tensions between the Germans and the British in the years leading up to World War I.

Indians first migrated to Hong Kong as early as the British, which is no surprise as India was also a colony of the British, and Sepoys had been involved in the Opium War. Over the course of the 19th and 20th centuries, the numbers and types of Indians arriving in Hong Kong varied greatly. One group of Indian migrants, mostly Sikhs, were those in the employ of the British in their efforts to control Hong Kong. Other major groups included Parsees, Muslims, and Hindus. Caroline Pluss' chapter on the Indian migration to Hong Kong succeeds in sorting through all these groups: their motivations, concerns and interactions with the other Hong Kong communities: to give us a much clearer picture of the contributions of the Indian communities to Hong Kong history.

Another chapter that succeeds in clarifying what could have been a very complicated topic is the one by Cindy Yik-yi Chu on the Stanley civilian internment camp, set up by the Japanese occupiers during World War II. Chu traces the developments within the camp community and that community's relations with the Japanese (and, somewhat, with the local Chinese) during the war years, and demonstrates the extraordinary efforts of discipline and cooperation needed by the interned foreign community in order to survive. One aspect of the chapter that seemed puzzling concerned the Japanese engagement in what Chu refers to as "anti-foreign" activity while occupying Hong Kong. The implication of that statement is that the Japanese were just as native to Hong Kong as the Chinese residents, but that does not appear to be the argument Chu is making. Since the argument seems to be used to contrast the attitudes of the Japanese with the few instances of local Chinese anti-foreignism of prior decades, possibly "Anti-Western" would have been a better phrase to use in this case.

Chu also wrote the chapter detailing the activities of the Catholic Church between the world wars. Here she effectively demonstrates that the Catholic Church's most successful activities creating smooth and often warm relations with the local community during this period were not evangelisation, but provision of social services and social welfare.

The last chapter by Chi-kwan Mark concerns American consular officials in Hong Kong during the 1950's, especially those Mark calls "China Hands." Mark's discussion of the position of these experts in dutifully carrying out the policies of the United States government while also being almost uniquely (among Americans in Hong Kong) sympathetic to the precarious condition of Hong Kong in its relationship to mainland China deserves special commendation. Mark demonstrates that these officials had limited influence at the time, yet their reports on the actual conditions in China during the early years of Communist rule, with the likelihood of this rule becoming more not less secure, eventually provided for more realistic and effective American policies.

While there are some quibbles with the organisation and parameters of some of the topics of various chapters (e.g. how "foreign" exactly was the Catholic Church by the 1920's; should the Indians in the employ of the British army and administration be lumped in with the Indians who actually settled in Hong Kong; is it too limited to separate the American consular officials from the American business and academic interests resident in Hong Kong, etc.), overall this edited book provides a very good overview of a few of the foreign communities resident in Hong Kong, their development over time, and their relations with other foreign and local communities.

Paul Lococo Jr. University of Hawaii-Leeward

*Life is elsewhere: Stories of the Indonesian Chinese in Hong Kong* (in Chinese), by Wang Cangbai. Hong Kong: Centre of Asian Studies, The University of Hong Kong, 2006. 306pp. ISBN: 9–6282–6947–X.

The study of the Indonesian Chinese (or Chinese Indonesians) is a fertile one. A rich body of literature covering all aspects of Indonesian migration has been published, e.g., their migration history, economic activities, integration process, transnational network, etc. However, this book, by carefully recording life stories of ten Indonesian Chinese in Hong Kong and by exploring the identity puzzle of this ethnic group, has provided valuable data that will undoubtedly be beneficial to further studies in this area. Moreover, illustrated by dozens of historical photos, the book has helped readers to get vivid pictures of the lives of these migrants and the historical contexts of their moves.

The core chapters of the book are composed of ten life stories. The ten participants have moved several times in their life from Indonesia to mainland China, and then, to Hong Kong. It is their special re-migration and re-settlement experiences that have made this group quite special. Of the ten participants, all but one was born and grew up in Indonesia. One was born in China but was brought to Indonesia in his teens by his foster father. Having spent their childhood in Indonesia but received education in Chinese schools there, they were socialized in an environment which had integrated both Indonesian and Chinese cultures. This experience made them a bicultural group, and had shaped their philosophy of life.

In the 1950s, our story tellers were young, with youthful spirits and beautiful dreams about the future. Their newly founded socialist motherland China became a fantastic destination in which to have their personal dreams come true. They decided to "return" to their "motherland," that is, their ancestors' motherland—China. Their determination to return was so strong that they gave up their property in Indonesia and some even severed all ties with their parents if they did not understand or accept their decision to return. They imagined that their new life in the socialist motherland would be like going back home. Their plan was to first attend university in China, and then, they could make a special contribution to the motherland's socialist construction.

However, the gap between their expectation and the reality they encountered was very big. At that time, the living standard in the newly founded People's Republic was very low and soon after their return, between 1960 and 1962, the country faced an economic crisis. To make things worse, besides economic difficulties, discrimination against people with "overseas relationship" made all returnees feel uncomfortable and marginalized. This harsh reality inexorably broke the returnees' dream. However, according to the participants, they adjusted themselves to this new environment because of two primary reasons. The first was that they were young and they did not want to give up their dreams easily; the second reason was that they had no way of going back to Indonesia. Overtime, they became doctors, teachers, actresses, employees of state-owned enterprise, etc. Their life was stable but the psychological burden was heavy, particularly after the Cultural Revolution broke out in 1966.

The second turning point in their life appeared in the early 1970s, when the authorities in China began to allow them to leave China. Under the pretence of applying for visas to return to their birth-place, Indonesia, they went to Hong Kong, and ended up staying in Hong Kong, which was something they had never thought about before. It is worth noting that, unlike their enthusiastic description of their return to China, their representation of the second migration was full of disappointment and bitterness. This time, in order to "come to Hong Kong", they had to give up not only their properties, which were not that much, but the social status that they had built up in mainland China. However, they felt that they had no choice.

Their new life in Hong Kong was very difficult. They had to re-establish a home with empty hands and they were all middle aged by then. One participant said, "Life was so tough that I almost decided to run back to mainland" (p. 115); and from another participant, "If you see the situation of peasant workers in mainland China today, you would understand how difficult it was for us at that time" (p. 60). Migration from the mainland to Hong Kong meant sacrificing social status for a life of more freedom and fewer restrictions. After working hard for decades, they settled down in Hong Kong, and became to be known as "Indonesian Chinese in Hong Kong."

These unusual life stories mirror the political development in mainland China and its foreign relationship with Indonesia over the last half century. Moreover, besides presenting primary data in the core chapters, the author has made an impressive effort in exploring the issue of identity in the introductory and concluding chapters in the book. It is not surprising that these Indonesian Chinese in Hong Kong form a special group. When they were in Indonesia, they identified themselves as Chinese because they were of Chinese blood; when they returned to their motherland China, they were labeled as "returned overseas Chinese" or even as "foreigners," because they kept some Indonesian traits. In Hong Kong, they were regarded as "mainlanders," because they spoke Mandarin not Cantonese. They were never accepted as "purely Chinese" anywhere. Wang shows how this group of people has made efforts to rid themselves of psychological ambivalence. Wang argues that these people have constructed an "extra territorial identity." Their identity does not relate to any particular location or a particular culture. Their "imagined community" is based on a transnational space. Their cultural and relational patterns are not wholly from Indonesia, mainland China, or Hong Kong, but have developed in all places over time. In fact, as Wang argues, this is quite liberating—it liberates people from the sense of being marginal.

The other theoretical issue explored by Wang is about "pseudo-clanship" that is created on the basis of Chinese school schoolmate relationship. Indonesian Chinese in Hong Kong started to organize themselves in the 1990s. Among the Chinese migrants abroad, associations are often based on shared provenance, on the same clan, on the same dialect, or on shared profession. The associations of the Indonesian Chinese in Hong Kong are mostly based on school ties that they have developed when they were attending Chinese school in Indonesia (located in Palembang) before they returned to mainland China. In fact, Wang argues that it is almost like a clanship in the traditional Chinese society. Wang points out that, more than anything else, the days these Indonesian Chinese spent in the Chinese schools in Palembang had a major impact on their lives. As mentioned in their life stories, it was the education in Chinese schools that had guided them to "return to the motherland," and this move changed their life forever. Regardless of whether such change evoked positive or negative memories, it is an unforgettable experience that only the schoolmates could understand and relate to. As a result, they have invented a pseudo-clanship, a home.

Finally, in terms of methodology, there is a difference between recording oral data and building up an academic study based on oral resources. The current book is something in between. For instance, when studying the oral data, it is important to note that oral life story is a compressed history. Moreover, just as Alessandro Portelli (1991) has pointed out, the first thing that makes oral history different is that "they tell us not just what people did, but what they wanted to do, what they believed they were doing, what they now think they did. Oral sources may not add much to what we know of, for instance, the material cost of a given strike to the workers involved; but they tell us a good deal about its psychological costs" (p. 50). Elizabeth Tonkin (1992) argues that "the past" is not only a resource to deploy or support a case or to assert a social claim, it also enters memory in different ways and helps to structure it; therefore, "we are our memories" (p. 1). Also, she argues that personal narratives cannot be taken as accurate historical documents but should be approached "as literature" that itself is "part of social action," and "it is a dynamic process and also a situational one" (p. 51). From this point of view, further exploration still can be developed on the basis of the current oral data, although Wang has already made an admirable effort.

## *References*

Portelli, Alessandro. 1991. *The Death of Luigi Trastulli and Other Stories, Form and Meaning in Oral History*. New York: State University of New York Press.

Tonkin, Elizabeth. 1992. *Narrating Our Past, the Social Construction of Oral History*. Cambridge: Cambridge University Press.

Li Minghuan — Xiamen University, China

*Social Survey Research in Practice: Chinese Experience and Analysis* (in Chinese), edited by Bian Yanjie, Li Lulu and Cai He. Hong Kong: Oxford University Press, 2004. 262pp. ISBN: 0–1959–7492–1.

Survey research in the People's Republic of China started in the early 1980's, about the same time when sociology re-emerged in China after a 20-year absence as a social science discipline. Today, the survey research method is widely used within and beyond the academic world in China. However, as China has undergone tremendous social changes in the past two decades, it is becoming increasingly difficult to conduct surveys in China for academic purposes. The book being reviewed here addresses these difficulties and offers some solutions.

The book is, essentially, a documentation of the first general social survey for urban China, which was conducted in 2003 (China GSS 2003). In the book, the entire process, from questionnaire design, sampling design, survey implementation to data entry, cleaning, and coding, is described and discussed in details. The editors of the book are the main organizers of the survey, and the majority of the chapter contributors have been fully involved in the design and implementation of the survey. Most of them also have rich experiences in conducting surveys in China.

For students of sociology in China, this is an extremely helpful book for them to learn how to conduct a survey, even though they may have read some textbooks, taken a method course or have participated in some surveys. For researchers from outside China, the book is also very helpful. In fact, if one is going to conduct a survey in China for the first time, this book is a must-read.

The book begins with a chapter about the questionnaire design for China GSS 2003. It stresses the theoretical rationales of the survey, which tends to be lacking in many academic surveys in China. In particular, it discusses the Chinese contexts and the application of general sociological theories and concepts adopted in the survey. It also discusses the details in the operationalization of the basic concepts and of the instrument design.

Chapters 3–5 address the issue of sampling, an important stage in a survey research, which is not well understood by many researchers in China. For example, Chapter 3 shows that, between 1990 and 2001, a total of 141 empirical papers based on survey data were published in the two most important academic journals in the discipline of sociology in

China, *Sociological Research* and *Social Sciences in China* (about 12 empirical papers a year on average); and only about 40% of these papers provide a description of the sampling procedure used in the survey.

While Chapter 3 identifies methodological problems in the previous empirical work regarding sampling, Chapter 4 deals with two common problems faced by survey researchers in recently years. In the past, researchers have relied on the household registration list to draw a representative sample from the general population in a given Chinese city. Apparently, this approach is quite problematic now. First of all, migrants account for a great proportion of the urban population today, and many of them are not registered. Secondly, within the registered local population, many do not live in the place of their registration. The author compares the probability proportionate to size sampling technique (PPS) with the map-based sampling technique and discusses their strength and weakness in solving the two problems.

Chapter 5 addresses the same problems as Chapter 4 does; but Chapter 5 uses a concrete example—China GSS 2003. It describes the difficulties encountered, and measures taken in the sampling and implementation of China GSS 2003. It also goes beyond the sampling stage, and discusses problems in the interview stage; for example, the problem of not being able to enter the chosen household, and the problem of respondent refusal, both are major problems in conducting surveys in China today.

Chapters 7–10 are concerned with data quality. Specifically, they discuss the measures taken to ensure the quality of the data collected in China GSS 2003. Chapter 7, about the interviewer effect, examines the extent to which interviewers may affect the quality of the data in China GSS 2003, which had employed more than 300 interviewers. Chapter 8 is about the factors that influence the willingness of the respondents to answer questions truthfully. Chapter 9 describes the data entry and cleaning process, and Chapter 10 provides a detailed description on the coding of the open-ended questions, in particular, the coding of the occupations.

Chapter 6 discusses the role of the government (at different levels) in the implementation of a survey. This is an issue that anyone, who has done an academic survey in China, knows about; but few have bothered to discuss it in a systematic fashion, even though it is crucial for conducting a successful academic survey in China.

Chapter 6 begins with a general discussion on the role of the government in carrying out a survey in China. Then, it describes how China GSS 2003 has been "assisted" by various government offices. It ranges from getting the basic information on the population from a city or district government to being accompanied by a staff of a neighborhood committee to carry out the actual interviews. As Table 6.1 shows, the local government is involved in the survey work in all of the 47 primary sampling units in 39 cities, and only in 13% of the cases that the government offered nothing beyond an endorsement. In terms of the involvement of neighborhood committees, only 5 out of 47 units did not receive help from the neighborhood committee in carrying out the interviews. Indeed, this kind of help from the local government is almost indispensable. For example, the basic information on the population (e.g., household registration list) is not publicly available and cannot be purchased. In all 47 primary sampling units, the basic information has been obtained through the government office (in 36% of the cases, with payments), and through (direct or indirect) personal ties. This last part about personal ties shows the arbitrary nature of the assistance/endorsement from the local government, which is not surprising to anyone with a basic knowledge about China.

In sum, this book offers a comprehensive and systematic discussion about how to conduct a survey in China today; and it does so by analyzing concrete examples from a large-scaled survey recently conducted in China. The book is not simply a how-to book—it reveals a society in rapid transition—a society which is fascinating and challenging to study. I recommend it to all students and researchers, who are interested in conducting a survey in China. In fact, I hope that, at least, some parts of the book, e.g., Chapter 6, can be published in English to make it available to more researchers.

Ruan Danching Hong Kong Baptist University

*Childrearing Values in the United States and China: A Comparison of Belief Systems and Social Structure*, by Xiao Hong, 2001. Westport, CT: Praeger, 161pp. ISBN: 0-275-97313-1.

This book studies how social class, gender and culture influence childrearing values (parental preference for values developed in children) in the United States and China. In addition to analysis performed on the individual countries, cross-country comparisons were also made. While the traditional literature has focused on a single class-value dimension of autonomy versus conformity, the author argued that childrearing values are multidimensional. On a very general level, class theory argues that middle class parents tend to value autonomy while working class parents value conformity; gender theory suggests that women will emphasize care orientation; and some studies of parental values from a cultural perspective imply that American parents would value autonomy more than Chinese parents. Furthermore, how class and gender might affect childrearing values could well vary across different cultures.

The data used in the book were taken from the World Values Survey (WVS), which was designed primarily for making cross-national comparisons of values and norms in a wide range of areas. The data were collected during 1990–1993. The US sample was a national representative sample while the Chinese data came from a representative sample of the urban population only. As part of the survey, respondents were asked to choose up to five items from a list of 11 items pertaining to childrearing values, namely, good manners, independence, hard work, feeling of responsibility, imagination, tolerance/respect for others, thrift, perseverance, religious faith, unselfishness, and obedience. The author applied factor analysis to the data in generating three value domains, namely, autonomy, conformity, and an orientation to care. Multivariate analysis of variance and regressions were then applied to discern how various independent variables relating to gender as well as social, economic, educational, demographic, and religious backgrounds affect on childrearing values.

The book finds that gender, culture, and social class affect childrearing values in some unexpected ways. The underlying structures of childrearing values in the US and China are strikingly similar, but they are not identical. This is shown in the clusters of value items making up the three dimensions of childrearing values in each country. The autonomy and care orientation dimensions are made up of similar clusters in the two countries, but not so for the conformity dimension. Also, autonomy and conformity are found to be not necessarily opposing values, as it has often been cast in the traditional literature. Instead, people may see positive aspects in both attributes. This is most readily seen among American women in the advantaged classes, which are composed of female owners/managers, professionals, and foremen/supervisors. Furthermore, while the book supports previous research, which shows that childrearing values are affected by a number of social, familial, and personal characteristics, it also uncovers substantial and consistent gender differences in the effects of parental education and occupation on child socialization values.

The book makes a number of important and original contributions. It claims to be the first to systematically analyze the link between social structure and childrearing values in China. It also provides cross-country comparisons whereby one could examine how social class and gender exert their influence on childrearing values in different ways depending on the specific cultural context. In doing so the book underscores the care that is needed in doing cross-country comparisons. For example, the conventional view is that Americans value autonomy while Chinese emphasize conformity. The reality is probably much more complicated than this caricature. To start with, words like "autonomy" and "conformity" could mean different things in different cultures. And indeed the book finds that while Americans tend to value independence more than obedience, rather paradoxically they also value independence much less and obedience much more than Chinese. Another example is that of the effect of occupational autonomy on value orientations. The book finds that occupational autonomy is not related to any of the value orientations, which is contrary to previous results. But the real surprise is that among those Chinese who have greater occupational autonomy, they are found to value conformity more and autonomy less. The author attributes this surprising finding to the fact that the ruling Chinese Communist Party tends to reward cadres who demonstrate greater loyalty and reliability with the more desirable job positions; therefore, people in advantaged job positions could actually value conformity more.

The book has produced many new and interesting results. However, many of the results are not easy to interpret. Indeed, due to the lack of a theoretical framework serving as the basis of the empirical analyses, only ad hoc rationalizations could be rendered to many of the findings.

This field of research remains a promising one. The author has done some original, pioneering work; but, much remains to be done. Some possible directions for further research were pointed out by the author herself. For example, due to limitation of the data, the author did not take into consideration the age and sex of the children. In addition, because of the great variations in cultures and social structures across countries, there is a need to design country-specific questionnaire. While uniformity of questionnaire facilitates comparisons as is the case in the current study, in some cases, country-specific questionnaires are needed. An example is that it may make sense to measure religiosity in the US with church attendance. But in a country like China, a relevant measure of religiosity could well involve how frequently the respondents engage in rituals such as ancestor worship. Finally, because much of the findings are contrary to those in the existing literature and a little counter-intuitive, further research leading to a greater body of evidence would be useful.

Odalia M. H. Wong Hong Kong Baptist University

*Marriage, Divorce and Remarriage: Professional Practice in the Hong Kong Cultural Context*, edited by Young, Katherine P. H. and Anita Y. L. Fok. Hong Kong: Hong Kong University Press, 2005. 299pp. ISBN: 9-6220-9741-3.

Readers with an interest in social work and marriage counseling will find this book offers some fine examples of effective counseling practice. Other readers will generally find that this book raises some important questions about the relationship between the practices of counselors and social workers and Hong Kong cultural accounts of marriage and family. In posing these questions, the book sometimes exhibits the particular difficulties of a values approach to social problems, but overall, it does an important service; it brings culture back into the discussion of marriage and family.

For while family is not the ostensible subject of *Marriage, Divorce and Remarriage*, it hovers just behind most of the twelve articles which make up the collection. In that regard, those who deal with marriage in Hong Kong find themselves caught between two cultural worlds. One is ancient, now gone, in which marriage was viewed as an aspect of the patriarchal family, which in turn, was then seen as holding together state and society in a stable whole. The other world is the present, in which marriage is construed as a contract between two individuals to supply each other with particular goods and services, albeit ones that may go far beyond material support. Such marriages appear rootless because they are no longer embedded in a set of practices that clearly articulate with kin group and community, although they may be construed. As such, its relative instability creates problems, both for children and the state.

Enter the practices of modern marriage counseling and the yearning for some kind of public policy that would, once again, place marriage, even a radically-changed construct of non-patriarchal marriage, in a stable context. For the writers of *Marriage, Divorce and Remarriage*, that is the critical question: can the techniques of modern, Amero-European counseling, literally, be "married" with a re-interpreted Confucian tradition? And, in turn, comes my question: if that can be done, will it suffice?

Anthropologist Clifford Geertz says of such efforts, "Ideology bridges the emotional gap between things as they are and as one would have them be, thus ensuring the performance of roles that might otherwise be abandoned in despair or apathy" (1964:50). In *Marriage, Divorce and Remarriage*, the contributors work to construct the kind of ideology that will allow them both to deal with the pain of their clients and to give their clients an account of marriage that will support changes in behavior. They want also to gain a following for such a new account in the community, so that marriages may receive more appropriate support from state and other civic bodies.

In this book, that account of marriage is clearly still a work in progress, but we can see emerging the outline of a new marital ideal. In its concern with companionship and support, it partakes of the New Domestic Ideal, as described by C. H. Ng (1995), but it goes far more deeply into the social construction of self than previous work on marriage in Hong Kong. The work of therapy in marriage, divorce and remarriage is seen to be the reconstruction of selves around new principles of self-differentiation. Since the self is largely constructed around accounts of how the individual is to make sense of, and go on in the world, it seems logical to offer clients a new kind of individualism. This kind of individualism will then make it possible for a spouse to work with his or her partner on the marriage project in ways that develop the relationship into something larger and better connected with meanings still important to the community as a whole.

Quite rightly, the writers question the kind of individualism this should be, and look to Confucian sources for better grounding than that apparently offered by Western culture. Julia Tao Lai Poh-Wah's discussion of this potential ground is engaging, but still very tentative, particularly with respect to women. Perhaps counseling techniques that develop self-differentiation can be married with a story from the Analects about the duty to self, but the weavers of the new ideology still face significant hurdles.

The ghost of the patriarchal family lurks in a number of the articles of *Marriage, Divorce, and Remarriage*. For that ghost, women's assertion of their individuality is deeply problematic. For example, in "The Changing Nature and Ideology of Marriage in Hong Kong, "Lam Chui Wan, Lam Wai Man, and Timothy Y. K. Leung take for granted that women's education and employment can be tagged with the blame for much of the rise in Hong Kong's divorce rate. It seems that these writers not only ignore the analytical error this position represents (correlation is not causation), they are also content to present women's aspirations as some kind of social problem. Hence, the article fails to ask key questions: why do women want to leave certain kinds of marriages when they have the ability to exercise the option? Is there really something wrong with marriage itself, per se? Or does it rest more with those men (as well as women) who apparently face such difficulties in developing the kind of individuality now seen as necessary to carry on a positive marital relationship?

*Marriage, Divorce and Remarriage* is replete with examples of men's particular struggles with attempts to become self-aware, to reveal themselves more fully to their partners, and to move into a kind of shared self-development within marriage. Much of the time they are seen simply to avoid the whole process, much to the concern of social workers and therapists alike—see "Gender Considerations in Couple Work," by Timothy Y. K. Leung, Monica L. T. Ng, Yeung Ka Ching, and Ivan T. Y. Yau. But in that article no one asks the further question: why is it so hard for many men to open up? Instead, the writers take refuge in the concept of face, which is seen to require no explanation.

Social workers and social scientists alike must take up the greater challenge: to address the concept of individualism Hong Kong men are forced to embrace in the world of commerce. (The same one women now struggle with as they attempt to keep their attention on meaningful relationships as well.)

The kind of raw individualism at the heart of modern consumer capitalism takes no prisoners. It asks a man to put his personal feelings aside in order to engage in a massive competition, where the measure of his value is the degree to which he succeeds in overcoming others to make money. One may co-operate with one's corporate team, but since one has to compete even within that team to maintain a place, there is little room for the expression of any emotion that may render one vulnerable. When older, Chinese prescriptions for masculine stoicism in the face of pain (for the extension and honour of the lineage) are added to this, it is little wonder that men find it difficult to embrace another kind of individualism—one which requires compassion for both self and others.

To embrace this "new" individualism is to ask men either to compartmentalize their lives in ways that have already proven largely unworkable, or, to begin to resist the present culture of capitalism.

The interests of Hong Kong's business and governmental elite are entirely served by the kind of individualism that renders men incapable of dealing with feelings of pain and vulnerability. And while it may seem easier for social workers to avoid any sort of challenge to such an elite, they must eventually face the necessity of engaging the men they counsel with an understanding of the employment culture in which they, as men, must survive. If such a culture requires a construct of masculinity that avoids dealing with emotion, hard questions must be asked about it—and not only of individual men.

Social workers must begin by understanding that to question the roots of men's behaviors is not necessarily to blame them, as a number of writers in *Marriage, Divorce and Remarriage* seem to fear. Instead, such questioning requires those who think about a new ideology of marriage to consider and respond to the larger institutional constraints on men's abilities to re-conceptualize themselves. A functional account of marriage requires no less. Moreover, Hong Kong's social thinkers will then be treating men as the moral agents Confucius wished.

Indeed, understanding culture is critical to the re-development of marriage, but grappling with its many manifestations requires a wider outlook across social institutions. It is not sufficient to take one aspect of culture in isolation and hope that a re-interpretation of that aspect will do all that is necessary. Nonetheless, the writers of *Marriage, Divorce, and Remarriage* are to be commended for opening up questions about culture and marriage that need to be asked and for beginning to provide some answers, however provisional. It is now up to the readers of this provocative volume to join the dialogue. For many people, in Hong Kong and elsewhere, marriage is still too important to be abandoned.

### *References*

Geertz, C. (1964). "Ideology as a Cultural System." Pp. 47–76 in *Ideology and Discontent*, edited by D. E. Apter. New York: Free Press of Glencoe.

Ng, C. H. (1995). "New Directions in Cultural Studies." Pp. 1–22 in *Culture & Society in Hong Kong*, edited by E. Sinn. Hong Kong: The Centre of Asian Studies, the University of Hong Kong.

May Partridge Sociologist

(Currently an independent researcher at Cedar, British Columbia)

# NOTICE TO CONTRIBUTORS

## *Editorial Procedures*

*Social Transformations in Chinese Societies* (STCS), previously known as *Hong Kong Journal of Sociology*, is the official annual of the Hong Kong Sociological Association. All manuscripts considered appropriate for this annual are reviewed anonymously by at least two outside reviewers. The review process usually takes two months.

Manuscripts accepted for publication are subject to nonsubstantive, stylistic editing. A copy of the edited manuscript will be sent to the corresponding author for proofreading. It should be corrected and returned to the Brill Academic Publishers within seven days. Once the final version of the manuscript has been accepted, authors are requested not to make further changes to the manuscript.

## *Manuscript Submission*

Authors should submit their manuscript either by post or electronically (preferred mode) to one of the following editors.

CHAN KWOK-BUN, Department of Sociology, Hong Kong Baptist University, Kowloon Tong, Hong Kong. Email: ckb@hkbu.edu.hk

AGNES S. KU, Division of Social Science, Hong Kong University of Science and Technology, Clear Water Bay, Hong Kong. Email: soagnes@ust.hk

CHU YIN-WAH, Department of Sociology, Hong Kong Baptist University, Kowloon Tong, Hong Kong. Email: ywchu@hkbu.edu.hk

The package should include:

(1) a cover letter giving the address, e-mail address, telephone, and fax numbers of the corresponding author, the title of and the word count for the manuscript, and a statement that the manuscript has not been previously published and that it is not under consideration for publication in any other journal or book;

(2) three copies of the manuscript; and
(3) a copy of the manuscript on computer diskette.
(4) Both the cover letter and the manuscript can be sent as attached MS-Word or PDF files if electronic submission is chosen.

The acceptance of a manuscript by the STCS implies an understanding by the author(s) that the STCS will have the sole publication rights over the manuscript. Authors are responsible for securing permission to reproduce all copyrighted tables, figures, illustrations, etc., before they are submitted to the STCS.

### *Manuscript Preparation*

Manuscript pages must be printed double-spaced in a clear typeface on 21 × 29.7 cm paper, with 3.5 cm margins and justified to the left margin.

The length of an English manuscript should not be more than 10,000 words.

Manuscripts should meet the format guidelines that are specified in the Notice to Contributors published in the February and August issues of the *American Sociological Review or the ASA Style Guide* (2d ed., 1997). Your manuscript can have up to eight separate sections.

(1) The **title page** should include the full title of the article, the author or authors' name(s) and institutional affiliation(s).
(2) An **abstract** of 150–200 words. This should be printed on a separate page headed by the title.
(3) Begin the **text** on a new page headed by the title. Omit author name(s). STCS uses anonymous peer reviewers to evaluate manuscripts, so please keep the text of your manuscript anonymous. For example, if you cite your own work, write "Chan (1999) concluded…," but not "I concluded (Chan 1999)…"
    1. The hierarchy of headings and subheadings should be clear.
    2. Citations in the text give the last name of the author(s) and year of publication. Include page number(s) whenever you quote directly from a work or refer to specific passages. In the following examples of text citations, ellipses (…) indicate manuscript text.
        – If an author's name is in the text, then follow it with the year in parentheses: …Chan (1999). If an author's name is not in

the text, then enclose the last name and year in parentheses: ...(Chan 1999).
- Page(s) cited follow the year of publication after a colon: ...(Chan 1999: 239–40).
- Give both last names for joint authors: ...(Chan and Lee 1999).
- For works with three authors, list all three last names in the first citation in the text: ...(Chan, Lee, and Cheung 1999). For all subsequent citations use "et al.": ...(Chan et al. 1999). For works with four or more authors, use "et al." throughout.
- List a series of citations in date order separated by semicolons: ...(Chan 1995; Lee 1998; Cheung 2000).
- Use "forthcoming" to cite sources scheduled for publication. For dissertations and unpublished papers, cite the date. If no date is available, then use "n.d." in place of the date: ...Chan (forthcoming) and Lee (n.d.).

3. Number notes consecutively throughout the text using superscript Arabic numerals.

(4) **Notes** should be printed, double-spaced in a separate "Notes" section. Begin each note with the numeral to which it is keyed in the text.

(5) **References** should be presented in a separate "References" section. All references cited in the text must be listed in the reference section, and vice versa. Publication information for each must be complete and correct.

1. List the references in alphabetical order by authors' last names; include first names and middle initials for all authors when available.
2. List two or more entries by the same author(s) in order of the year of publication.
3. If two or more cited works are by the same author(s) within the same year, then list them in alphabetical order by title and distinguish them by adding the letters a, b, c, etc., to the year.
4. For works with more than one author, list all authors.

Examples

*Books*: Inglehart, Ronald. (1990). *Culture Shift in Advanced Industrial Society*. Princeton, NJ: Princeton University Press.

Tilly, Charles, Louise Tilly, and Richard Tilly. 1975. *The Rebellious Century, 1830–1930*. Cambridge, MA: Harvard University Press.

*Periodicals*: Portes, Alejandro. (2000). "The Hidden Abode: Sociology as Analysis of the Unexpected." *American Sociological Review* 65:1–18.

*Collections*: Coleman, James S. (1994). "A Rational Choice Perspective on Economic Sociology." Pp. 166–80 in *The Handbook of Economic Sociology*, edited by Neil J. Smelser and Richard Swedberg. Princeton, NJ: Princeton University Press.

(6) **Tables** should be numbered consecutively throughout the text and printed on separate sheets. Insert a note in the text to indicate table placement (e.g., "Table 1 about here"). Each table must include a descriptive title and headings for all columns and rows.

(7) **Figures** should be numbered consecutively throughout the text and printed on separate sheets. Insert a note in the text to indicate figure placement (e.g., "Figure 1 about here"). Each figure must include a title or caption and be submitted on diskette or in camera-ready form.

(8) **Appendices** should be lettered and attached at the end of the manuscript. Each appendix must include a descriptive title.

NOTICE TO SUBSCRIBERS

Subscription orders may be sent to
Brill, c/o Turpin Distribution, Stratton Business Park, Pegasus Drive, Biggleswade
Bedfordshire SG 18 8TQ, United Kingdom
Tel +44 (0)1767 604–954
Fax +44 (0)1767 601–640
E-mail brill@turpin-distribution.com

www.ingramcontent.com/pod-product-compliance
Lightning Source LLC
LaVergne TN
LVHW080646011026
849160LV00014B/1340
*9789004168244*